Blended Learning
Tools for teaching and training

Barbara Allan

facet publishing

© Barbara Allan 2007

Published by Facet Publishing,
7 Ridgmount Street, London WC1E 7AE
www.facetpublishing.co.uk

Facet Publishing is wholly owned by CILIP: the Chartered
Institute of Library and Information Professionals.

British Library Cataloguing in Publication Data
A catalogue record for this book is available from the British
Library.

ISBN 978-1-85604-614-5

First published 2007

Typeset from author's disk in 9/13 pt Revival 565 and Franklin
Gothic by Facet Publishing.
Printed and made in Great Britain by Cromwell Press Ltd,
Trowbridge, Wiltshire.

Blen

Tools fo

Also by Barbara Allan

Project Management: tools and techniques for today's ILS professional (2004)
978-1-85604-504-9

Supervising and Leading Teams in ILS (2006) 978-1-85604-587-2

Contents

List of figures

List of tables

Acknowledgements

Thank you to the many people in the library and information profession who have shared ideas, answered queries and generally discussed their blended learning experiences with me. Thank you to Dr Cecilia Loureiro-Koechlin for reading and commenting on Chapter 2, 'Tools and Technologies'. In addition, Cecilia provided technical support throughout this project and our discussions enhanced the content of this book. I would like to acknowledge the work of Dina Lewis as our book, *Virtual Learning Communities* (Open University Press, 2005), helped to inform the content of Chapter 8, 'Communities of Practice'. An earlier work of mine, *Project Management: tools and techniques for today's ILS professional* (Facet Publishing, 2004), helped to inform Chapter 9, 'Managing Blended Learning Projects'. Finally, thank you to Denis and Sarah for providing me with their constant support during this project.

Barbara Allan

1 Introduction

The aim of this chapter is to introduce blended learning in the context of information and library services (ILS), and also to introduce the book and its structure. Following this introduction, the chapter considers the following topics: teaching and training in the 21st century; what is blended learning?; and the structure of the book.

The aim of the book is to provide a practical guide to library and information workers who are involved in education and training, and who are interested in designing and delivering blended learning experiences to their colleagues and customers. The term 'blended learning' has risen in popularity from around 2000 and, in the context of this book, it is used to mean a holistic approach to learning that involves a blend of different approaches, e.g. face-to-face and e-learning, the use of different technology-based tools, or the blending of classroom-based and work-based learning. This is explored in more detail in the next section.

One of the challenges of writing this book is that this is a rapidly developing field so my focus is on providing the underpinning theories behind good-quality blended learning and a range of practical examples. In addition, I consider some of the many challenges currently faced by ILS staff, including the need to work with very large groups and also with diverse groups. In taking this approach, I hope that this book will provide a useful resource for both experienced practitioners and those who are relatively new to the design and delivery of blended learning. I also consider project management in the context of the design and delivery of new or adapted blended learning programmes. Many ILS establish projects, sometimes using external funding, as a means of developing their education and training provision. The chapter on project management (Chapter 9) provides a practical overview to this subject using examples from current practice.

I have based this book on information and knowledge gained from:

- my experiences in the design and delivery of traditional training programmes, e-learning programmes and also blended learning programmes
- discussions with colleagues working in ILS
- feedback from colleagues who have attended my workshops (based at CILIP) and ILS conferences

- visits (both real and virtual) to a wide range of ILS
- professional networks and conferences, and also the literature.

This book is aimed at a wide range of ILS professionals, e.g. staff involved in end-user education, students of library and information management, staff developers, independent consultants and trainers, and information providers, e.g. database providers. In common with other authors, I found it difficult to decide on a term to describe accurately the concept of 'the learner' and, as a result, I have used a variety of words that reflect the current terminology used within the sector, including 'students', 'end-users' and 'participants'.

Teaching and training in the 21st century

The landscapes of education and training have been transformed in the past decade as a result of drivers such as rapid developments in information and communications technology, the move to a 24/7 culture, changing patterns of work and leisure, globalization, increased and changing expectations of stakeholders, and the constant demand to work in a manner that is 'smart, lean and agile'. Education and training programmes are constantly changing and developing, and in recent years the rising interest in e-learning has expanded and shifted its focus so that many practitioners are now concerned with blended learning programmes. Reasons for developing blended learning programmes include:

- making learning more accessible, engaging and relevant
- providing more flexible learning opportunities
- reducing the amount of time spent on face-to-face learning activities by shifting the balance to more blended learning activities
- integrating practitioner-based experiences with classroom-based learning
- developing programmes that are relatively cheap to repeat or use with large groups of learners
- exploiting ICT and training facilities
- demonstrating the use of leading-edge technologies
- demand from users or other stakeholders
- interest at senior management level
- availability of external funding
- to explore new approaches to learning and teaching
- to keep up with other ILS.

The needs and expectations of learners are constantly changing and, increasingly, they expect technology-rich and flexible learning opportunities. In addition, many end-users and other learners are working in the context of increased work and time pressures, and so demand a shift in balance from face-to-face training sessions to ones that involve a more flexible blend of face-to-face and e-learning activities. In addition, many people want flexible training opportunities that are explicitly related to their work experiences and so they require programmes that provide an opportunity to develop their knowledge and skills with reference to their practitioner needs.

The parent organization or ILS may require the development of blended e-learning programmes in response to changes in their overall strategy, including their human resource management practices. In addition, they may want to exploit their ICT and training facilities, and also demonstrate the use of leading-edge technologies. In the past few years ILS have seen a period of rapid change and they are increasingly becoming realigned with new visions of teaching and learning. For example, there is now a shift towards expanding the traditional library and IT facilities and services to developing 'learning spaces' which include:

- individual study spaces
- group study spaces
- meeting rooms and lecture rooms
- more networked PCs
- spaces for laptops and wireless use
- cafés
- relaxation zones with armchairs and settees
- noisy zones where mobile phones are allowed
- flexible furniture that enables spaces to be reorganized for different kinds of activities
- an increasing array of self-service facilities
- 24-hour access.

An example of an innovative way of staffing a new learning space, a LearningZone, is outlined in Chapter 3. Underpinning these changes is a recognition of a changing vision for ILS and one that is more actively engaged in learning and teaching. Consequently more and more ILS workers are becoming involved in different approaches to designing and delivering blended learning opportunities to their students, end-users or colleagues.

There are many other reasons for developing blended learning programmes. For example, they may be developed as a result of the individual interests and aspirations of library and information workers. In addition, interest in blended learning by senior managers may result in them initiating a project. Individual practitioners may see the opportunity to develop a blended learning programme as a means of enhancing their knowledge and skills (and *curriculum vitae*) with the possibility of new employment opportunities. Finally, blended learning programmes may be initiated as a result of new opportunities, e.g. access to development funds from the parent organization or an external funding agency. Sometimes, ILS go down the route of blended learning as they want to look up-to-date and professional, or they want to 'keep up with the Joneses'.

The development of e-learning and, more recently, blended learning, is located in changes in work and society. Theorists such as Eriksen (2001) and Virilio (2000) argue that society today is characterized by the acceleration and compression of time and space. Eriksen (2001) characterizes this in terms of 'fast time' and 'slow time'. 'Fast time' is linked to the rise in information and communications technology, resulting in increased access to information at ever increasing speeds. Eriksen suggests that this brings advantages to the senders of virtual communications but that it reduces the freedom and flexibility of the recipient. An example of this phenomenon occurs when we open up our e-mail system, particularly after a holiday break, and discover perhaps hundreds of e-mails waiting to be answered. Informal discussions with library and information colleagues often move to concerns about rising workloads, increased demands from customers and other stakeholders, the pressure to become 100% available during working hours via e-mail, discussion groups, chat rooms, messenger systems, landline and mobile phones, as well as in person. One consequence of 'fast time' is that it creates a demand for more flexible approaches to learning and teaching so that the learners may fit it into their busy lives. Another effect of this 'fast time' is that it replaces 'slow time', which is required for certain kinds of emotional and intellectual experiences including reflection (Land, 2006). This is particularly relevant to practitioners who are concerned with introducing e-learning or blended learning as a means of combating work, travel and time pressures. These initiatives may falter or even fail as they increase the pressures on an individual or group, and so produce an additional time burden resulting in less time for reflection and learning. This concept is considered later in this book, e.g. in Chapters 4, 5 and 7.

In many respects, this book has been written in response to these changing demands on library and information workers, and it will provide guidance on managing and delivering good-quality learning and teaching experiences.

What is blended learning?

The term 'blended learning' has risen in popularity in the past five years and is used in a variety of ways both in the literature and also in ILS practice. Informal discussions with colleagues revealed that 'blended learning' was used to mean:

A mixture of face-to-face and e-learning.

The use of different internet-based tools including chat rooms, discussion groups, podcasts and self-assessment tools to support a traditional course.

These quotations provide an impression that blended learning involves a rich mixture of technology-based approaches to teaching and learning, and sometimes a combination of technology-based and classroom-based learning, and this is represented in Figure 1.1.

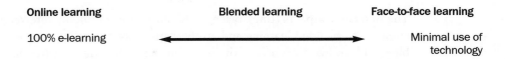

Figure 1.1 Overview of blended learning

A more detailed analysis of blended learning is provided by Sharpe et al. (2006) and adapted here (Figure 1.2), and this identifies the different aspects of learning and teaching which may be blended together:

- time, e.g. synchronous or asynchronous learning activities and communications (see Chapter 2 for a definition of these terms)
- a place where learning takes place, e.g. on campus, in workplace, at home
- different information and communication technologies (ICTs), e.g. CD/DVD, first-generation internet technologies, social-networking software or Web 2.0, or developing technologies
- context of learning, e.g. academic or workplace
- pedagogy, e.g. tutor- or student-centred, behaviourist or constructivist (see Chapter 3 for a definition of these terms)
- focus, e.g. aims of learning process presented by tutors or aims negotiated and agreed by individuals, groups or communities
- types of learner, e.g. learners with different roles, such as student or practitioners, or multi-disciplinary or professional groupings of learners and teachers
- relationships with others in the learning process, e.g. individual learning, group learning, or development of a learning community.

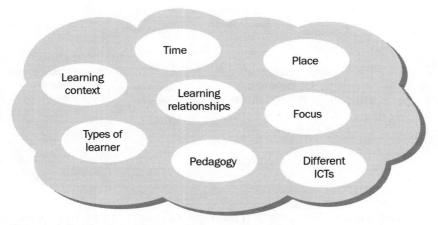

Figure 1.2 The landscape of blended learning

The first three aspects (time, place, technology) are commonly referred to in discussions on blended learning and are perhaps more typical of early examples of blended learning. In contrast, the next four items broaden out the discussion of blended learning and means that this concept could include a combination of work-based and classroom-based activities. For example, a blended learning programme on the topic of project management could involve the introduction of standard tools and techniques in the classroom and then individuals developing their own project based on the needs of their workplace, with support from their tutor and peers via an online discussion group and e-mail. This is illustrated in Figure 1.3. Another approach, illustrated in Figure 1.4, is that of an information-literacy undergraduate programme which uses a wide range of ICTs.

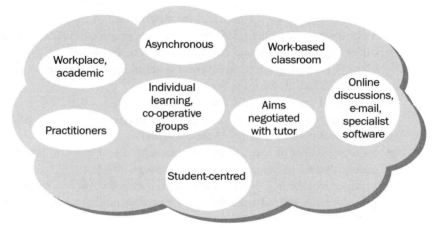

Figure 1.3 Features of a blended learning programme on project management

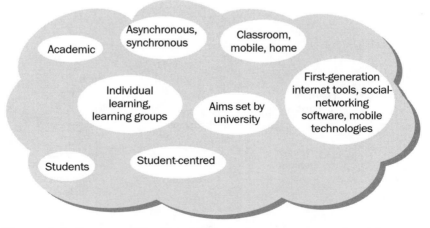

Figure 1.4 Features of a blended learning programme involving a range of technologies

Another approach to thinking about blended learning is to consider it from a historical perspective and Sharpe et al. (2006) offer three distinct models. The first of these is blended learning as a supplement to traditional programmes, e.g. the provision of additional materials and guidance through a virtual learning environment, e-mailing PowerPoint slides to delegates, use of online communication tools such as chat rooms or discussion boards, use of social software such as wiki or blogs, use of online quizzes, or additional resources provided via CD-ROMs or DVDs. This model is linked to the ideas presented by Littlejohn and Pegler (2007), who talk about 'wraparound' activity blending, where face-to-face (F2F) activities are wrapped around e-activities or resources and vice versa. This is illustrated in Figure 1.5.

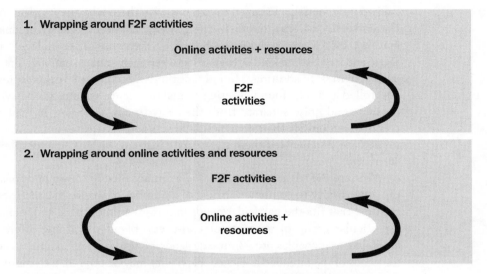

Figure 1.5 Two approaches to 'wraparound' blended learning

The second model is a transformative approach where new or previously existing programmes are designed or redesigned to integrate a wide range of approaches to learning and teaching relevant to the learners and the context of learning. This is the approach considered in Chapters 4 to 6 in this book and it is illustrated in Figures 1.2, 1.3 and 1.4 in this chapter.

The third approach is the learner-led one, which is holistic and typified by the use of a wide range of technologies, including mobile phones and iPods. These are tools that are commonly used on a day-to-day basis, e.g. for social reasons, and are often the preferred communication tools of different groups of learners, e.g. students. How can we engage students (and others) in learning through their preferred technologies (these are described in Chapter 2) – e-mail, social-networking software such as MySpace or Facebook, weblogs, iPods, mobile phones and message systems? My own experiences of students indicate that they use technology in a highly sophisticated way and this often bypasses many formal learning systems (Allan, 2007). They use their mobile phones and message systems, and some have even established weblogs and wikis to carry out parts of their course work, e.g. group work, and produce high-quality products such as reports or websites. They use these technologies not only to exchange information, documents and files, and to plan their face-to-face meetings, but also to discuss and explore ideas and to develop and construct their own knowledge. They appear to continually engage with each other using social-networking software (see Chapter 2) in a way that is radically different from how many people involved in education and training envision learning. What I learnt from these students, probably a fairly typical group of full-time undergraduates, is that they are managing their own technologies and are resourceful and independent. I started to explore with them why they appeared to bypass the university's formal online learning systems. I found that by linking and integrating their learning activities with their everyday use of technologies, they could juggle and strike some kind of balance between their studies, employment and socializing activities. In addition, I found that they wanted to use technologies that they controlled and they found entering formal university systems via passwords cumbersome and quite separate from their day-to-day activities. In contrast, direct communications via their own handheld sets and social sites online was quick and immediate, and enabled them to integrate learning within their complex everyday activities.

What are the advantages of blended learning? Blended learning appears to offer the opportunity to combine the best of a number of worlds in constructing a programme that fits the particular needs in terms of time, space and technologies of a particular group of students or end-users. Blended learning offers increased flexibility, as it enables programme designers to use a variety of approaches to meet the needs of the intended audience. Flexibility may be offered in terms of the organization and delivery of the programme as well as learning and teaching methods. Blended learning programmes may include:

- a rich mixture of face-to-face and/or e-learning
- use of different media including text, audio or video podcasts
- alternative approaches to learning, e.g. choice of reading materials, media, face-to-face and online activities
- alternative approaches to assessment, e.g. written assignments, group assignments, multiple choice tests
- alternative approaches to contacting and working with tutors, including face-to-face sessions, e-mail and message systems, phone, online discussion groups.

Blended learning also offers flexibility of time and space to both learners and tutors. For example, the time involved in physically attending a course may be reduced through the utilization of e-learning activities. Individuals may choose when they engage with their e-learning and select from a menu of opportunities to create an individualized learning experience that meets their needs and interests. One of the great advantages of blended learning is that it offers possibilities of new types of learning groups, e.g. multi-professional and/or international groups, that enable people to learn and work together across traditional boundaries of professions, organizations, geography or time.

One of the rationales for using blended learning is that it will enhance the engagement of learners by providing a rich mixture of learning opportunities. This view acknowledges that individual learners are likely to be interested in and motivated by different approaches to teaching and learning. The different models of learning styles, e.g. Dunn and Dunn (1999) and Honey and Mumford (1992), may be used to support this explanation (see Chapter 3). A recent example, recounted by a colleague, involved a student trip to two very different styles of ILS, a recently refurbished public library and an information centre in a voluntary organization. Following this trip, the students discussed their experiences and developed a detailed online discussion that involved them in comparing and contrasting their impressions, and involved an in-depth discussion about maintaining a quality service. This online discussion opened within two hours of the end of the trip and continued for 11 days. In total the 14 students posted 212 messages about their experience and some of their messages showed that they had visited and evaluated the websites of their host organizations as well as reading the academic literature. This example demonstrates that by using a combination of learning and teaching methods it is possible to engage individuals in a learning experience so that they become motivated to explore and discuss their experiences beyond a specific time-framed activity such as a trip.

There are challenges with blended learning. My own experience is that the planning and design of blended learning programmes is more challenging than that of traditional programmes, e.g. face-to-face workshops, as it is likely to bring together a wider range of people, resources and technologies. This all takes time and sometimes requires detailed negotiations. Another issue is student or end-user expectations, as individuals who sign up for a course may have certain expectations, about the types of learning experiences that they are going to engage in, and if these are not met then they may be disappointed. Other issues may arise in terms of access to and availability of appropriate technologies. Sometimes the firewalls of the participants' employing organizations limit access to aspects of the e-learning systems and this may cause delays and frustration for the learner. If the technology fails, then this may cause major problems with the ability to deliver the programme. I was once involved in the delivery of a blended learning programme which involved extensive use of ICT. A flood in the computing centre that hosted the online learning system meant that we had an unexpected disruption to the course, which was frustrating for both the participants and e-tutors. Issues may arise as a result of unrealistic expectations of stakeholders, e.g. managers may expect blended learning to be a cheap way of delivering training and there is little evidence to suggest that this is the case.

In addition, there is an issue about the use of the term 'blended learning' and this issue is thoroughly explored by Oliver and Trigwell (2005). One question that arises is whether or not you can blend pedagogies. My own view is that a particular blended learning programme will be underpinned by one particular pedagogy but that it is possible to introduce specific activities that are located within another pedagogy. For example, I am currently involved in delivering a management development programme that is underpinned by social theories of learning and where much of the student experience is based around collaborative group work. Within this programme there are two learning activities which are based on a different approach, i.e. we have recorded interviews with guest speakers and these are available as audio files (an example of a didactic approach to teaching and learning) and we also use a formative and summative multiple-choice quiz as a means of enabling the students to develop their use of technical jargon (a behaviourist approach). In theory, this programme presents a pedagogic blend of learning activities but, in reality, it is clearly located within social theories of learning and the students work together and support each other as a learning community throughout the programme. Finally, the language of teaching and learning is in a state of change and flux. At the time of writing, the term 'blended learning' is commonly used in the way in which it is used in this book. However, I anticipate that in a relatively short time the use of the word 'blended' will be dropped. It will become unnecessary, as it will be generally accepted that education and training programmes integrate an appropriate blend of learning activities and experiences.

Structure of the book

The overall aim of this book is to provide a practical guide to library and information workers who are involved in education and training, and who are interested in designing and delivering blended learning experiences to their colleagues and customers. While the focus of subsequent chapters is on the practice of blended learning, relevant underpinning theories of learning are also considered to enable the reader to gain a holistic view of this subject. The chapters in this book have been written so that they can be read in any order.

Following on from this introductory chapter, Chapter 2 presents an overview of the tools and technologies that may be involved in blended learning. The chapter begins by looking at technologies in the classroom and considers tools such as PowerPoint, interactive whiteboards and audience response systems. This is followed by a section that looks at virtual communication tools, starting with a brief history of the development of these tools. A number of communication tools are then outlined and these include: audio files; bulletin boards, discussion lists or e-lists; chat or conferencing facilities; e-mail; instant messaging; news digests and news groups; polling and questionnaire software or webforms; and video-conferencing. Next there is a section on social-networking software which covers instant messaging and phone calls; podcasts, social-networking sites; video clips; weblogs; wikis; virtual tours; and virtual worlds. The next section considers e-learning systems and focuses on subscription-based educational services such as WebCT and Blackboard, which are often called virtual learning environments (VLEs), and freely available e-learning technologies such as Moodle, which is increasingly becoming popular as a means of providing a VLE; subscription-based generic services such as iCohere; group-collaboration software such as Lotus Notes; and freely available group facilities such as Google groups. One of the challenges of writing this chapter has been that the technology is rapidly changing and there is an ever-increasing range of options that may be used within a blended learning programme. Some tools, e.g. standard virtual communication tools, are well established within learning and training activities, while others such as weblogs, wikis and social-networking software are slowly becoming adopted within mainstream education and training programmes. The chapter ends with a brief overview of mobile technologies used to support mobile or m-learning.

Chapter 3 provides an overview of different approaches to teaching and learning, and this is the most theoretical chapter in the book. The first section provides an overview of the physical, virtual and social environments in which learning and teaching takes place. This is followed by a section that considers individual approaches to learning by presenting two different approaches to individual learning styles. Next there is a brief discussion on tutor-centred and learner-centred approaches to teaching and learning. As many blended learning programmes are based on learner-centred approaches this concept is explored in some depth, including the idea that knowledge is socially constructed and that learning is socially situated. Finally, this chapter provides an overview of a range of specific approaches to teaching and learning, including action learning, inquiry-based learning (including problem-based learning, project-based learning and work-based learning) and reflective practice.

Chapter 4 starts with an overview of the design and development cycle and this involves the following stages: needs analysis; design; development; delivery; and evaluation. This is followed by sections that consider a range of topics including: integrating face-to-face and e-learning activities; technical issues; copyright and other intellectual property issues; and finally evaluation. The overall purpose of the chapter is to provide guidance on the factors that need to be taken into account when designing and developing blended learning programmes.

Chapter 5 provides an introduction to the design and use of individual learning activities and this is followed by an alphabetical list and discussion on different learning activities, ranging from action planning to visits. The next chapter, Chapter 6, considers group learning activities and starts by exploring a number of specialist group learning activities, including team building and inquiry-based learning. The latter includes problem-based learning, project-based learning and work-based learning. This is followed by sections on group processes, including the group development process and also team roles; online group learning processes;

working with diverse learning groups; working with large groups; and, finally, working with challenging learners.

Chapter 7 explores working as a tutor and looks at some of the special demands of e-tutoring. It is divided into the following topics: principles of tutoring; e-tutoring; presentations; working with a co-tutor; and managing virtual communications.

In recent years there has been much research in the development of learning communities, particularly with respect to online communities. The concept of a 'community of practice' has become popular and the purpose of Chapter 8 is to introduce and explore this idea and the ways in which it offers opportunities for blended learning. The chapter starts by exploring the concept of communities of practice and these are distinguished from communities of interest. This is followed by an outline of the processes involved in establishing and facilitating a community of practice. Mentoring is an important activity within communities of practice, and a description of the mentoring process concludes the chapter.

Project management is relevant to practitioners involved in blended learning, as they may be asked to manage or contribute as team members to a project. Particularly in the public sector, learning innovations and innovative programmes are frequently developed as a result of gaining external funding, and so they need to be managed as projects. Chapter 9 starts by considering the principles of project management and this is followed by sections on gaining approval and getting going, and managing the project. In addition, this chapter considers gaining accreditation for your programme and also documenting the project. Finally, there is a discussion on working with the project team.

References

Allan, B. (2007) Developing the Best Blend? From blended e-learning to blended learning, *Library and Information Update*, **6** (3), 26–8.

Dunn, R. and Dunn, K. (1999) *The Complete Guide to Learning Styles*, Boston MA, Allyn & Bacon.

Eriksen, T. H. (2001) *Tyranny of the Moment: fast and slow time in the information age*, London, Pluto.

Honey, P. and Mumford, A. (1992) *The Manual of Learning Styles*, Maidenhead, Peter Honey.

Land, R. (2006) Networked Learning and the Politics of Speed: a dromological perspective, *Networked Learning 2006*, Lancaster, University of Lancaster, www.networkedlearningconference.org.uk/ [accessed 21/06/06].

Littlejohn, A. and Pegler, C. (2007) *Prepared for Blended E-learning*, London, Routledge.

Oliver, M. and Trigwell, K. (2005) Can 'blended learning' be redeemed? *E-learning*, **2** (1), 17–26.

Sharpe, R., Benfield, G., Roberts, G. and Francis, R. (2006) *The Undergraduate*

Experience of Blended E-learning: a review of UK literature and practice, York, Higher Education Academy.

Virilio, P. (2000) *The Information Bomb*, translated by Chris Turner, London, Verso.

2 Tools and technologies

Introduction

The purpose of this chapter is to introduce a range of tools and technologies and to consider their application in blended learning. It is divided into five main parts: technologies in the classroom; virtual communication tools; social-networking software; e-learning systems; and mobile learning. As a result of reading this chapter, readers will have an overview of the range of technologies that may be used to support their customers, end-users or colleagues.

Technologies in the classroom

This section considers technologies that are commonly used in face-to-face learning situations. The technologies covered are PowerPoint, interactive whiteboards and audience response systems.

PowerPoint

PowerPoint is a relatively easy communications tool to use but it is too often misused. Its main purpose is to support a presentation rather than to replace the presenter. PowerPoint presentations often include example screen-shots, links to websites or databases, and supplementary materials, e.g. access to audio or video clips. Common problems with the preparation of PowerPoint presentations include the production of too many slides, presentation of too much detail on each slide, and the over-use of sound and other effects. Problems with the use of PowerPoint in the support of presentations include reading off the slides, and its use as a replacement for cue cards.

Well produced PowerPoint presentations tend to:

- be used to present supplementary materials, e.g. images, screen-shots
- use an appropriate level of detail, e.g. no more than seven words per line and seven lines per slide
- use a range of professional images, e.g. photographs
- not use dissolves, spins and other transitions

- make limited and appropriate use of sound effects.

Software such as SnagIT may be used to capture and edit screen images and this enables very professional-looking presentations to be constructed with examples of online searches or the use of specific ICT tools (see www.techsmith.com/snag-it/). In the absence of such tools, it is possible to edit screen-shots using tools, such as Paint, which are available in the accessories folder on most computers. Increasingly PowerPoint presentations are used with interactive whiteboards and/or audience response systems.

Interactive whiteboards

An interactive whiteboard, sometimes called an IWB, is a touch-sensitive whiteboard normally mounted on a wall that allows students and their tutors to participate interactively in taught sessions. It consists of three pieces of equipment: a computer, a data projector, and a touch-sensitive screen or whiteboard. The computer can be controlled from the whiteboard, e.g. by individuals pointing at icons with their finger or through the use of a special electronic 'pen'. These actions are then transmitted to the computer.

> The key feature of this technology is that it emphasises whole-class teaching strategies. These include teacher modelling and demonstration, prompting, probing and promoting questioning, managed whole-class discussions, review of work in progress to reinforce key points emerging from individual and group work, and whole-class evaluation in plenary sessions.
>
> (Becta, 2004a)

In the context of ILS, interactive whiteboards may be used to:

- demonstrate searching techniques, e.g. of a library catalogue, commercial database or the internet
- encourage reading and enhance literacy skills.

Case study 2.1   Research into interactive whiteboard use

Bell (2001) carried out research into whiteboard use and found that 'between 50 and 90 per cent of use of the electronic whiteboard in their institution was for demonstrations such as searching the school library catalogue or commercial databases; however, many of the teachers encouraged or required student input into those demonstrations ("it allows students to interact with instruction – they can come up to the board" and add information to the screen). It was reported that students enjoyed this interactivity and found it interesting and even motivational. It was also reported that the electronic whiteboard was better in this regard than the more familiar computer with digital projector set-up, which, it was said, did not encourage students to provide input to the same extent. On the down side, it was difficult to move the electronic whiteboard equipment and re-calibrate it in a new setting, so that unless all classrooms could be equipped with the technology, then teachers would have to take their class to a room in which the electronic whiteboard was already set up.'

The combination of the use of an interactive whiteboard and an audience response system is described in the next section.

Audience response systems

Audience response systems are commonly seen on TV games programmes where members of the audience use a hand-held set to answer multiple-choice questions or vote on an issue. The use of these systems is becoming increasingly popular in educational settings, where lecture rooms are fitted out with the appropriate technology.

Case study 2.2   Use of interactive whiteboards (IWBs) and an audience response system in information literacy training

This case study has been written up by Jones, Peters and Shields (2007).

IWBs have changed InfoSkills provision greatly as they have allowed a level of participation in training sessions that was not previously possible. Used in conjunction with the specialist software (ACTIVstudio 2 – see www.ioe.mmu.ac.uk/promethean/) they allow trainers to pre-prepare flipcharts (similar to PowerPoint slides) or to annotate over any application that is currently running. MMU Library is also piloting an audience participation voting system (ACTIVote) as part of this software which allows the trainer to conduct votes throughout the session. This keeps the event interactive and allows the trainer to assess if key concepts have been understood by the audience. . . . ACTIVstudio functions have been utilised in MMU InfoSkills sessions in the following ways:

- Using flipcharts to write up keywords from a search query, allowing interaction as students shout out the answers
- Highlighting areas in a PowerPoint presentation or on a website
- Using the timer facility to ensure that set exercises run to time
- Using ACTIVote for knowledge checks and evaluation
- Using ACTIVote to break up lectures and engage the audience.

Since IWBs have been used in InfoSkills sessions the benefits to the Library and the students have been sizeable. Library staff are conscious that the sessions they are running are far more interesting and interactive for the students and as a result the sessions are relaxed and enjoyable for both trainers and participants. Staff who use the boards regularly have stated that they would 'hate to go back to the old style projection units' (staff feedback form) as the boards allow more movement around the room to highlight important areas of a database and offer more chances to engage the audience. Feedback from students and academics has been equally positive. On evaluation forms students highlight the interaction of the sessions and several have mentioned the IWB as a specific reason for their enjoyment of the session.

Virtual communication tools

Virtual communication tools are extensively used in libraries as a means of communicating with their users and they enable many librarians and their end-users to engage in lively discussions and activities over the internet. Online communications provide an important channel for many information workers to communicate with their colleagues and also network across the profession and with other professions. Virtual communication tools are also important in enabling information professionals to exchange information and ideas, work together on a common theme or issue, and work collaboratively in teams. While this is a well-established aspect of library and information professional practice, it has received a new impetus in recent years with the recognition that these professional communities of interest and practice are an important source of individual, team and professional development. The terms 'communities of practice' and 'communities of interest' were coined by Wenger (1998) and this concept is described and discussed in some detail in Chapter 8.

There are two main types of online communication processes, asynchronous and synchronous, and these are described below.

- **Asynchronous tools** – enable people to communicate at a time that suits them. Individuals post a message that is held by the system. This message can be read and responded to as and when the recipient comes online. Asynchronous communications take place over time rather than at the same time. Examples include e-mail, discussion boards, weblogs.
- **Synchronous tools** – enable people to communicate when they log on to the same system at the same time, i.e. they are immediate and live communications. Unlike face-to-face communications, a transcript or record of the communication process is available in most systems. Examples include chat and conference rooms, telephony or phone calls supported by the internet, e.g. Skype, and videoconferencing.

The first generation of virtual communication tools became available during the 1990s and resulted in a range of tools including e-mail, e-lists or discussion lists, bulletin boards, online chat and conferencing, and videoconferencing. The availability of these tools revolutionized teaching and learning and led to the development of e-learning (see Allan, 2002). Many of these tools are available in virtual learning environments and other types of group communications software, and these are explored later in this chapter. These tools continue to form the bedrock of many blended learning programmes and they are described in the next section of this chapter.

In the past few years, the second generation of virtual communication tools, often referred to as social-networking software or Web 2.0, has developed and is now used regularly by millions of people. The aim of social-networking websites is to provide a space where individuals can meet. As its name suggests, social networking is concerned with individuals making connections with others using internet-based tools such as weblogs and wikis, and personal sites using facilities such as MySpace, Facebook and Flickr. Some of these tools, e.g. weblogs and wikis, are currently being integrated into blended learning programmes. At the time of writing, it is difficult to predict the impact that some social-networking software will have on the provision of blended learning programmes within ILS. However, millions of people, and particularly the under-25s, regularly use social-networking software as a way of keeping in touch with friends, making new friends and sharing ideas across the world. For this reason alone it is important that library and information workers know about social-networking software and consider its use within their professional practice. The innovative 'Five weeks to a social library', a free US-based online course for teaching librarians about social software (such as blogs, RSS, social bookmarking and wikis) and its use in libraries, was widely aclaimed in the professional literature in early 2007. All course materials are licensed under a Creative Commons Attribution-Non-Commercial-Share-Alike licence and this means that other libraries have access to these valuable resources (see www.sociallibraries.com/course/ about). This site is well worth visiting as it provides a good example of a blended learning programme that uses a diverse range of technologies. Social-networking software is considered later in this chapter.

Associated with these developments is the use of web feeds or news feeds, of which a common example is the Really Simple Syndication (RSS) feed (Sauers, 2006). This allows information from a variety of internet sources, including news services, information services, podcasts and weblogs (see later in this chapter) to be sent to an individual's website or e-mail account. These are read in readers or aggregators which individuals can use to organize and filter information. Each feed contains a news or information summary and if you wish to read further then clicking onto the headline will lead you to the original source. The advantage of RSS feeds is that they save visiting a variety of sites. The development of RSS feeds has meant that many websites now offer individuals the opportunity to set up a feed by simply clicking on a link labelled RSS or XML (these links are often orange). This means that it is possible to access up-to-date information as it is posted on the internet. While many news feeds are used to distribute text-based information other formats can also be delivered, e.g. audio or video files delivered ready to be played on a computer, iPod or MP3 player, or some mobile phones via podcasting.

First-generation virtual communication tools

A list of common first-generation virtual communication tools is presented with their key characteristics in Table 2.1 and they are explored below. Although these tools are presented individually, in practice they are used in combination, e.g. a blended learning programme may use a mixture of chat, discussion boards, e-mails, online questionnaires and video calls.

Table 2.1 Characteristics of first-generation virtual communication tools

Type of tool	Type of interaction	Asynchronous/ Synchronous	E-learning applications
Audio files	1 to many	Asynchronous	Exchange audio information
Bulletin boards, discussion lists or e-lists	1 to many	Asynchronous	Exchange information Detailed instruction Discussions Collaborative or project work Knowledge construction Follow-up, e.g. training sessions, coaching or mentoring sessions
Chat or conferencing	1 to 1, 1 to many	Synchronous	Exchange information Detailed instruction Discussions Collaborative or project work Knowledge construction Follow-up, e.g. training sessions, coaching or mentoring sessions
E-mail	1 to 1, 1 to many	Asynchronous	Exchange information Detailed instruction Follow-up, e.g. training sessions, coaching or mentoring sessions Knowledge construction Training delivery, e.g. use of e-mail Network
Instant messaging	1 to 1, 1 to many	Synchronous	Exchange information Detailed instruction
News digests and news groups	1 to many	Asynchronous	Exchange information
Polling and questionnaire software or webforms	1 to 1, 1 to many	Asynchronous	Collect information
Videoconferencing	1 to 1, 1 to a few	Synchronous	Exchange information Detailed instruction Discussions Knowledge construction Training events, meetings

Audio files

Embedding an audio file into a web page is a relatively quick and simple way of enhancing web-based learning and training activities. Katharine Widdows (2007) identifies the following potential uses of embedded audio files in her weblog:

- Audio to accompany floor plans on the web site (clickable maps which are synchronised with audio files so users could select, for example 'short loan' on the map, and the audio file would play basic information about short loan while they view a close up image).
- Clickable form layouts (say for inter-library loan forms) with audio files embedded in each section explaining how to fill it in and other relevant points (maybe copyright requirements in this example, etc.).
- Audio accompaniment to web-based tutorials.

In addition, audio files are commonly used as a means of disseminating mini-lectures or interviews with specialists. In particular, they provide an easily accessible tool for individuals who have missed a particular face-to-face session or who wish to listen to a session again. The availability of relatively cheap recording systems that can make high-quality recordings over the telephone means that it is simple and cheap to record telephone-based interviews or mini-lectures and make them accessible to a wider audience. One of the limitations of embedded audio files is that they need to be kept short, i.e. no longer than 15 minutes worth of listening time. They provide an alternative means of accessing information, e.g. for people with a visual impairment or dyslexia. In addition, their use can be supported by an accompanying PowerPoint presentation or transcript.

Discussion boards

As well as sending e-mails to individuals it is possible to send messages to groups via e-lists or discussion lists, bulletin boards and newsgroups. These are all examples of discussion boards at different stages of evolution. They are all organized around a particular topic of interest and they all enable dialogue between many people who share the same rights in terms of accessing and using the system. The technical differences between different types of systems are beyond the scope of this book and, from the perspective of the majority of users, to all intents and purposes they operate like mass group e-mail systems. Discussion groups may be open to any individual interested in the topic and disseminated via open e-mail systems or they may be closed to a small group of people and disseminated within a closed learning environment (see later in this chapter) or via a private e-mail system.

E-lists

There are thousands of e-lists available on the internet and each is devoted to a particular topic and aimed at a specific audience. Mail lists can be used in a variety of ways and, in general, they provide a forum for:

- requests for factual information
- requests for advice and opinions or experiences
- information about new websites, products and publications
- assistance with software or hardware problems
- advice on buying or using new systems
- conference and meeting announcements
- staff development announcements
- information about job vacancies.

Joining or leaving a mail list is a simple matter of sending an e-mail to the relevant subscription service. Information about these lists is available from a number of sources including:

- Topica: www.topica.com/
- JISCmail: www.jiscmail.ac.uk.

For example, JISCmail supports the e-list ARLIS-LINK, of ARLIS/UK & Ireland: the Art Libraries Society. It is possible to search the e-list archives and this means that it provides an important information source.

There are a number of different types of mail lists. Some are open to anyone who wishes to join while others are closed to a specific clientèle. Some discussion groups are moderated, i.e. messages are vetted before being posted to the list, while others are not moderated. Many discussion lists maintain a database of previous discussions and these can be a useful source of information and advice. Some discussion lists develop a FAQ, as this enables new members to tap into key questions and answers without established list members needing to revisit old topics. In order to survive and thrive discussion lists depend on four vital ingredients: content, participation, IT support and management. If one of these elements goes wrong, the mail list may flounder and fizzle out.

Some lists are very active and may generate 100+ messages a day. Two useful facilities for managing this situation include digest messages and mail filtering:

- Digest messages
  Many discussion lists have the ability to send you a digest message. This collates all the messages received that day and sends it out as one e-mail. An index or contents page may be included in the digest.
- Mail filtering
  Most e-mail software has a facility for filtering mail into folders. This means that incoming mail, e.g. from a discussion list, is directed into a separate

folder. This keeps your main inbox clear and means that you can look at these messages when it is convenient for you.

Table 2.2 summarizes the advantages and disadvantages of e-lists.

Table 2.2 Advantages and disadvantages of e-lists	
Advantages	**Disadvantages**
Quick and easy method of communication	Can be difficult to separate out facts from opinions
Provides access to wide group of people	Can waste a lot of time e.g. reading irrelevant messages
Speedy response – sometimes within minutes!	May be overwhelmed by e-mails
Good method of keeping up-to-date	Discussions may be on very specific topics and not relevant to your particular interests
Good method of tapping into practical experience and expertise	Discussion list may be dominated by a few people
Good method of networking	Personal disputes may dominate or sour discussion list
Based on e-mail so doesn't require specialist software	May be used to distribute SPAM

There are thousands of e-lists relevant to library and information, e.g. in Australia the Australian Library and Information Association (ALIA) manages the ALIAnet e-lists, which serve the entire library and information sector in Australia (and overseas) (see www.alia.org.au/alianet/e-lists/). Examples of some of the lists supported by ALIA include:

- **aliaAURORA** Aurora Leadership Institutes and Aurora Foundation e-list
- **aliaBUILD** a discussion list for all aspects of planning library buildings
- **aliaCAREER** a list where librarians can discuss their career issues
- **aliaCATLIBS** ALIAnet list for discussion of cataloguing and related issues
- **aliaCIAN** ALIAnet e-list for community information networkers Australia.

The Chartered Institute of Library and Information Professionals (CILIP) in the UK supports an equally diverse group of e-lists, as does the American Library Association (ALA). Further examples of e-lists can be found at http://lists.topica.com/ or by visiting the websites of professional associations.

These e-lists all offer professional staff the opportunity to share ideas and information, and also network with each other. For staff working in isolation, e.g. solo information workers and many workplace information professionals, they offer a valuable opportunity to break down the isolation that can occur. They also offer an opportunity to gain professional help of the kind that is available from experienced colleagues in large libraries and information services, e.g. specific queries, say, about copyright issues, are likely to be answered with sound professional advice. For information workers who are working towards professional qualifications they offer an opportunity to share ideas and experiences about the qualification process and, again, they can offer a valuable source of support and motivation. This is particularly important to people who are relatively new to the profession and who have not yet built up their own network, as the e-mail discussion list offers a valuable and ready-made network.

An example of a general bulletin board for information and library workers is on the Free Pint website, where the Free Pint Bar enables individuals to post questions and comments. A Student Bar helps students on information courses with academic queries, job search and general career queries. It can be accessed at www.freepint.com.

Bulletin boards or discussion groups

Bulletin boards enable individuals to enter and use a shared e-list feature that may be hosted on a website or as part of a learning environment. Closed bulletin boards are a key component of many blended learning programmes and using a bulletin board or discussion group enables people to come together in different groupings to explore a topic. They may work online to produce a group product, such as a presentation or report. An example screen-shot of a discussion group is presented in Figure 2.1.

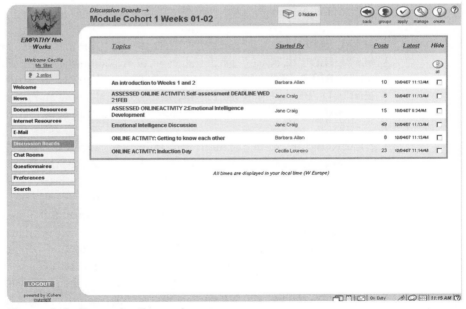

Figure 2.1 Example discussion group

One of the advantages of using a discussion group is that they are asynchronous and so different people can log in and respond to messages or create new messages at a time that suits them. A typical learning environment provides discussion lists with the following features:

- indexes
- a basic search facility, e.g. by topic, author, keywords
- tools to enable you to view bulletins in a hierarchical format (often called threaded or unthreaded) where they are sorted by date/time
- facilities to enable messages to be selected, saved and downloaded
- facilities to indicate whether or not the user has read a particular message, e.g. red flags for unread messages.

While many discussion lists are private closed groups, e.g. to staff working within a particular organization, others are public. It is important to be aware that some people who use them may be using a false name and may have ulterior (possibly sinister) motives for using the bulletin board.

Many discussion groups or bulletin boards provide features whereby messages sent to the board are then forwarded to the private e-mail addresses of individual subscribers. This may occur as and when they arrive at the bulletin board, or as a daily, weekly or monthly digest. Recipients may then have to re-enter the bulletin board to respond to the message or they may be able to send a message to the bulletin board from their private e-mail address.

Chat or conferencing

Chat or conference software enables individuals to hold 'live' discussions by sending each other short written messages. The live discussion could involve two people (chat) or a group (conferencing). Chat software may be used to support individual users, provide quick advice and guidance to a member of staff, e.g. someone at a remote library, or as a coaching tool. Chat software normally enables public and/or private conversations to take place and, depending on the software, these may be with individuals or groups. Chats may take place in public chat arenas or else in private. Some chat software enables individual chat rooms to be set up so that different people can meet in different virtual places. Virtual learning environments include chat or conference software that enables these synchronous conversations to take place and they may be supported by tools such as whiteboards. In addition, they may have a facility for recording or archiving the chat sessions. An example chat room is presented in Figure 2.2.

Chatting online has a number of advantages: it is often a private form of communication, it is immediate and the text can be saved for future reference. Chatting online can be helpful for people with hearing or speech impairments and it can also ease communication among those for whom English is a second language.

Figure 2.2 Example chat room

In addition, the text of chat sessions can be used for training purposes. As with most tools, there are disadvantages to online chat and these include the absence of non-verbal signals and the need to learn how to send and be comfortable with short telegraphic messages between two or more people. Some people don't feel comfortable with this form of communication and there is the potential danger that the other person may log off and 'disappear'. However, an increasing number of people are becoming very experienced with this form of communication and there is an entire internet subculture built around chat.

Many library and information services offer reference services based on chat tools and a list of libraries offering chat services is available at http://liswiki.org/wiki/Chat_reference_libraries. One example is that of the National Library of Australia's AskNow!, a chat online service that is staffed by librarians across Australia (www.nla.gov.au/infoserv/askus.html). In the context of blended learning programmes, chat services provide a valuable way of enabling individuals to have quick conversations, e.g. e-tutor and individual students, student-to-student chat sessions, mentee and mentor discussions.

Conference software provides a facility for a group of people to get together and work in a virtual space by chatting online. This facility is becoming increasingly popular as part of a blended learning programme because it enables large and small groups to work together with or without a tutor. As with one-to-one chat, it does take a while to become comfortable with working in this type of environment.

E-mails

E-mails are a common and simple method of exchanging information. E-mail is regularly used by information workers for both formal and informal learning and teaching activities. E-mail may be used in a variety of ways in blended learning programmes as a means of:

- starting off a programme by sending delegates information about login procedures so that they can access a specialist website
- distributing learning materials
- distributing diagnostic tools, e.g. pre-course self-assessment activities
- enabling learners to gain individual support from their tutor during the life of a course
- enabling one-to-one communications in coaching or mentoring programmes.

The advantages of e-mail are that it is a relatively cheap and accessible approach to contacting individual learners and one that they can access as part of their day-to-day work activities rather than through a special site. It can be used to provide training to large numbers of people in diverse locations, e.g. as a means of providing training activities or materials to library and information workers in a multisite organization.

Case study 2.3 illustrates a blended learning programme that involves minimal use of technology, as it is dependent on the availability of PowerPoint and e-mail. In addition, this example illustrates the blending of a classroom-based workshop with professional practice.

Case study 2.3 Training end-users

I regularly run a two day workshop on training end-users for the professional association, CILIP. The objectives of this workshop are to enable participants to:

- understand the principles of designing successful training events
- identify approaches to running successful training events
- identify a range of strategies for ensuring that their training events include a variety of interesting and memorable activities.

The first day of this course covers the following topics:

- characteristics of effective end-user training sessions
- individual learners and their learning styles
- designing successful training sessions
- running training sessions
- preparation, including contingency planning
- getting off to a good start
- managing the session
- assessing learning
- closing the session

- follow-up activities
- setting up micro-teaching.

There is then a three-week gap during which delegates produce a training plan for a one-hour training session and prepare to deliver one activity or aspect of that plan on the second day of the workshop. Delegates use this as an opportunity to develop a training event that they will then use in their workplace and the opportunity to deliver one aspect of the plan provides a chance to experiment in front of a supportive group of learners.

In between the two days of the course, delegates send their draft training plans and activities to the workshop leader for feedback and comment. This blend of face-to-face workshops with e-mail feedback on work carried out between the two separate workshop days enables delegates to develop high-quality training plans and activities that are relevant to the needs of their workplace.

The second day of the workshop involves delegates sharing their training plan and receiving feedback from their peers, who take on the role of critical friends, and they then deliver one activity or aspect of the plan to the whole group. Again, they receive feedback from their peers. The course closes after sessions on dealing with tricky situations, action planning and evaluation.

E-mail communications may also be used to support informal coaching arrangements and this is explored in Case Study 2.4, where e-mail provided a pragmatic solution to overcoming time and travel limitations.

Case study 2.4 E-mail as part of a coaching process

A few years ago I coached a colleague, whom I shall call Jane, who wanted to gain promotion from her current position in a workplace information unit in the food industry. The overall aim of the coaching process was to enable Jane to be successful in interviews. The structure of the coaching process was a blended solution of face-to-face and online elements. This was for pragmatic reasons, i.e. pressure of time and need to complete the process within four weeks.

The first coaching session was face-to-face and involved identifying specific outcomes and time was also spent reviewing the interview process and good practice. Jane left with a series of specific actions to complete. She kept in touch with me by e-mail and, during this period, I gave her constructive feedback on her curriculum vitae. The next stage involved a practice interview session and it was impossible to arrange a time to meet. So we went online and held the interview using chat software. This enabled me to set up a 'formal' interview process and lead the questioning. Another colleague supported the activity by playing the part of the second interviewer. It was a challenging process for all of us! It required extremely detailed preparation. As we prepared and saved the interview questions on a Word file, this enabled us to cut and paste individual questions into the chat session. The actual interview was extremely intense and required great concentration. In this respect it mirrored the experience of a face-to-face interview. Overall, it was a very effective activity and one of the benefits was the transcript, which enabled us to identify extremely good answers as well as answers that could be improved. We discussed these by e-mail over the next few days.

The final part of the coaching process involved preparation for a presentation. Again, much of the preparatory work was carried out by e-mail and this resulted in the production of a professional presentation. The final stage involved a practice presentation session and this was carried out face-to-face. After three interviews Jane was offered a new position.

Overall, this was an extremely intensive process and it would have been much easier to carry out face-to-face. However, the pressures of our respective schedules and workloads meant that this wasn't possible and the blended solution worked well. One benefit of the experience was that we both gained experience and skills in working through e-mail.

News digests and news groups

News digests may be distributed via e-mail or RSS feeds. One particularly useful example can be found on the prize-winning www.freepint.com site, which offers the following digests via e-mail:

- FreePint Newsletter, which is sent fortnightly and contains tips, features and resources. It is available in PDF format, in plain text with links to HTML version, or subscribers may opt for a brief notification that the newsletter is available online.
- The Weekly Bar Digest provides latest research, and information and questions are published twice a week. It is available in plain text and HTML.
- The Student Bar Digest provides a round-up of the latest postings from the student bar and is only available in plain text.
- The Author Update is a quarterly newsletter for authors interested in contributing to the FreePint Newsletter. It is available in plain text.

Newsgroups have developed from being communications-based on e-mail-like systems to utilizing RSS feeds with a web-based structure, which means that the overall look of the feed tends to be more inviting than an e-mail or e-list. In addition, it is possible to use a tool called an aggregator to combine the feeds from your favourite sites.

Polling, questionnaires and webforms

Increasingly libraries are using online forms or webforms that individuals fill in to request information or help, or in response to a survey. Webforms have a number of learning applications, and common uses include reference services, administration of a training or development programme such as a mentoring scheme, and also as a tool for obtaining information from participants in a blended learning programme.

Webforms are often used as a means of providing a reference service within a library or information unit. Examples of libraries with webforms for reference services include:

- the Library of Congress Ask a Librarian scheme at www.loc.gov/rr/askalib/
- The People's Network in the UK at www.peoplesnetwork.gov.uk/
- The National Library of Australia at www.nla.gov.au/infoserv/askus.html.

Webforms may be used as a tool within staff development processes, for example in a mentoring scheme to enable mentors and mentees to apply to be part of a mentoring programme. An example of this type of application is considered in Chapter 8. Webforms are also sometimes used within blended learning programmes, e.g. as a means of evaluating the programme or obtaining information from participants. Webforms have the advantage that they include a series of prompts, enabling the designer to ask specific questions and so obtain structured information from the respondent. They can also be printed out by the respondent, who may want to use the printed record in a portfolio of evidence. In addition, the responses are normally easy to download into other tools, e.g. database or spreadsheet, so that they can be analysed further.

A more sophisticated approach to obtaining information online is through the use of polling and questionnaire software, which enables you to quickly set up a survey or questionnaire and obtain feedback from a wide range of people. It has a wide range of uses in blended learning, including:

- obtaining feedback from e-learners or e-tutors
- setting up and running simple assessment activities
- organizing meeting times, e.g. online chat or face-to-face sessions.

Polling software is available from a number of sources including SurveyMonkey (www.surveymonkey.com/), which describes its features as:

> Using just your web browser, create your survey with our intuitive survey editor. Select from over a dozen types of questions (single choice, multiple choice, rating scales, drop-down menus, and more . . .). Powerful options allow you to require answers to any question, control the flow with custom skip logic, and even randomise answer choices to eliminate bias. In addition, you have complete control over the colours and layout of your survey.

A wide range of games software is also available over the internet and this may be used to create and disseminate teaching and training games, e.g. quizzes and crosswords. A popular example is Hot Potatoes (http://hotpot.uvic.ca/), which provides six applications that enable you

> to create interactive multiple-choice, short-answer, jumbled-sentence, crossword, matching/ordering and gap-fill exercises for the World Wide Web. Hot Potatoes is not freeware, but it is free of charge for those working for publicly-funded non-profit-making educational institutions, who make their pages available on the web.

Videoconferencing

Videoconferencing has been available for years but previously required specialist and very expensive equipment installed in specialist rooms. In recent years videoconferencing packages have been developed for use on standard desktop computers but, in the context of blended learning, the use of desktop videoconferencing doesn't yet appear to be widely spread in ILS. The use of video calls as part of instant messaging and internet phone services is a relatively new service which has yet to be widely used as part of blended learning programmes. The main advantage of videoconferencing is that it may be used to facilitate meetings or training sessions when the participants are unable to attend a particular venue. It can also save travel costs and time. As with the use of other technologies, it does take some time to become accustomed to managing and running sessions with a number of participants via videoconferencing.

Social-networking software

As mentioned previously, and as its name suggests, social-networking software is now extensively used for networking purposes by friends and families. It is increasingly becoming used in the context of learning and teaching and it is likely that this use will continue to expand rapidly in coming years. Valuable resources on social-networking software or Web 2.0 include the book by Phil Bradley (2007), *How to Use Web 2.0 in your Library*, and his Web 2.0 resources available at www.philb.com/iwantto.htm, and also Karen Blakeman's links at www.rba.co.uk/wordpress.

Instant messaging and phone calls

Instant messaging and phone calls (or internet telephony) used to be quite separate communication tools but the boundaries between the two have recently become blurred, as most messaging systems now let you make voice and video phone calls between other computers and sometimes between landline or mobile phones. Some services that focus on telephony also offer instant messaging.

Instant messaging enables you to send and display a message on someone's screen in a matter of seconds. It is a free service but you may have to accept intrusive adverts.

Instant message systems commonly have friend or buddy lists that watch to see when one of the people on your contact list comes online and then alert you with a small pop-up message so that you can start messaging them. For some people this may sound like a nightmare scenario, although it does offer the opportunity of providing immediate access to help and support. One example of an ILS training application of instant messaging is to provide additional support to staff learning to use a new system. It means that staff working on a busy reference or help desk can message a colleague with a question and obtain an instant response. It obviously depends on both people being online or the relevant instant messaging system. One real advantage of this type of communication is that it doesn't take staff away from their service points and users don't need to know that additional help is being requested. One trainer can support a number of people using this type of system.

Examples of instant messaging software include Windows Messenger (available on PCs running Windows XP), MSN Messenger, AIM (AOL Instant Messenger), Yahoo! Messenger and ICQ. See:

- MSN Messenger: http://webmessenger.msn.com/
- AOL Instant Messenger: www.aim.com
- Yahoo! Messenger: www.messenger.yahoo.com
- ICQ: www.icq.com.

All of these services offer extras such as video and voice calls to other computers, as well as messaging to mobile phones. Skype provides instant messaging, voice calls and video calls. It has the advantage of enabling you to use standard phones as well as other computers, and it doesn't have the disadvantage of pushing adverts at you.

Synchronous communications now include internet telephony, which is the ability to make phone calls via the internet. The advantage of internet telephony is that it enables individuals to make long-distance phone calls through the computer and the internet without incurring expensive phone charges. In addition, it now enables individuals to call regular phones (landlines and mobiles) via an internet connection. It works through technology called VoIP (Voice over Internet Protocol), sometimes also called 'broadband phone'. Individuals using the internet for phone calls need to obtain a microphone for their computer, install internet telephone software and also sort out payment (pay-as-you-go or flat-rate subscription).

A commonly used system is Skype (see www.skype.com), which is rather like a regular instant messaging system with free computer-to-computer phone calls between users. It also allows you to call landline and mobile phones anywhere around the world as well as to make video calls. You can receive calls to your computer from other computers provided that you have a special SkypeIn subscription. Other providers include Net2Phone, DialPad and Babble (see www.net2phone.com, http://voice.yahoo.com/, www.babble.net). Increasingly, organizations are combining internet telephony, e-mail, traditional phones, voice mail, video calls and facsimile transmissions into powerful new, unified messaging services.

Podcasts

Podcasts are a useful tool in a blended learning programme as they may be used as a means of recording guest speakers or interviews, or offering an alternative method of disseminating information through mini-presentations. A podcast is a standalone audio or video file with an RSS feed. They are relatively easy to set up as all that is required is a microphone, computer and appropriate software (e.g. an audio editor such as Audacity, available at www.audacity.sourceforge.net). Once you have recorded and edited your audio file you need to convert it into an MP3 file, e.g. using iTunes (see www.itunes.com). It can then be uploaded and an RSS feed created either manually (e.g. see www.audiofeeds.org) or automatically (e.g. see www.feedburner.com). Finally, you need to publish your podcast and make it available on your website or learning environment.

Social-networking sites

Communication tools such as MySpace (www.myspace.com), Friendster (www.friendster.com) and FaceBook (www.facebook.com) enable individuals to create a personalized website where they post photographs, text, weblinks, collect their personal e-mail, and host chat sessions and bulletin boards. Depending on the provider, individuals may restrict access to their website to named contacts or the website may be open to anyone. These sites are extensively used by millions of people and they provide a lively online community. In addition to these general sites there are specialist sites focused on a specific topic, e.g. online book clubs at www.librarything.com/ and www.bookcrossing.com/. A number of libraries have made use of this facility, including Brooklyn College Library (www.myspace.com/brooklyncollegelibrary), University of Texas Library (www.myspace.com/utlibraries), and Westmont Public Library (www.myspace.com/westmontlibrary), whose website in MySpace is presented in Figure 2.3.

Another example of social-networking sites is specialist photographic sites such as Flickr (www.flickr.com/), which is a site that enables individuals to store, search, sort and share photographs. Within this site there is a specialist site for librarians (e.g. www.flickr.com/groups/librariesandlibrarians/discuss/169806/), which acts as a focus for sharing experience with Flickr, with discussions on topics such as privacy issues raised by sharing photographs of library events on the site. Stephens (2006) identifies ten ways of using Flickr in public libraries, via his weblog at http://tametheweb.com, as follows:

1 To highlight new materials
2 To show the face of the teen advisory board
3 To highlight programs and some young library users
4 To create a presence in the site itself
5 To create an easy virtual tour for users and staff!
6 To store and use images for wikis, etc

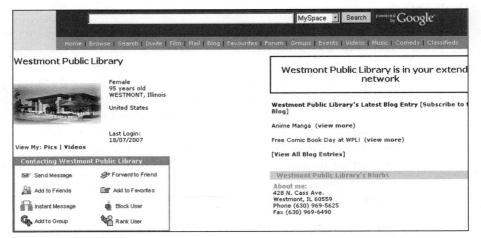

Figure 2.3 Example of the use of social-networking software, MySpace, by a public library

7   To promote what your teens are doing at the library and a book sale!
8   To share the library's history
9   To commemorate the first patron of the new bookmobile!
10   To celebrate Harry Potter Day!

Videoclips

A popular site that enables individuals to disseminate their videos across the internet is YouTube (www.youtube.com). The array of videos available via YouTube is immense and their quality varies accordingly. Other similar sites include www.video.aol.com and http://video.google.co.uk/. Increasingly, ILS are using this type of facility as a means of disseminating brief guides to their users, and popular examples include library tours, library guides by students for students and short topics on general themes such as study skills or time management. An example is given in Figure 2.4. YouTube is a well-used resource and I have used it in two main ways: identifying video clips that are relevant to a particular teaching situation and sending the web links to students via e-mail so that they can view the clips before or after a class; and as a means of disseminating short talks or guest lectures. I find it particularly useful for adding a novelty factor to blended learning programmes and activities, and for engaging students by using a tool that they access in their leisure time.

Virtual tours

Many library and information services offer virtual tours and these may be incorporated into blended learning programmes, e.g. induction talks and activities.
It is possible to create virtual tours without having access to sophisticated

Figure 2.4   Example library welcome video disseminated via YouTube

technology, e.g. using a weblog with video clips, photographs and commentaries. Alternatively, some libraries have the resources to develop 3D computer simulations of their ILS. Good examples of virtual tours include:

- 3-D tour of the Saint Cross Building and Bodleian Law Library at www.chem.ox.ac.uk/oxfordtour/stcrossbuilding/
- 3-D tour of the Library of Congress at www.loc.gov/jefftour/
- Southern Cross University at www.scu.edu.au/students/virtualtour/pages/library.php.

Virtual worlds

Some of the earliest forms of internet synchronous activity were online games through the creation of virtual worlds. These are often referred to by names such as MOO, MUD, MUXe, MUSE or MUSH. These names related to various forms of 'multiple user' environments, which often involve individuals in assuming a character and then becoming involved in virtual role-play. Starting points for exploring these virtual worlds include: MUD Connector (www.mudconnector.com) and MUD Central (www.mudcentral.com).

In recent years the development of large, collaborative online games called 'massively multiplayer online games' (MMOGs) means that it is possible to access three-dimensional virtual worlds and act out or explore a particular character or process. Second Life is a 3-D virtual world for adults aged 18 and over where one can create an avatar or persona and interact with others in a variety of different settings. There is a Second Life library, Infoisland, at www.infoisland.org/. For teenagers aged between 14 and 18 years there is also a Teen Second Life, where no adults are allowed.

Bell, Peters and Pope (2007) write about a Second Life Library project based on the Alliance Library System (www.alliancelibrarysystem.com/), a regional library system with 259 member libraries in Illinois, USA. They write:

> Although gaming is becoming more popular in libraries to attract teens, we only have a couple of libraries offering gaming activities. More libraries are interested, but most people do not understand the relationship gaming has to literacy, learning, digital storytelling, and content creation. Obtaining grant-funded support for gaming in libraries has been difficult, perhaps in part because funding agencies cannot discern the connection between gaming and other aspects of literacy, content creation, and social interaction. Since then, we have been waiting and looking for the right opportunity to get our libraries involved in gaming and virtual worlds – to make library collections and services available. . . .
>
> Since we put out a call for participation, over 150 librarians from all over the world have joined our Google group, which is used for project communication and discussion. Approximately three dozen volunteers are actively involved in developing library services and programs. Our need for virtual space has blossomed. We have gone from a rental space to a small plot of land to an island from an anonymous donor. A builder is working on our main library building, which should be ready in July [2006]. Second Life Library is now part of Info Island, which includes partners such as TechSoup.org, World Bridges, and the ICT (Information Communications and Technology) Library, which provides information on education tools in Second Life for educators.

Again, this is a rapidly developing area and many library and information workers are currently exploring the opportunities that virtual worlds offer to ILS.

Weblogs

Weblogs (blogs) provide a means of personal expression and sharing information via the internet. In some respects a weblog is rather like an online diary or journal owned by an individual who uses it to share their experiences. The structure of weblogs varies but typically they are divided into two or three columns. One column (the central one) normally includes postings or brief paragraphs of opinion, information or personal diary entries, and these are arranged chronologically with the most recent first. In addition, they may contain a contents list, a space for visitors to add a comment below a specific blog entry, and other features, e.g. search tool, favourite web links, etc. Example weblogs include Sheila Webber's information literacy blog, available at http://information-literacy.blogspot.com/; and

Steven Cohen's blog, which is dedicated to resources for professional development, at www.librarystuff.net. They are extensively used within libraries and Sauers (2007) provides a useful summary although, given the nature of the subject, this is likely to become dated quickly.

Weblogs may be used in a variety of ways within a blended learning programme. They may be used as an additional information source, as some weblogs provide access to high-quality information provided by experts. A classic example is Phil Bradley's weblog at www.philbradley.typepad.com/ (Figure 2.5) and I visit this weblog regularly as a means of updating myself on internet and ICT developments. Weblogs may be used as a learning journal and as part of the blended learning process, e.g. individual participants may be asked to keep a blog about their learning experiences, with their colleagues having an opportunity to comment on them. The final blog may then be submitted as part of an assessment activity. Foggo (2007) provides a case study on the use of blogs in teaching and assessing students' bibliographic skills. Foggo writes: 'The blog worked well in that it engaged all the students in considering their objectives for the session. However, it took up too much time and meant that it was hard to get them to re-focus on their group work.' Weblogs may also be used as a means of capturing and reflecting on continuous professional development and working towards becoming a chartered member of a professional association such as CILIP. Two examples of this type of weblog are available at http://charteringbookmouse.wordpress.com/ and http://blogs.warwick.ac.uk/kwiddows/entry/podcast_workshop/.

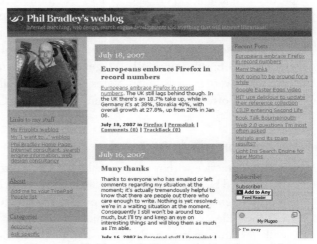

Figure 2.5 Example home page of a weblog

Wikis

A wiki is a web page that can be edited by any reader. One of the commonest examples of a wiki is Wikipedia, which is described as follows:

> Wikipedia is a multilingual, web-based, free content encyclopedia project. Wikipedia is written collaboratively by volunteers from all around the world. With rare exceptions, its articles can be edited by anyone with access to the Internet, simply by clicking the *edit this page* link. The name Wikipedia is a portmanteau of the words wiki (a type of collaborative website) and *encyclopedia*. Since its creation in 2001, Wikipedia has grown rapidly into one of the largest reference Web sites on the Internet.
>
> (www.wikipedia.org)

One of the strengths of wikis is that they provide an opportunity for a large number of people to contribute to a set of ideas and develop a resource. The obvious disadvantage is that there is no editorial control over the material, so the quality of the information is variable. Wikis are relevant to blended learning programmes as they may be used as learning tools by course members. Developing a wiki in a learning environment that is only open to programme members means that it can be used to develop and build a communal resource.

E-learning systems

The previous sections provided an overview of different types of virtual communication tools and social-networking software. This section provides an overview of e-learning systems, i.e. online environments that bring together a range of tools to support e-learning; in some respects they can be considered as 'one-stop shops' for particular learning experiences. There are a number of different approaches to providing an e-learning system: subscription-based educational services such as WebCT and Blackboard, which are often called virtual learning environments (VLEs); open-source systems such as Moodle that offer another approach to developing a VLE; subscription-based generic services such as iCohere; group collaboration software such as Lotus Notes; and freely available software such as the group facilities offered by many internet services, e.g. Google groups.

Virtual learning environments (VLEs)

It is common practice within educational organizations to use an e-learning system or VLE provided by a specialist educational supplier (on either a subscription basis or as a free open-source system) and examples include Blackboard, Bodington, Desire2Learn, Fle3, Moodle, Sakari Project and WebCT. VLEs have revolutionized how colleges, universities and, increasingly, schools deliver their learning and teaching and they are widely used across the world. They support the learning and teaching process within a single software environment. These learning environments are typically owned by the whole institution and supported by a specialist team who manage and administer these large and complex systems.

VLEs typically provide access to the following tools (see also Figure 2.6), which may be organized in such a way that learners only have access to the tools linked

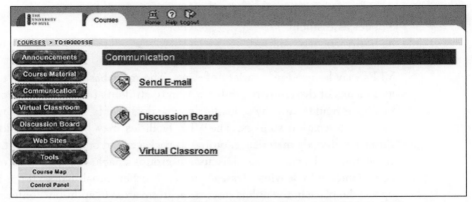

Figure 2.6 Typical set of facilities available in a virtual learning environment such as Blackboard

to their particular programme of study:

- structured learning programmes
- information sources
- communication tools
- assessment tools
- personal management tools
- administrator and tutor tools.

The systems are normally linked to the parent organization's management information systems and this enables data to be transferred between systems, providing automatic enrolment of students onto the VLE and transfer of assessment marks between systems. This type of connected system is often referred to as a managed learning environment.

A growing trend appears to be a shift towards systems such as Moodle (www.moodle.org), which is free, open-source software. Open-source software is freely available to download and adapt to suit a particular institution's needs. One of the main features of systems such as Moodle is that they are incredibly flexible and offer users freedom as to which aspects of the system they wish to use. Moodle has many features expected of an e-learning platform including:

- discussion groups
- chat rooms
- resource management
- quizzes and surveys
- blogs
- wikis
- database activities

- glossaries
- peer assessment
- multi-language support.

VLEs may be used in a variety of ways. The most basic approach is to use them as a means of disseminating information to students through the announcements facility, e-mail facility, by uploading course documents, and providing web links to useful information sources. The VLE facilities may be used to guide students through self-study materials, multimedia packages and online assessment tools, questionnaires and inventories. Discussion groups enable students and/or tutors to communicate by leaving messages for each other. Small work groups may be set up to take place in the online discussion group area. In addition, conference or chat rooms enable pairs or groups of students to hold live chat sessions with each other and/or their tutor.

VLEs provide assessment tools which enable e-tutors to create interactive learning activities, diagnose students' knowledge and skills, monitor student progress, and formally assess student learning. The tutor designs and plans the assessment activity and this can then be input into the assessment tool, e.g. as a set of questions. The types of set that are normally available include:

- select from drop-down-list boxes
- four radio-button responses
- fill-in-the-blanks
- short text
- true-and-false-statements.

Responses are automatically assessed and appropriate feedback is given to both the student and the tutor. The tutor has access to summaries of the students' performances and these may be transferred to a spreadsheet or institutional management information system. Assessment tools enable the tutor to:

- create questions using a set of question types
- arrange questions into sets to be delivered together
- assign attributes to the question set, such as
  — whether the questions are presented in a random order
  — whether the question set is time constrained
  — the pass mark for the question set
- provide feedback on a per-question and/or question-set basis
- provide a copy of the feedback for the student.

The personal management facility enables individual learners to keep a diary, update their user details (if the VLE is part of a MLE then this will update all relevant records), keep track of online results from self-diagnostic tests and formal assessments, and change their password and other personal information.

The tools facility is normally only available to specific users, such as library and information staff, tutors and instructors, and system administrators. It enables individuals to:

- create and manage groups of students
- update and manage the virtual learning environment
- set up and create online assessment tools and activities
- monitor student activity, e.g. login, length of time online, results of online assignments
- view enrolment information.

VLEs typically allow different types and levels of access:

- student or guest access
- tutor access
- administrator or manager access.

Each of these types of access enables the user to work in and manipulate the virtual environment. For example, students are typically allowed access to specific learning materials and resources, they will be able to communicate with other students in their group, and take specific online assessments. Tutors normally have access to student tracking information, e.g. details of logins and online work, and assessment results. Administrators' or managers' access privileges enable them to add new courses and provide access to the system for students and tutors.

As can be seen, VLEs provide an extensive range of facilities, and individual library and information workers will need to spend some time exploring and learning how to use the facilities available on their organization's VLE. Typically a VLE contains online tutorials for students and for tutors or instructors. Working through these is likely to take a couple of hours and will provide a good overview of the system and its capability. In addition, the home websites of these VLEs often provide excellent tutorial and demonstration features as well as product news and FAQ sections.

Conferencing systems

Another range of products that may be used to support blended learning programmes has developed from conferencing systems. These are often subscription-based services and the example used here is iCohere (see www.iCohere.com). iCohere provides a conferencing system with the following range of facilities:

- Relationship building
  — searchable member directory
  — member networking profiles

— *Who's online* with instant messaging
— private group workspaces and discussion areas
— private threads within online discussions
- Collaborative learning
  — online meetings
  — online discussions with group process tools
  — integration of narrated PowerPoint presentations
  — templates for collaborative learning activities
  — integration of web conferencing tools such as LiveMeeting or Webex
- Collaborative knowledge-sharing
  — expert database
  — idea/innovation bank
  — unlimited configurable databases for capturing and sharing structured data
  — integration of *digital stories* (audio, video or narrated PowerPoint)
  — document and link sharing
  — full site-search including active and archived materials
  — project collaboration
- Project management tools
  — task management tools
  — document version tracking
  — document check-in and check-out
  — individual, group and community calendars.

Figure 2.1 shows a discussion thread in iCohere and also shows the range of facilities (see column on left-hand side of screen-shot) and Figure 2.2 shows an iCohere chat room. In general, there is an overlap between the facilities of a VLE such as Blackboard or WebCT and a conferencing system such as iCohere. Perhaps one of the main differences is the 'look and feel' of the different systems, with iCohere presenting a more corporate or business-like image than the educational systems such as Blackboard and WebCT. In addition, systems such as iCohere offer a wider range of facilities aimed at sharing expertise through an experts' database, sharing and developing documents through document systems, and also project management tools.

Group collaboration software

One approach to developing an e-learning site is to use a commercial software product such as Lotus Notes (www.lotus.com), which is a collaborative application owned by the IBM Software Group. Library and information workers in the private sector may have access to this or similar software products within their own organization. Lotus Notes provides a range of facilities including e-mail, threaded discussions, instant messenger, document management, project management and contact management databases. Today Notes also provides blogs, wikis, RSS aggregators and online help systems. Additionally, Lotus provides an extension range of resources which means that it can be tailored to meet the needs of a specific group of learners or community of practice. Group collaborative sofware offers similar facilities to the conferencing systems and it offers easy access to the types of tools required to support a blended learning or e-learning programme, particularly for library and information professionals working in the private sector.

Group sites

Library and information workers who work in a context where they don't have access to a VLE or group collaborative software such as Lotus Notes, and who don't have a budget to purchase or subscribe to an e-learning system, will find that there are many freely available group sites on the internet. These sites have a range of features and, in general, they provide access to noticeboards, space for sharing documents and photographs, blog facilities, e-mail facilities, discussion boards and chat rooms. Unlike the VLEs they don't provide online assessment tools but these could be incorporated using tools such as SurveyMonkey.

Wilson (2007) provides an evaluation of group sites, and highly rated the Windows Live Spaces (http://spaces.live.com), but notes that while this site is particularly useful for disseminating information, its collaborative features are relatively weak. This is in contrast to Nexo (www.nexo.com), which provides excellent collaborative features with group editorship. Other sites include Google groups (http://groups.google.com), Mailspaces (www.mailspaces.com) and Yahoo! groups (http://group.yahoo.com); and even MySpace (www.myspace.com) could be used as a group site for e-learning. This is an area that is rapidly developing, so it is well worthwhile reviewing a range of group sites before deciding on using a particular one.

Mobile learning or m-learning

Increasingly, students and end-users are using mobile technologies such as mobile phones, laptops with integrated wireless cards, personal digital assistants (PDAs) and tablet PCs. The widespread availability of technologies such as Bluetooth devices, digital cameras and MP3 music players such as the iPod is also increasingly being used to support learning. Examples of mobile learning include:

- students using hand-held computers, PDAs or hand-held audience response or voting systems in a lecture room
- students and end-users using mobile technologies such as a pocket PC or mobile phone to enhance group collaboration
- on-the-job training for someone who accesses training on a mobile device, e.g. using a PDA
- hand-held or wearable devices in museums, galleries and libraries, e.g. to provide a guided tour

- MP3 devices such as an iPod to listen to podcasts containing lectures or recordings of interviews, watch short video clips, or listen to audio books and newspapers
- mobile phones with online services to enable tutors to send text messages, quizzes and other learning activities
- hand-held dictionaries.

This is a rapidly changing field and new mobile technologies are becoming available on the high street at competitive prices.

Summary

There is an extensive and continuously growing range of tools and technologies that may be used within a blended learning programme. This chapter has provided an overview of commonly used tools and technologies including: technologies in the classroom; virtual communication tools and learning environments; social software; and mobile learning. This is a rapidly growing and changing field, and library and information workers are constantly incorporating new technologies into their teaching and learning activities within blended learning programmes.

References

Allan, B. (2002) *E-learning and Teaching in Library and Information Services*, London, Facet Publishing.

Becta (2004a) *Getting the Most From Your Interactive Whiteboard: a guide for primary schools*, www.becta.org.uk/ [accessed 12 May 2007].

Becta (2004b) *ICT in Schools Survey 2004*, www.becta.org.uk/ [accessed 12 May 2007].

Bell, L., Peters, T. and Pope, K. (2007) Get a Second Life! Prospecting for gold in a 3-D world, *Computers in Libraries*, **27** (1), 10–15.

Bell, M. A. (2001) *Update to Survey of Use of Interactive Electronic Whiteboard in Instruction*, www.shsu.edu/~lis_mah/documents/updateboardindex.htm [accessed on 12 May 2007].

Bradley, P. (2007) *How to Use Web 2.0 in Your Library*, London, Facet Publishing.

Foggo, L. (2007) Using Blogs for Formative Assessment and Interactive Teaching, *Ariadne*, 51, http://ariadne.ac.uk/issue51/foggo [accessed 10 July 2007].

Jones, R., Peters, K. and Shields, E. (2007) Transform Your Training: practical approaches to interactive information literacy teaching, *Journal of Information Literacy*, **1** (1), 35–42.

Sauers, M. (2007) Blogging and RSS: a librarian's guide, *Information Today*.

Stephens, M. (2006) *10 Ways to Use Flickr in Your Libraries*, http://tametheweb.com/2006/11/ [accessed 5 June 2007].

Wenger, E. (1998) Communities of Practice: learning as a social system, *Systems Thinker*, www.co-i-l.com/coil/knowledge-garden/cop/lss.shtml [accessed 12 May 2007].

Widdows, K. (2007) *When I Grow Up I Want to be a Librarian*, http://blogs.warwick.ac.uk/kwiddows [accessed 10 July 2007].

Wilson, M. (2007) Online Community Tools Round Up, *Webuser*, www.webuser.co.uk/products/online_community_tools_3135_index.html [accessed 10 July 2007].

3 Models of teaching and learning

Introduction

The purpose of this chapter is to provide an overview of those theories of learning that are particularly relevant to blended learning. This is an important topic, as understanding the theoretical ideas that underpin learning enables librarians and information workers to design, develop and deliver effective blended programmes and activities. In addition, library and information workers may be involved in working in partnership with colleagues who have a different understanding of learning and teaching; consequently, understanding different pedagogies is sometimes very helpful when working in multi-disciplinary teams.

Learning is a complex and messy business, and it is difficult to summarize learning theories without risking over-simplifying the topic. In addition, although the topics presented in this chapter are organized under separate headings there is much overlap between different ideas. The first topic considers the context of learning, i.e. the physical, virtual and social environments in which learning and teaching takes place. The context of learning helps to shape the types of learning processes that occur and may contribute to motivating or de-motivating learners (and also tutors). This is followed by a section that considers individual approaches to learning by presenting two different approaches to individual learning styles. There is an active debate about the value of the concept of learning styles and some of the research in this area is vigorously critiqued. Learning styles are included here because the concept is widely used in many educational institutions. In addition, it provides a valuable metaphor for thinking about individual approaches to learning and one that enables tutors to understand the need to provide a varied learning experience.

The next section provides a brief overview of teacher- or tutor-centred approaches to learning and teaching. Increasingly, education and training providers, and also individual tutors, are moving from a tutor-centred to a learner-centred approach to teaching and learning. Learner-centred approaches to teaching and learning are explored in more depth, including the idea that knowledge is socially constructed and learning is socially situated. Finally, the chapter provides an overview of a range of specific approaches to teaching and learning that are commonly associated with blended learning and these include action learning, inquiry-based learning (including problem-based learning, project-based learning and work-based learning) and reflective practice.

Context of learning

The context of learning includes factors such as the learning environment (both physical and virtual) and the people involved in the learning process, e.g. the students, tutors and support staff in an educational organization, or colleagues, managers and trainers in the workplace. While some of the elements contained within these factors will be outside the control of individual tutors or programme designers, there are some aspects that need to be taken into account during the design and delivery process.

The environment, both face-to-face and online, is crucial to the success of any learning programme. It is important to provide a comfortable physical environment for face-to-face activities such as lectures and workshops. This view is supported by well-established research by psychologists on motivation (Mullins, 2007) and also some learning style theorists, e.g. Dunn and Dunn (see below). At a very basic level, it is important to ensure that the learning environment is physically comfortable, visually attractive and equipped with an appropriate range of information and communications technologies. Many ILS within the education sector are redesigning their library buildings and moving to providing a variety of learning spaces that support the shift from traditional tutor-centred approaches to learning and teaching to a student-centred approach that involves different types of learning activities (see Chapter 1). Logan and Starr (2005) identify the attributes associated with these changes as including:

- hi-tech facilities
- information arcades
- faculty support centres
- library cafés
- portable and ubiquitous computing
- ample access to public computing
- places for people and their activities.

In addition, modern learning environments include more traditional spaces for accessing and using learning resources such as books, journals and DVDs, as well as printed reference tools.

The design and layout of the online environment is important too. Entering and using a virtual learning environment may be daunting for some people. As a result, it is important to provide clear and uncluttered online guidance, and to design the site so that it is simple to use. If individual learners find the site overwhelming and difficult to use, then they may be tempted to log out, leave the site and do something else. It is much easier to leave an e-learning site than it is to walk out of a classroom. In both physical and virtual learning environments it is important to provide clear guidance and support systems. These may be provided at help desks, via student helpers or learning assistants, via virtual reference desks, or through telephone help lines. Alternatively, they may be provided through handouts and help sheets, which may be paper-based and/or online.

Many factors affect individual motivation to learn and some key ones include a clear reason for learning, e.g. desire to gain a new skill or to obtain a qualification or new job. Providing transparent access to a blended learning programme that clearly identifies the benefits to learners and also the ways in which their learning will be useful to them will help to motivate individual learners. Increasing or maintaining a student's sense of self-esteem and pleasure are strong secondary motivators for engaging in learning experiences. This means that it is important to provide regular feedback so that learners can measure their progress within the learning process.

The attitudes of friends, tutors and support staff will have an important impact on the learners' ability to engage with their blended learning programme. Individuals working within an organization where there is a positive attitude to learning and innovative approaches to learning are more likely to find it easy to engage in and participate in a programme. Tutors who are enthusiastic about and committed to the programme will enable the learners to become active participants. In contrast, negative or cynical attitudes can really inhibit learning. This has important implications for the selection of staff who are involved in the design and delivery of blended learning programmes. Increasingly, student helpers or assistants are providing support in learning zones and their value is illustrated in the following quotations from a student user and a student assistant in the LearningZone at the new learning space at the University of the Arts, London (Christie and Everitt, 2007, 35):

> The student assistants are excellent, friendly and knowledgeable. I think it is good that there is no information desk so there isn't a barrier. And it makes the assistants seem more friendly and helpful. Because the staff are helpful, I have made friends with a few of them as well. (Student user)

> The role of the LearningZone Assistant is to help students with their work by solving their software problems and making them feel more confident about getting on with their work. . . . Before we got our LearningZone t-shirts, students had difficulty finding us for help. Now they find us more easily. Since I started work in the LearningZone, I feel more confident in my own work as I now realize how to find the information even if I don't know the answer when I am helping someone.
>
> (Student assistant)

Learning styles

There are many different models of learning styles and two of them are considered here: the Honey and Mumford (1992) model is selected because it is widely used in schools and colleges and is often referred to in discussions about reflection and reflective practice; the Dunn and Dunn (1999) model is included because it provides a very broad perspective on individual approaches to teaching and learning. There are extensive academic debates about the reliability and validity of different models of learning styles and, in the context of this book, I think they offer a valuable metaphor and framework for thinking about individual approaches to learning.

The Honey and Mumford model (1992) was based on the ideas of Kolb (1984) and is now widely used in both academic and commercial learning and teaching situations. Peter Honey and Alan Mumford found that different people prefer different ways of learning and that most people are unaware of their preferences. They identified four main learning styles (activist, pragmatist, reflector, theorist) and produced tools for identifying them. These tools are widely available online (www.peterhoney.com). Learning about learning styles gives tutors or developers an insight into the range of learning style preferences in a group of learners. The Honey and Mumford model of the learning cycle is shown in Figure 3.1 and Table 3.1 summarizes the main characteristics of the different learning styles.

There are limitations to this model, e.g. it was developed in the context of western approaches to management training in organizations rather than in the context used in this book. The model offers an over-simplification of the learning process, e.g. the diagram suggests that learners move around a cyclical process in a linear manner. My own experience is that learning is a more complex process than is implied by the model; individuals may move around the cycle in a variety of directions and spend varying amounts of time at different stages. In addition, individual learners may be involved in a number of processes at the same time, e.g. my own style of reflection is through activities such as writing or talking. Despite these limitations, this does have the benefit of providing a simple model that learners may

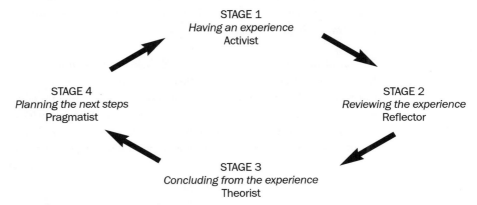

Figure 3.1 Honey and Mumford model of learning styles

Table 3.1   Summary of the main characteristics of the different learning styles (description by John Fewings, Humberside Training and Enterprise Council, 1999)

Activists	Pragmatists	Reflectors	Theorists
Activists are 'here and now' people who are keen to try anything once. They tend to act first and think about the problems afterwards (if at all). They are gregarious people who enjoy being the centre of attention. They are excited by anything lively and vibrant but quickly get bored with the routine and mundane. They are creative in their thinking and come up with innovative solutions to problems but lose interest with the implementation or long term consolidation of plans.	Pragmatists enjoy new theories and techniques. They can often see instant applications and are keen to try out their ideas in practice. They enjoy the challenge of having a problem to solve and quickly come up with practical solutions. They are rather impatient with long-winded planning and discussion, preferring to 'get on with the job'. They are tightly focused – concentrating on the job in hand until it is completed. This can sometimes result in tunnel vision. Pragmatists are often task-oriented rather than people oriented.	Reflectors like time and space to think things through carefully before coming to a conclusion. They listen carefully and gather information to help them make rational and considered judgements. They prefer to act as observers rather than be involved in the thick of things. Because they often adopt a low profile, they may be thought of as quiet or shy. Nevertheless 'still waters run deep' and their considered opinions should not be ignored. Reflectors often find it difficult to make decisions.	Theorists have a methodical and logical approach to most things. They like to analyse ideas in a detached way, asking questions and making mental connections until they have integrated new theories into a comprehensive overview. They are not usually happy with intuitive thinking or subjective judgements. They are often perfectionists with set ways of doing things. Theorists pay attention to detail, which can be of great benefit – or may serve to slow them down and stand in the way of creativity.

use to explore and reflect on their own experiences.

The Dunn and Dunn (1999) model of learning styles (Table 3.2) was developed by researchers in the USA who identified seven dimensions of learning: perceptual, information processing, problem solving, environmental, physiological, emotional and sociological. This model incorporates ideas from Honey and Mumford, and also other researchers. It may be used by developers of blended learning programmes to ensure that they provide a variety of different types of learning situations so that, at the very least, they meet the needs of some of the learners some of the time. The learning style preferences identified by Dunn and Dunn and their implications for course developers are outlined in Table 3.2.

These two models of learning styles are relevant to the design and delivery of blended learning programmes as they provide insights into the diversity of learners and their range of learning needs. Successful programmes will enable learners to take their preferred route through a rich mixture of learning activities that will appeal to a wide range of learning styles. In practice, it is probably impossible to design a blended learning programme that covers all the learning style preferences at all times. So, most programme designers attempt to meet the needs of different learning style preferences at some stage in the learning process. The design of varied blended learning programmes is explored in Chapter 4.

Table 3.2   Dunn and Dunn learning style preferences

Learning dimension	Learning style preferences	Implications for course developers
Perceptual	Auditory Visual – picture Visual – text Tactile +/or kinaesthetic Verbal kinaesthetic	Provide learning and teaching materials in a variety of alternative formats.
Information processing	Analytical – step-by-step Global – metaphor, 'big picture' Integrated – analytical + global	Provide alternative routes through the learning process so that individuals may start with the big picture or develop their understanding a step at a time.
Problem solving	Reflective Impulsive	Provide space for reflection in the course as well as opportunities for action.
Environmental	Sound Light Temperature Seating	Ensure that the learning environment is comfortable and that it is possible to alter the physical environment. Provide the learners with choices about where they learn.
Physiological	Time of day Intake Mobility	Provide the learners with choices about when they they learn. Provide spaces where they may eat and drink while they learn. Enable them to move about.
Emotional	Motivation Persistence Conformity Structure	Acknowledge that different learners are motivated in different ways. Provide positive feedback. Provide structure and scaffolding for learners.
Sociological	Team Authority Variety	Enable learners to work in different groupings, e.g. individually, in pairs, small and large groups. Provide them with access to a tutor or facilitator. Provide variety, e.g. guest speakers, different types of learning activities.

Approaches to learning

There is a vast literature on approaches to learning and, rather than attempt to provide a detailed review of research on this topic, I have identified and explored tutor-centred and learner-centred approaches, and this is followed by a section that considers learner-centred pedagogies in some depth.

Tutor-centred pedagogies

Traditional approaches to teaching were based on the idea that learning involves 'filling up' the learner with knowledge; this is sometimes referred to as the transmission or banking model of education and training. Typical examples of tutor-centred learning and teaching activities include didactic lectures and also traditional computer-aided learning packages that were based on the idea of 'drill and practice'. Examples of learning programmes that are underpinned with this approach to learning include some web-based training programmes that transmit chunks of knowledge to the learner and then use question-and-answer techniques or activities to reinforce the learning. One common feature of this approach to learning is that learners have little choice about what they will learn.

Tutor-centred approaches are sometimes linked to an underlying theory of teaching and learning called behaviourism, in which learning activities and processes are clearly labelled, observed and measured. These are typified by:

- a very specific definition of learning objectives
- material broken down into small chunks and linked in a clear, logical sequence
- emphasis on knowledge and skill reproduction
- learning activities sequenced by the tutor
- frequent tests or reviews; the use of 'model' answers
- regular feedback based on students' ability to achieve outcomes set in the programme
- little awareness or allowance for personal learning needs, interests or negotiation.

The design of many interactive web-based learning packages intended for independent learners working with minimal or no support from a tutor is based on behaviourist principles. This approach to teaching and learning is relevant in certain types of situation where students are required to learn specific information, e.g. definitions of terms or scientific equations. Interactive learning activities based on tutor-centred principles, which enable students to test their specific knowledge and identify gaps that need further work, may be delivered via online or face-to-face activities as part of a blended learning programme.

Learner-centred pedagogies

The past decade has seen a shift in thinking about teaching and learning from a transmission-oriented pedagogy to one that is more open and involves students as active participants in the construction of knowledge and meaning. This approach is linked to the concept of deep and surface approaches to learning (for example see Entwistle, 1981). Individuals who adopt a deep approach to learning are concerned with the meaning of what they are studying and the ways in which an idea will fit into existing knowledge structures. Consequently, they develop a much deeper and more complex understanding of their subject. In contrast, individuals who adopt a surface approach to learning are concerned with remembering the topic, e.g. for an examination, and so have a limited grasp of the subject. This is an important set of ideas, as the implications for individuals who are involved in the design and delivery of blended learning programmes is that they need to build in activities that will help to engage learners in deep rather than surface learning activities. A wide range of group learning processes is used to encourage deep learning, and examples covered later in this chapter include action learning, inquiry-based learning, problem-based learning, project-based learning, work-based learning and reflective practice.

Learner-centred pedagogies are concerned with enabling individuals to experience active and relevant learning experiences. This is illustrated in Figure 3.2.

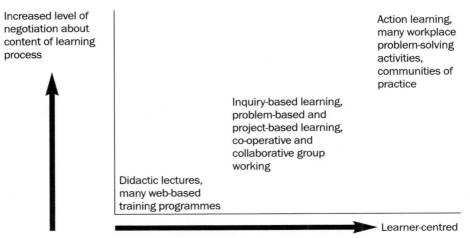

Figure 3.2 Learner-centred approaches

Figure 3.2 illustrates three of the basic tenets of learner-centred pedagogies:

- The learner is actively involved in the learning process.
- Learning is based on real-life and authentic situations that are relevant.
- Learning is a social process.

Actively engaging learners in the learning process means that they are more likely to become motivated to learn and to fully participate in the learning activities. This set of ideas underpins approaches to learning such as inquiry-based learning, problem-based learning, project-based learning, and co-operative and collaborative group learning, and also communities of practice. These approaches to learning tend to involve real-life problems and group work. Learner-centred pedagogies place the learners and their interests at the heart of the learning process. This means that learning programmes are likely to begin by establishing the learners' starting positions, e.g. their current knowledge and skills, and then go on to identify their goals and outcomes. The learning process is likely to be based on real-life and authentic situations that are relevant to the individual learners. This process may involve the learners in discussions about their starting points and learning requirements, and it may mean that they identify how they will achieve their learning goals.

Consequently, learning becomes a negotiated process that involves dialogue between learners and tutors. In the learner-centred model of learning, individuals learn as a result of interactions with others, and what we learn depends on who we are, what we want to become and what we value. This means that learning is placed within the context of a group or a community. Goodyear (2000) summarized this view in the following 'principles of learning', adapted from Darrouzet and Lynn (1999):

- Learning is fundamentally social.
- Learning is integrated into the life of communities.
- Learning is an act of participation.
- Knowing depends on engagement in practice.
- Engagement is inseparable from empowerment.
- Failure to learn is the result of exclusion from participation.
- People are natural lifelong learners.

There is a vast literature base on socially oriented theories of learning and it can be divided into three main movements: constructivism, Soviet socio-cultural theory and situated cognition. These three approaches to learning are not mutually exclusive and there is some overlap between them. One theoretical model that is now closely linked with student-centred learning is constructivist theory. Alexander (1999) describes the three basic characteristics common to constructivist theory as:

- Knowledge is not a product to be accumulated but an active process in which the learner attempts to make sense out of the world.
- People acquire knowledge in forms that make sense to them and enable them to use it in a meaningful way in their lives.
- The construction of knowledge is based on collaboration and social negotiation of meaning. Common understandings and shared meaning are developed through discussions with peers and tutors.

This suggests that in discussions it is important to create a learning environment that will enable students to work in learning groups and:

- exchange their own world maps or mental models
- explore their own ideas and meaning of a topic
- identify and explore ideas between theory and practice
- share their work and academic experiences with each other.

Constructivist theory views knowledge as something which is actively constructed by learners through discussion and negotiation with their peers and tutors, and this process results in common understandings and shared meanings. Many learning activities, including discussions, inquiry-based and problem-based learning, provide a means by which learners can engage in knowledge construction and exchange their own world maps or mental models, explore their own ideas and the meaning of a topic, identify and explore ideas between theory and the practice, and share their work and academic experiences with each other.

The concept of knowledge construction is often linked to collaborative group work that Dillenbourg (1999) broadly defines as 'a situation in which two or more people attempt to learn something together'. He interprets this definition in the following way:

- 'Two or more' may mean a pair, a small group (3–5), a class (20–30), a community (100s or 1000s of people), or a society (10,000s or 1,000,000).
- 'Learn something' means a variety of learning situations including 'follow a course', 'study course material', 'perform learning activities such as problem solving', 'learn from lifelong work practice', etc.
- 'Together' may involve different forms of interaction: face-to-face; computer-mediated – synchronous or asynchronous, frequent in time or not, a truly joint effort or involving the division of labour.

Dillenbourg also suggests that a learning situation is collaborative if the learners are peers at more or less the same level, working towards a common goal, and also working together. He highlights the importance of shared goals negotiated by learners rather than goals that are set by an external agent. The research literature on collaborative learning is complex, as different researchers use different theoretical perspectives and research paradigms. There is a very large literature on collaborative and co-operative learning and it is worth noting that many people seem to use the terms interchangeably. One set of definitions that reflect the concepts of co-operative and collaborative learning is presented as follows:

> Co-operative working includes sharing resources, exchanging information and giving and receiving feedback. Typically co-operative working involves individuals working towards individual goals and outcomes but benefiting from working in a supportive group. If there is an end product it is often possible to identify who contributed to different parts of it.
>
> Collaborative learning groups are likely to involve e-learners working together on a shared goal. This may be a goal that they have agreed and negotiated themselves, or it may be a goal set up by a tutor or other person. Examples include learners working on a joint project, practitioners working together on a joint report or academic article, or colleagues working together on a joint workplace project. If there is an end product it is extremely difficult to differentiate different people's contributions.
>
> (Lewis and Allan, 2005, 132)

An example of a co-operative learning experience is three student librarians co-authoring learning materials. Working co-operatively they decide who will be responsible for writing each section. Although each may obtain feedback from their colleagues, that section will be 'theirs'. In contrast, if they were working together collaboratively then they would discuss the contents of each section together and although one person might lead on each section the others would edit and add their ideas and perspectives to it. In the final product it would be difficult to identify who wrote which part of the learning materials, i.e. they would have achieved a seamless collaborative product. The benefits of co-operative and collaborative learning include increased motivation due to sharing of ideas, support from other learners and 'sparking off ideas'. Additionally research (e.g. McConnell, 2005) suggests that these approaches to structuring learning result in individual learners having a deeper understanding of the material and develop high-quality thinking strategies. McConnell concludes that achievement is generally higher in co-operative situations rather than individualistic or competitive ones.

The use of collaborative group activities in e-learning is common practice and there is an extensive body of literature that illuminates the processes involved in this approach to supporting learning (e.g. Dillenbourg and Schneider, 1994; Hodgson and Reynolds, 2005; McConnell, 2005). Increasingly, a more critical perspective on communities is developing, e.g. Hodgson and Reynolds (2005) critique the notion of 'community' and suggest that it is often applied unquestioningly and is associated with consensus and pressures to conform. They argue that individuals who do not conform to community expectations may become isolated and marginalized.

Vygotsky (1978) suggests that learners are capable of performing at higher intellectual levels when they are asked to work in group situations than when they work individually. Vygotsky talks about the 'zone of proximal development' and suggests that learners' learning is enhanced when working with someone who is more skilled. This idea is supported by other researchers, e.g. McConnell (2000), speaking in respect of collaborative group work in virtual environments, indicated that co-operative methods led to higher achievement than competitive or individualistic ones. He used four indices of achievement: mastery and retention of material; quality of reasoning strategies; process gains, e.g. new ideas and solutions that are generated in a group situation; and transference of learning, i.e. peer learning.

The concept of cognitive apprenticeship, i.e. learning from someone who is more skilled, may be located within socio-cultural theories of learning. The idea is based on traditional apprenticeship and it explores learning from the viewpoint of a new practitioner developing their knowledge and skills by observing and learning from expert practice. Cognitive apprenticeship may involve face-to-face and/or virtual communication processes; it is embedded into authentic work practices and involves a range of instructional methods as well as social activities. Collins, Brown and Newman (1989) provide a framework of six instructional methods of cognitive apprenticeship:

1 Modelling, where the new practitioner learns from observing and copying an expert's practices.

2 Coaching, where the new practitioner is supported through one-to-one support that is likely to include goal setting, instruction, practice, feedback.

3 Scaffolding, where the experienced practitioner provides temporary support to the learner for those parts of the task that they find difficult. This support may initially be extremely active and then the experienced practitioner may fade out as they gradually remove their support in response to the new practitioner developing competence and confidence.

4 Articulation, where the new practitioner discusses their issue or problem and explores it with the guidance of the more experienced practitioner.

5 Reflection, which enables the new practitioner to externalize their internal thinking processes and discuss them with the more experienced practitioner. This is likely to involve a process that includes evaluation, exploring other options or ways of behaving, and action planning.

6 Exploration, where the new practitioner is involved in work-based problem solving. The more experienced practitioner may set guidelines, make suggestions for action, and enable the learner to understand and appreciate the complexity of the problem, underlying issues and its context.

Increasingly virtual communication tools are playing an important role in cognitive apprenticeship and this is explored by Wang and Bonk (2001). Virtual communication tools such as e-mail, message systems, discussion groups and chat rooms provide a medium through which new entrants to the profession can learn from more experienced practitioners. This process is often managed through formal coaching and mentoring schemes or takes place within a community of practice (see Chapter 8). In the context of professional training programmes the concept of cognitive apprenticeship provides a framework for the development of work-based learning activities, e.g. through the use of case studies or problem-solving activities in both face-to-face and e-learning situations. Finally, the process of cognitive apprenticeship may also lead individual practitioners to become actively participating members of communities of practice as they are introduced to and become part of a professional community.

The concept of situated cognition relates to the entry of learners into a community, and learning to learn and work within that community. The community may be located within an educational institution or, as Lave and Wenger (1991 and 2002) suggest, it may take place outside educational contexts, e.g. within professional communities. These learning communities must be in existence over a period of time to enable the participants to interact and learn. Wenger states:

> The development of practice takes time, but what defines a community of practice in its temporal dimension is not just a specific minimum of time . . . [but] . . . sustaining enough mutual engagement in pursuing an enterprise together to share some significant learning . . . communities of practice can be thought of as shared histories of learning.

(Wenger, 1998, 86)

The work of Lave and Wenger (1991 and 2002) is based on a number of assumptions about learning, learners, knowledge, and knowing and learners.

1 **Learners are social beings** and interactions with others are a core component of learning activities and situations.
2 **Knowledge** is a matter of competence with respect to valued enterprises.
3 **Knowing** is a matter of participating in the pursuit of such enterprises, that is, of active engagement in the world.
4 **Meaning** – our ability to make connections between ideas and individual experience – is ultimately what learning is to produce.

Wenger (1998) develops this model further and identifies four components that are required for situated cognition:

1 **Meaning**: a way of talking about our (changing) ability – individually and collectively – to experience our life and the world as meaningful.
2 **Practice**: a way of talking about shared historical and social resources, frameworks and perspectives that can sustain mutual engagement in action.
3 **Community**: a way of talking about the social configurations in which our enterprises are defined as worth pursuing and our participation is recognizable as competence.
4 **Identity**: a way of talking about how learning changes who we are and creates personal histories of becoming in the context of our communities.

The subject of communities of practice is considered in more detail in Chapter 8, which explores ways of facilitating communities so that individuals engage in meaningful acts, e.g. working on real-life problems and then developing a shared practice as a result of engaging with the real-life problems, which is likely to create a shared history, e.g. of successes and failures. This process appears to enable the development of a community which, in turn, provides a means by which individuals may develop their professional identify as members of that community.

Specific approaches to teaching and learning

This section explores a number of specific approaches to teaching and learning, including action learning, inquiry-based learning (including problem-based learning, project-based learning and work-based learning) and reflective practice.

Action learning

Action learning was developed from the work of Revans (1980) and it is commonly associated with management education and development (Pedler, Burgoyne and Boydell, 2001). It involves a small group of people coming together and working on a specific 'live' problem or issue; action learning emphasizes the importance of experience and action. Figure 3.3 provides an overview of the action learning process.

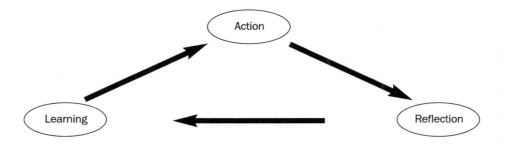

Figure 3.3 The action learning process

Action learning is a process that is frequently used for working on real-life, complex and 'messy' problems, and it is not uncommon to hear of a group of senior managers who have set up an action learning set as a means of working on a common problem. An important part of action learning is reflection and a small, dedicated group working together, using a mixture of face-to-face and online communication tools, accelerates this reflective process. The stages in action learning include:

- forming an action learning set of six to eight members
- deciding whether or not to have a facilitator who may be a group member or an external facilitator
- deciding how often to meet and how to communicate with each other, e.g. face-to-face and/or online using e-mail, discussion groups and/or computer conferencing
- reaching agreement on the problem(s) to be tackled
- working on the problem(s) within the learning set including reflection-in-action and reflection-on-action (see later in this chapter)
- developing solution(s)
- reflecting on the whole process and its outcomes.

The advantages of action learning are that it enables individuals to share their expertise and gain different perspectives on the particular problem or context. In addition, individuals are likely to learn new approaches to problem solving and also develop their ability to reflect. However, there are some disadvantages to action learning as it is quite a time-consuming process and it is normally limited to problems that have a medium- or long-term solution. In addition, the whole process depends on the skill of the facilitator and the capabilities of the members of the action learning set.

Case study 3.1 Action learning

A number of law librarians working in private-sector law practices came together on a management training course. As a result of this course they realized that they shared a number of work-based problems and they decided to set up an action learning set to work together on these issues. In their first meeting they decided that each member would take responsibility for one of the problems and would lead and co-ordinate activities relating to that problem. The group met once a month in a wine bar and in between meetings they worked together in an online environment using Google groups. Over time they gradually resolved their common work problems. After 18 months, the group decided that they had dealt with their original common issues and closed the action learning set. They continued to meet for an occasional night out in a wine bar!

Inquiry-based learning (IBL)

This term is used to describe a variety of learning and teaching methods that are student-centred and may include problem-based learning, project-based learning and work-based learning. Kahn and O'Rourke (2005) identify the characteristics of inquiry-based learning as:

- students engage with a complex problem or scenario that is sufficiently open-ended to allow a variety of responses or solutions
- students direct the lines of inquiry and the methods employed
- the inquiry requires students to draw on existing knowledge and identify their required learning needs
- the tasks stimulate curiosity in the students, encouraging them to actively explore and seek out new evidence
- responsibility falls to the students for analysing and presenting that evidence in appropriate ways and in support of their own responses to the problem.

IBL enables students to develop a range of transferable skills, including research skills, information and ICT skills, team working, problem solving, critical thinking and reflection, and also self-management. Bruce and Davidson (1996) provide a model for inquiry-based learning which indicates its cyclical nature. This is illustrated in Figure 3.4.

Problem-based learning

Problem-based learning (PBL), an example of inquiry-based learning, is extensively

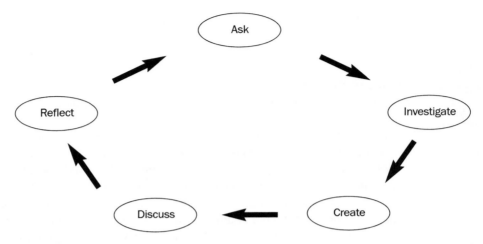

Figure 3.4 Inquiry-based learning

used as a means of enhancing student learning and the basic idea is that the starting point or trigger for learning is a problem, a query or puzzle that the learner wishes to solve (Boud and Feletti, 1991). It is extensively used as an underpinning pedagogy in health and social care education as well as other disciplines. Rankin (1992) found that students who had experienced PBL developed their information literacy skills more quickly than non-PBL students. Rankin's findings suggested that PBL students made increased use of the library and that they also used a much wider variety of information resources. PBL students also became more independent as learners and this was illustrated by their more effective use of reference services.

PBL depends on the availability of realistic scenarios or problem situations that are then used as the focus for student group-work. The problem situations are typically complex and the students may be presented with a wide variety of data, including irrelevant data. In addition, they may be required to search for information using a variety of sources and/or generate their own data, e.g. from experiments or calculations. They are then required to create a possible solution or solutions to the problem, and discuss this in their group and with their tutor or guest speaker. Finally, they are required to reflect on their problem-solving process and their learning. In many respects, PBL attempts to imitate the types of complex situations that professional workers experience in their working lives.

Case study 3.2 Problem-based learning

Penn State University in the USA uses PBL across a wide range of subjects and faculties. Debora Cheney, a librarian at Penn State University, developed a course which aimed to introduce students to PBL and information-literacy skills (Cheney, 2004). She developed a list of specific resources which students could use when they began the information retrieval part of their PBL learning exercise. Students attended a library session where each PBL group was asked to use and critically evaluate different databases as a means of answering a question related to their PBL activity. The librarian's role was that of facilitator and at the end of the activity each PBL group presented its findings to the entire group. An evaluation of this activity indicated that it was extremely effective.

Savin-Baden (2003 and 2006) describes the process of PBL as involving the students or practitioners in working through the following stages, which may take place over a number of weeks or months:

- Initial group activities
  1. Study the problem.
  2. Identify what you need to know to be able to solve the problem.
  3. Identify the group learning needs.
  4. Allocate the learning needs to individuals.
- Individual activity
  5. Research and achieve learning needs.
- Group activities
  6. Peer teach outcomes of individual research.
  7. Reassess overall goals in light of outcomes of individual research and group discussions.
  8. Formulate action plan for managing or resolving the problem. This may result in the production of a specific output, e.g. proposal, fact sheet, presentation or report.

Another way of thinking about PBL is to imagine that the problem is at the centre of the learning process and that the students or practitioners develop their solution to the problem by accessing a variety of learning and information opportunities. Once they have resolved the problem this is demonstrated by the students or practitioners producing an appropriate output, e.g. report or presentation. In an academic context, this output may form the basis of an assessment process. This process is illustrated in Figure 3.5. One aspect of the PBL process that isn't illustrated in this diagram is the communication processes, and the learners may use a variety of means, including face-to-face meetings and also online communications using tools such as e-mail, discussion groups, chat rooms, wikis, mobile phones and message systems. PBL is also considered in Chapter 4, where the design issues arising from this approach are briefly considered.

Project-based learning

Project-based learning involves students working on a specific project carried out

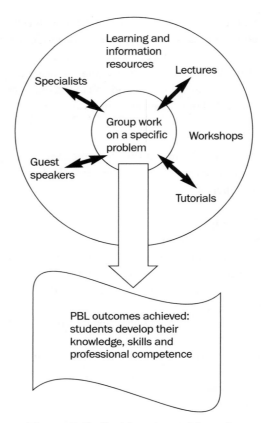

Figure 3.5 Problem-based learning

either independently or as part of a group. Savin-Baden (2003) differentiates between project-based learning and problem-based learning, as shown in Table 3.3. Project-based learning is commonly used in schools, e.g. for history projects on the Romans or Egyptians, or science projects on recycling or global warming, and these are often carried out in the school library with the support of the librarian or teacher, or at home with the support of parents. In colleges and universities project-based learning may be used as an opportunity to enable individuals or groups of students to select and work on a project that is of interest to them. For example, as part of a first-year undergraduate Academic and Professional Skills module at the University of Hull Business School (UK) students are asked to select a topic (from a list provided by their tutor) and use this as the basis of a group research project that enables them to develop their information literacy, team working skills and presentation skills. Tutors provide support via lectures and tutorials, and additional resources, e.g. a guide to business and management information sources, are provided via a virtual learning environment.

Table 3.3 Differences between project-based learning and problem-based learning	
Project-based learning	**Problem-based learning**
Project is used as a means of delivering and enabling student to understand a particular topic.	Problem is core of learning process and student(s) identify their own learning needs.
Project is task-oriented and frequently set by the tutor.	Problem originates from tutor, student and/or workplace.
Tutor supervises and defines project process.	Tutor facilitates.
Students may be required to follow a set process and they are required to produce a solution or strategy to solve the problem.	Students may be provided with problem-solving methodologies but the focus is on problem management rather than producing the 'right' answer.
The tutor may provide supporting lectures that enable the students to carry out the project.	The tutor may provide guidance on problem-based learning. If the whole curriculum is based on PBL then there is likely to be an extensive induction on this approach to teaching and learning.
Students are expected to draw on their existing knowledge and they may be provided with additional lectures that focus on the specific knowledge requirements for the project-based learning activities.	Students are expected to identify and search for the information that they require to solve the problem.

Work-based learning

In this section, the term work-based learning (WBL) is used to mean inquiry-based learning where the focus is on working with and learning from a work-based issue or problem. WBL is commonly used as a focus for continuous professional development, as it enables individuals to work with real problems that are relevant to them and their work. They enable people to share ideas and expertise and perhaps develop innovative solutions to problems.

Case study 3.3 Blended project management course for information workers

I ran a blended learning programme on project management for information workers and this involved a blended mix of face-to-face and virtual workshops. The structure of the programme involved three one-day workshops and in between these days co-operative groups were set up in which participants worked in small groups on their own workplace projects. They used standard project management tools, e.g. MS Project, and gained help, support and encouragement from each other as well as their tutor. The types of projects that participants worked on included:

- implementation of a new integrated information system
- development of a digital learning resource centre
- development of a departmental website
- production of a new set of printed resources
- closure of a learning resource centre.

Overall, the participants achieved the following outcomes:

- They learnt standard project management skills and techniques.
- They applied their new knowledge and skills to workplace information projects.
- They developed new virtual communication skills.
- They internalized the experiences of an e-learner.
- They developed as a community of practice.

Reflective practice

An important component of many student-centred approaches to teaching and learning is the concept of reflection. The Honey and Mumford (1992) and the Dunn and Dunn (1999) learning styles models both include the concept of reflection, and this is considered to be an important aspect of learning processes. It also forms an important aspect of both action learning and inquiry-based learning (including problem-based learning, project-based learning and work-based learning). Practical approaches to reflective practice are considered in more detail in Chapter 5.

Reflection is a natural human activity and typically we reflect on our daily activities, our successes and failures, relationships and careers. This reflective process may take place during other activities – walking, swimming, showering, washing up – and our thoughts and conclusions may be lost as we move on to another activity. The importance of reflective practice is that it helps learners to improve their studying and learning skills. One study of reflective practice (Morrison, 1995) found that learners who were actively involved in formal reflective activities, e.g. by keeping a learning journal, reported:

- increased motivation and confidence – in studying, learning, reflecting, questioning
- greater self-awareness, leading to self-fulfilment
- better-developed professional skills and career self-awareness
- greater understanding of the links between theory and practice.

Reflective practice is used by many professional groups as the basis of their continuing professional development. The current interest in reflective practice has developed from the work of Schon (1991), which focused on developing professional practice, e.g. in the fields of medicine, music, architecture and art. It is used within the ILS profession as a vehicle for professional development through the preparation and presentation of individual learning journals or statements of professional development. While there is an increasing number of approaches and attempts to explore reflective practice, a useful starting point is the idea of reflection-in-action and reflection-on-action. Reflection-in-action is the process of reflecting while the learner is on task. It is a short-term activity and the findings may be used to improve the quality of the outcome of the task. Reflection-in-action tends to be an instrumental activity, which is focused on the immediate task (and its set of routines, strategies or practices) as a means of improving the outcome. The use of a longer-term lens through reflection-on-action enables the learner to look back on a completed task, e.g. an assignment or project, and question, analyse, criticize and evaluate their work. The outcome of this process may then be used to inform the next stage in the learning process, e.g. the next assignment or project.

One of the main difficulties with both reflection-in-action and reflection-on-action is that they require learners to reflect critically on their work. Research suggests that learners find it difficult objectively to reflect on their own work and this idea has been developed further by Schon (1991), who made the important distinction between 'theories-in-use' and 'espoused theories'. This is the difference between what we say (our espoused theory) and what we do (our theory-in-use). The espoused theories include our publicly proclaimed values and beliefs while the theories-in-use include our unconscious values and beliefs and the strategies that arise from them. One of the purposes of reflection is to help learners to uncover their theories-in-use as a means of helping them to improve their performance. Schon suggests that the role of the observer (tutor, peer or even a video recording) is crucial in helping learners shift from identifying their well-known espoused theories to uncovering their theories-in-use. This process may be challenging for the learner and there needs to be a positive relationship between tutor and learner if it is to be successful.

Summary

Learning is a complex, individual and messy business. This chapter started with an overview of the context of learning and this was followed by a summary of two approaches to thinking about individual learning styles. Thinking about learning styles helps programme designers and tutors to consider individual approaches to learning and the importance of providing a varied learning experience. The main focus of this chapter was student- or learner-centred approaches to teaching and learning. In particular, the importance of the people side of learning and the concepts of knowledge construction and group or community approaches to learning were outlined. Associated with these social theories of learning is the current rise in interest in specific approaches to teaching and learning, such as action learning, inquiry-based learning (including problem-based learning, project-based learning and work-based learning) and reflective practice. The use of these social theories of learning underpins many approaches to blended learning and, in particular, the examples that will be presented in Chapters 5 and 8.

References

Alexander, J. O. (1999) *Collaborative Design, Constructivist Learning, Information-Technology Immersion and Electronic Communities*, www.emoderators.com/ipct-j/1999/n1-2/alexander.html [accessed 23 June 2005].

Boud, D. and Feletti, G. (eds) (1991) *The Challenges of Problem Based Learning*, London, Kogan Page.

Bruce, B. C. and Davidson, J. (1996) An Inquiry Model for Literacy Across the Curriculum, *Journal of Curriculum Studies*, **28**, 281–300.

Cheney, D. (2004) Problem-based Learning: librarians as collaborators and consultants, *Portal: libraries and the academy*, **4** (4) 495–508.

Christie, P. and Everitt, R. (2007) No Rules: managing a flexible learning space, *Library & Information Update*, **6** (6), 32–5.

Collins, A., Brown, J. S. and Newman, S. (1989) Cognitive Apprenticeship. In Resnick, L. B. (ed.), *Knowing, Learning and Instruction*, Hillsdale NJ, Lawrence Erlbaum Associates, Inc., 453–94.

Darrouzet, C. and Lynn, C. (1999) *Creating a New Architecture for Learning*. Summary of the outcomes of the Asian Bank Capability Workshop, 9–18 August, Tokyo, Japan, 674–81,www2.nesu.edu/ [accessed 26 February 2002].

Dillenbourg, P. (1999) What Do You Mean By Collaborative Learning? In Dillenbourg, P. (ed.), *Collaborative-Learning: cognitive and computational approaches*, 1–16, London, Elsevier.

Dillenbourg, P. and Schneider, D. (1994) Collaborative Learning in the Internet, Proceedings, *Fourth International Conference on Computer Assisted Instruction*, Taiwan, S10-6–S10-13.

Dunn, R. and Dunn, K. (1999) *The Complete Guide to the Learning Style In-service System*, Boston MA, Allyn and Bacon.

Entwistle, N. (1981) *Styles of Learning and Meaning*, New York, John Wiley.

Goodyear, P. (2000) *Effective Networked Learning in Higher Education: notes and guidelines*, Networked Learning in Higher Education (JISC/CALT), csalt.lancs.ac.uk/jisc [accessed 23 February 2003].

Hodgson, V. and Reynolds, M. (2005) Consensus, Difference and 'Multiple Communities'. In networked learning, *Studies in Higher Education*, **30** (1), 1–24.

Honey, P. and Mumford, A. (1992) *The Manual of Learning Styles*, Maidenhead, Peter Honey.

Kahn, P. and O'Rourke, K. (2005) *Understanding Enquiry Based Learning*, www.aishe.org/readings/2005-2/contents.html [accessed 12 May 2007].

Kolb, D. A. (1984) *Experiential Learning: experience as the source of learning and development*, Englewood Cliffs NJ, Prentice-Hall.

Lave, J. and Wenger, E. (1991) *Situated Learning: legitimate peripheral participation*, Cambridge, Cambridge University Press.

Lave, J. and Wenger, E. (2002) Legitimate Peripheral Participation in Communities of Practice. In Harrison, R. et al. (eds) *Supporting Lifelong Learning*, Volume 1, *Perspectives on Learning*, London, Routledge, 111–26.

Lewis, D. and Allan, B. (2005) *Facilitating Virtual Learning Communities*, Maidenhead, Open University.

Logan, L. and Starr, S. (2005) Library as Place: results of a Delphi study, *Journal of the Medical Library Association*, **93**, 315–27.

McConnell, D. (2000) *Implementing Computer Supported Cooperative Learning*, 2nd edn, London, Kogan Page.

McConnell, D. (2005) Examining the Dynamics of Networked eLearning Groups and Communities, *Studies in Higher Education*, **30** (1), 25–42.

Morrison, K. (1995) Dewey, Habermas and Reflective Practice, *Curriculum*, **16** (2), 82–130.

Mullins, L. J. (2007) *Management and Organisational Behaviour*, Harlow, Prentice Hall.

Pedler, M., Burgoyne, J. and Boydell, T. (2001) *A Manager's Guide to Self Development*, 4th edn, Maidenhead, McGraw-Hill.

Rankin, J. A. (1992) Problem-based Medical Education: effect on library use, *Bulletin of the Medical Library Association*, **80** (1), 36–43.

Revans, R. W. (1980) *The ABC of Action Learning*, Bromley, Chartwell-Bratt.

Savin-Baden, M. (2003) *Facilitating Problem-based Learning: the other side of silence*, SRHE/Open University Press, Buckingham.

Savin-Baden, M. (2006) *Problem-based Learning Online*, Open University Press, Buckingham.

Schon, D. (1991) *The Reflective Practitioner*, San Francisco, Jossey-Bass.

Vygotsky, L. S. (1978) *Mind in Society: the development of higher psychological processes*, Cambridge MA, Harvard University Press.

Wang, F.-K. and Bonk, C. J. (2001) A Design Framework for Electronic Cognitive Apprenticeship, *Journal of Asynchronous Learning Networks*, **5** (2), www.aln.org/alnweb/journal [accessed 8 July 2007].

Wenger, E. (1998) *Communities of Practice: learning, meaning and identity*, Cambridge, Cambridge University Press.

4 Planning and designing blended learning programmes

Introduction

The purpose of this chapter is to provide guidance on the design and development of blended learning programmes. Library and information workers are frequently involved in the development of blended learning programmes and they may be working with ILS colleagues or in multi-professional teams.

This chapter is divided into five main sections. The first section provides an overview of the design and development cycle, and this is followed by sections that consider: developing a blended learning experience including the use of learning objects and developing detailed documentation; technical issues; copyright and other intellectual property issues; and, finally, delivery and evaluation.

Design and development cycle

Spending time on the design and development cycle enables you to focus on developing a blended learning experience that is responsive to the learners and their needs. It enables you to explore and design a programme that provides an appropriate combination of the features of blended learning programmes that were first presented in Chapter 1 and are repeated here:

- time, e.g. synchronous or asynchronous learning activities and communications
- place where learning occurs, e.g. on campus, in workplace, at home
- different information and communication technologies (ICTs), e.g. CD/DVD, first-generation internet technologies, social-networking software or Web 2.0, or new developing technologies
- context of learning, e.g. academic or workplace
- pedagogy, e.g. tutor- or student-centred, behaviourist or constructivist
- focus, e.g. aims of learning process presented by tutors or aims negotiated and agreed by individuals, groups or communities
- types of learner, e.g. learners with different roles, such as student or practitioners, or multi-disciplinary or professional groupings of learners and teachers

- relationships with others in the learning process, e.g. individual learning, group learning, or development of a learning community.

The design and development process for a blended learning programme is cyclical and involves five stages (Figure 4.1):

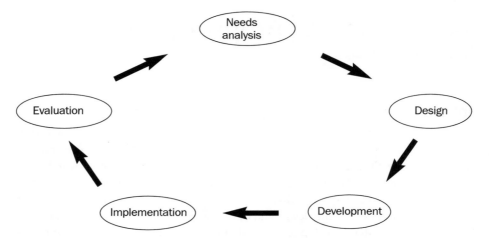

Figure 4.1 Stages of the design and development process

Each of these stages is considered in detail below. Whether the blended learning project is a major one that will run over a number of years and involve a multi-professional project team and hundreds of students or a small-scale project involving an individual information worker, the project leader will need to work through the design and development cycle. This will help to ensure that the blended learning provision is relevant to the needs of the organization/unit/individual and appropriately designed, developed and delivered so that the learners have a relevant and effective blended learning experience, and that the programme is evaluated to ensure continuous improvement.

Needs analysis

The first stage in the design process involves researching the need for the programme and this is likely to produce valuable information. The following questions provide a useful starting point for the needs analysis.

1 Why is there a need to develop this blended learning programme?
2 How will the proposed programme meet the aims and objectives of the library and information service?
3 How would the development of the programme serve the needs of the

library and information service?

4 Who are the potential learners – numbers, their background, ICT background, entry knowledge and skills, special needs, e.g. related to a disability or language skills?

5 How will the programme serve the needs of the learners?

6 What are the draft aims and learning outcomes of the programme?

7 How will the programme be delivered? Face-to-face and/or e-learning?

8 What types of technology will be used, e.g. e-mail, discussion groups, chat rooms, web-based training materials?

9 Will synchronous and/or a-synchronous interventions be used?

10 What will be the balance between practice-based and classroom-based learning?

11 Who will be involved in the design and delivery of the programme?

12 What underlying pedagogical approach(es) will be used in the programme?

13 Will the learners be involved in negotiating their programme aims and outcomes?

14 Will the programme make use of tutor-directed and/or student-centred learning?

15 What time frame do you have in mind for the programme? Identify the duration of the programme. How much time do you think the learners must invest in the programme?

16 How will the programme fit in with other learning and training activities?

17 Does this type of programme exist elsewhere?

At this stage it is also worthwhile considering practical aspects of developing the blended learning programme. The following list of questions will help to clarify what needs to be done before you can move on to the design stage:

1 Who needs to give permission for work to start on the design of the programme?

2 Whom else would it be sensible to consult before you start working on the programme design?

3 Who is likely to be involved in the developing the programme?

4 Who is likely to be involved in delivering the programme?

5 Is there a budget? And if so, what is it?

6 How much time have you got? Work out a rough figure for the next six months.

7 What potential problems may arise in this project?

8 What contingency plans do you need to consider before you get started?

As you research the answers to these questions you are likely to find that you need to consult a wide range of people, including:

- senior managers
- middle managers, supervisors and team leaders
- colleagues
- customers
- intended participants
- colleagues in other ILS.

Once you have carried out this initial research it is worthwhile investing time into producing a brief specification or programme outline. This may then be used to inform the design process and as a briefing document. The specification is likely to contain the following information:

- the working title of programme
- a brief rationale
- information about the intended audience
- aims and indicative learning outcomes
- the level of programme
- the programme structure
- the learning and teaching methods
- the assessment strategy
- information about the duration of programme
- indicative learning hours
- pre-requisites
- links with other programmes
- resource requirements – provider, e.g. ICT teaching laboratory
- resource requirements – learner, e.g. iPod, access to computer and internet
- resource requirements – other, e.g. reading list.

The first stage in identifying the scope of any blended learning programme is to clarify the aims and indicative learning outcomes. If you are working in a team it is essential that the whole team is involved in the process and agrees with the final statement of aims and indicative learning outcomes.

The aims are a broad statement of what the blended learning programme is to achieve. They will answer questions such as:

- What is the purpose of this programme?
- What is the programme intended to achieve?

Example aims include:

- The aim of this programme is to enable new staff to use basic ICT tools.
- The aim of the programme is to encourage young people to read and use information resources.

- The aim of the induction programme is to enable new staff to find their way around the virtual learning environment.
- The aim of the workshop is to enable students to access and evaluate information resources.
- The aim of the workshop is to enable delegates to design and deliver effective end-user training sessions.
- The aim of the programme is to promote mentoring in the information and library community.

Indicative learning outcomes give an indication of the anticipated knowledge and skills that someone will gain from participating in the programme. The use of the word 'indicative' is starting to be used in relation to learning outcomes because the programme designers and trainers can only indicate what they anticipate students will learn if they participate in the programme. Learning outcomes are important because they form the basis for the content of the programme and for all assessment activities. Outcomes must describe things that you are able to demonstrate that you have learned, so it is therefore helpful to avoid using words that describe non-observable states of mind. It is important to specify learning outcomes that are measurable, as this makes it possible to assess what has been learnt. Examples of learning outcomes include:

- By the end of the unit, learners will be able to:
  — print out a report
  — explain how to carry out the issuing procedure
  — list the main functions of the system
  — send an e-mail with an attachment.

When you are writing learning outcomes it is useful to:

- use clear English
- use specific words such as 'explain', 'produce', 'write', 'evaluate'
- avoid general words such as 'develop', 'understand', 'know'.

Figure 4.2 provides useful guidance on words to use when you are writing indicative learning outcomes. Example 4.1 provides an example programme outline and brings together the ideas discussed above about aims, learning outcomes and developing a programme structure.

Analyse	Distinguish between	Identify	Represent graphically
Apply	Evaluate	List	State
Assess	Explain	Outline	Suggest reasons why
Describe	Give examples of	Produce	Summarize

Figure 4.2 Words to use when writing indicative learning outcomes

Example 4.1 Example programme outline

Working title of programme: Training end-users

Brief rationale: ILS staff are increasingly asked to deliver short training programmes to their readers. This programme will enable them to develop the skills needed to design and run an end-user workshop.

Intended audience: ILS staff involved in end user training

Number of participants: 12–16

Aims and indicative learning outcomes

Aims: The aim of this workshop is to enable participants to design and deliver effective end-user workshops.

Indicative learning outcomes:

By the end of the event participants will be able to:

- outline the principles of designing successful training events
- identify approaches to running successful training events
- identify a range of strategies for ensuring that their training events include a variety of interesting and memorable activities
- design and present an interactive exercise.

Level of programme: Introductory workshop

Programme structure

This is a two-day workshop. The second day takes place at least 14 days after the first day and participants will be expected to deliver a mini training session. There will be e-mail contact between trainer and participants between the two days.

Programme content

Characteristics of effective end-user training sessions

Individual learners and their learning styles

Designing successful training sessions

Use of e-learning and blended learning

Running training sessions

Dealing with ICT issues

Managing tricky situations

Action planning

Evaluation

Learning and teaching methods

This is an interactive workshop. The trainer will use a wide range of teaching methods, including presentations, case studies, small group activities, micro-teaching sessions.

Continued on next page

Example 4.1 *Continued*

Learning hours

Participants will attend for 6 hours for 2 days. In addition, they will need to spend up to 3 hours preparing their micro-teaching session for day 2. They will also be encouraged to make use of e-mail support between days 1 and 2.

Pre-requisites

Participants need to be able to use the basic features of PowerPoint and to have access to e-mail.

Links with other programmes

None

Resource requirements – ICT teaching laboratory

Trainer will need access to a general training room with PowerPoint and internet access, and also to an ICT training room.

Resource requirements – access to computer

Participants will need access to a computer and e-mail between days 1 and 2.

Resource requirements – reading list

Allan, B. (2003) *Developing Information and Library Staff Through Work-based Learning: 101 activities*, Scarecrow Press.

Allan, B. (2003) *Training Skills for Library and Information Workers*, Scarecrow Press.

Allan, B. (2002) *E-learning and Training for Library and Information Workers*, Facet Publishing.

Parkin, M. (1998) *Tales for Trainers: using stories and metaphors to facilitate learning*, Kogan Page.

Race, P. (2001) *2000 Tips for Trainers and Staff Developers*, Kogan Page.

In addition to the programme outline it is worthwhile considering how the programme will be managed and this is likely to involve considering the following factors:

- programme management
- recruitment and selection
- induction and learner support
- disability awareness
- technical requirements and support
- library and other learning resources
- accreditation details (if appropriate)
- quality assurance policies and procedures.

Another approach to developing blended learning programmes is to use existing programmes and packages, as this may save time, expense and potential stress. It also means that you are not reinventing the wheel and can build on and learn from other people's expertise. Professional associations such as CILIP sometimes provide pre-packaged training materials that may be used by an ILS. Commercial publishers also provide a wide range of resources. The main disadvantage of using existing programmes or packages is that they may not completely match your needs. However, they can be adapted to meet specific needs. The related topic of learning objects, which are self-contained learning resources or activities that may be re-used in different situations, are considered later in this chapter.

Design

The detailed design process involves taking the programme summary and then working out the detail. This involves considering the following:

1   The aims and learning outcomes
2   The level of flexibility with respect to aims and indicative learning outcomes
3   What the learner must do to achieve the learning outcomes
4   The topics or themes
5   Use of different delivery methods (face-to-face and e-learning)
6   Use of different media (text, sound, vision)
7   Use of learning objects
8   Use of technology, e.g. the type and mixtures of web-based technologies
9   Use of synchronous and asynchronous interventions
10   Use of work or practice-based and classroom-based learning
11   The underpinning pedagogical approach
12   The nature of the programme, i.e. tutor-directed, autonomous or learner-directed learning
13   The detailed learning and teaching strategy
14   The assessment strategy
15   The overall structure, e.g. breakdown into modules
16   The programme content, exercises and activities
17   Supporting materials, e.g. images, examples
18   The logical order and links between different activities and resources
19   How the programme will be delivered to learners – the mix between face-to-face and e-learning; and between independent, co-operative and collaborative learning processes
20   The total number of learner hours
21   The total number of tutor hours
22   The house style
23   Any intellectual property issues
24   Any pre- or corequisites of the learners
25   How the programme will fit in with other learning opportunities.

An important question in the design process is how to produce a programme that is integrated and provides an appropriate balance of different types of learning experience. In Table 4.1 I have developed a schema, presented in Allan (2002) and based on the original work of Alison Hardingham, for face-to-face training programmes and this has been expanded below to cover blended learning.

Table 4.1 14 fundamental design principles for blended programmes

Design principles	Key concepts					
	Credibility	Commitment	Risk		Attention	Flexibility
Maximize opportunities for social interactions		▓	▓	▓		
Maximize action		▓	▓	▓	▓	
Signpost, signpost and then signpost again	▓	▓	▓	▓		
Vary pace and rhythm		▓	▓	▓		
Chunk content			▓	▓		▓
Map the participants' world	▓	▓		▓		▓
Give the participants choices	▓	▓	▓		▓	▓
Surface objections		▓	▓	▓		
Balance theory and practice	▓			▓		
Design in reflective activities		▓	▓		▓	
Design for accessibility		▓		▓		▓
Design in feedback		▓	▓	▓		
Design for closure		▓		▓	▓	▓
Design for support		▓	▓		▓	

1 Maximize opportunities for social interactions

There is a growing body of theory that suggests that learning is a social process (see Chapter 3). The implication of this for designers of blended learning programmes is that is it important to build in opportunities for social interactions throughout the learning process. Typically, this will start at the induction stage of the programme by providing time (either online or offline) for introductions and some appropriate type of ice-breaker activity. This needs to be followed up by structuring the blended learning programme to include opportunities for interaction, e.g. through paired or small-group activities and through the provision of refreshment breaks or a virtual café. The end of the programme needs to include time for individuals to say their goodbyes to each other.

2 Maximize action

This is a key point and involves designing ALL elements of a blended learning programme so that they involve the participants in active learning either individually, in small groups or as a whole group. Online learning needs to be active and to include regular question and answer sessions or other activities. Paired or group work can achieve this. Traditional classroom learning needs to include opportunities for action and interaction, e.g. discussions, individual and small group activities, and whole-class activities, e.g. using audience response systems. The more the participants are involved in the session, the more likely they are to benefit from it. An extensive range of different learning and teaching activities is presented in Chapters 5 and 6.

3 Signpost

As the programme developer and deliverer you will know in detail what is going to happen in the blended learning programme and the design rationale behind it. The participants do not have this information. This is important to bear in mind in online learning, where the participants may be working by themselves.

At any stage in the online aspects of a blended learning programme learners need to know where they are, how they got there and where they can move to next. It is important that the materials are organized in a logical way and that guiding is available. The following facilities are often used to organize e-learning sites:

- a home page with site map
- search tools
- a help facility
- headings
- a menu of contents
- an index
- a glossary
- hotlinks
- bookmarks.

One useful practice is to present the whole programme and highlight completed units, work-in-progress and forthcoming units. This enables the learners to visualize their progress within the whole learning programme. Many virtual learning environments provide these facilities as a standard set of authoring or tutor tools. This means that it is relatively simple for information workers and e-tutors to prepare their learning programme and that they don't need to develop specialized technical skills.

Classroom-based sessions also need to be clearly signposted and guided, and it is important to signpost and guide the participants through the event. Signposting means letting the participants know:

- the structure of the day
- training methods and techniques
- housekeeping arrangements
- why they are doing what they are doing, i.e. the rationale behind each activity
- what is expected of them, i.e. what they will be asked to do

- how they will be working (individually, in pairs, in small groups, as a whole group)
- your expectations, e.g. use of questions, what to do if they don't understand.

One result of signposting in both online and co-located learning situations is that participants feel safe and comfortable. This helps to enhance their learning. A lack of signposting may cause some participants to become lost, confused, angry and/or irritated.

In blended learning programmes where participants are involved in a range of face-to-face and e-learning activities it is often useful to send a daily or weekly e-mail or e-bulletin outlining the learning and teaching activities that need to be completed during that time.

4 Vary pace and rhythm

A learning event is an experience and, as with plays, novels, football matches or music, varying the pace and rhythm will help to enhance the impact of the event. This means thinking through the learning plan and including a range of slow and faster-paced activities.

Slow-pace activities include:

- reading and writing
- small group discussions
- completing questionnaires
- storytelling
- watching a video
- practising a new skill.

Fast-pace activities include:

- high-energy mini-presentations
- jokes and humour
- fast-paced question-and-answer sessions
- activities carried out under a tight time schedule, e.g. an online or classroom-based quiz.

When you are planning the blended learning programme consider how you will create variety in pace and rhythm. You may want to start with a relatively slow activity to enable people to relax in the learning environment, move on to a faster-paced activity, and then end with a slower activity, e.g. a period of reflection. In e-learning activities it is worth bearing in mind that the learners will need to fit them into their day-to-day lives and that they may take much longer to complete than if they were taking place in a classroom. When you are designing face-to-face activities, consider the time of the session and its impact on the learners, e.g. many people have more energy in the morning. Do you want to go with the energy of a group, e.g. the famous after-lunch lull, by including a quiet activity, or do you want to change the energy at this point by including something more upbeat and exciting?

5 Chunk content

Chunking involves breaking down the content of your blended learning programme and presenting it in manageable chunks. This involves identifying how much content will be presented or worked through over a particular time frame. Typically, people's attention may wane in the middle of an activity rather than at the beginning or end of it. By building in lots of breaks (which generate new beginnings and endings) you build in many more learning points into your session.

6 Map the participants' world

This involves matching and moulding the programme so that it fits into the world of the participants. This is achieved by using the same type of language as the participants and by using examples that are relevant to them. It means knowing your learners and working to ensure that all aspects of the blended learning programme map their world. One of the disadvantages of using learning resources (either web-based or classroom-based) that have been developed for another audience is that the language and tone may not fit your group of learners. This can reduce the impact of the materials and mean that some individuals may dismiss the message they convey, so reducing the effectiveness of the learning activity.

7 Give the participants choices

The majority of learners are likely to feel more comfortable and in control of their learning processes if they are given choices during the learning programme. This helps to increase their commitment to the programme, as they feel they are being treated with respect and as adults. The types of choices that may be offered include:

- learning goals
- topics or themes
- learning process(es)
- methods of working, e.g. individual or group
- members for group work
- learning resources, e.g. text, audio or visual
- printed or electronic materials
- timing, e.g. for face-to-face sessions and online chat or conference sessions

- where to learn, e.g. in training room, outside, foyer, café or on computer at workplace or home
- routes through an e-learning programme
- methods of communicating with the tutor, e.g. face-to-face, e-mail, telephone, discussion group or chat room
- examples used on programme, e.g. use of own or prepared examples
- asking questions in private or in a group context
- assessment methods and topics
- different approaches to evaluation and feedback.

8 Surface objections

Sometimes people arrive on a blended learning programme with negative feelings or objections about it. This is particularly true if they have been sent on the programme by their supervisor or team leader. If they do not have an opportunity to voice these feelings, they are unlikely to fully engage in the learning process and they may even attempt to sabotage it. Building in time to surface these objections or criticisms is useful as it means they can be dealt with. Hopefully, the individual will then become engaged in the learning process. Surfacing of objections may be carried out at the start of a programme in either an online or a co-located environment by asking learners to share their hopes, fears and concerns about participating in the programme. Most people will use this as an opportunity to raise any objections or concerns that they have. The tutor can then respond and, hopefully, allay these objections or concerns.

9 Balance theory and practice

There needs to be an appropriate balance between theory and practice within an e-learning programme. A rough rule is 20:80 theory to practice, and for most skills-based training courses spending a maximum of 20% of the time on theory is sufficient. In contrast, if you are involved in delivering a more theoretical programme you will still need to ensure that the theory is broken up, e.g. by activities. If the programme is too dense and theory-driven the participants may quickly become bored and switch off.

10 Design in reflective activities

In Chapter 1, the concepts of 'fast' and 'slow' time were introduced and it is important to introduce time for reflective activities. This allows students and end-users to reflect on and integrate their learning activities. Further information about reflective activities is included in Chapter 5.

11 Design for accessibility

Another important issue is that of accessibility and ensuring that the blended programme is accessible to a diverse range of people. It is worthwhile quoting here from the UK Disabilities Discrimination Act, which states 'Wherever possible courses . . . should be accessible by design, so that only minimal adaptations need to be made for individuals' (DDA, Part 4, Learning and Teaching Good Practice Guide, Disabilities Right Commission). Seale (2006) provides a helpful overview of accessibility research and practice and, writing in the context of higher education, she argues that programmes need to be developed with a 'proactive and flexible design' and this 'involves thinking about the needs of students with disabilities at the beginning of the design process'. Most educational institutions now employ specialists in disability awareness and support, and it is worthwhile contacting them during the design process to ensure that you meet the needs of your students or end-users.

Useful sources on this important topic include:

- W3C (1999) Web Content Accessibility Guidelines at www.w3.org
- Disability Equality Duty (2006) at www.dotheduty.org
- TechDis, a JISC advisory service at www.techdis.ac.uk.

12 Design in feedback

Feedback is an essential part of the learning process. High-quality feedback enhances learning and will increase the motivation of the learner. It also helps to focus attention. Feedback can be built into e-learning events through multiple-choice quizzes that enable the participants to check their understanding. In addition, feedback may be provided by tutors and other participants in the same way as it is in a classroom-based session.

13 Design for closure

Well-designed learning programmes have a clear beginning, middle and end. The beginning and end of each element of a blended learning programme needs to be clearly identified so that the learner is clearly guided through the learning process. As the participants approach the formal end of the blended learning programme it needs to be structured in a manner that promotes a sense of achievement, completion and closure.

14 Design for support

At the design stage consideration needs to be given as to how learners will be supported through the learning process. The types of support that need to be considered include:

- induction support
- use of technical systems
- technical help support
- tutorial support
- peer support
- mentor support.

The types of support will vary depending on the kind of programme and the balance between face-to-face and blended learning. A number of different approaches may be used, e.g. face-to-face support from a trainer, student helper or volunteer, or help desk; or remote support based on the use of printed or electronic resources, telephone or e-mail support. It is important to identify and plan for the preparation of flexible learner support. The following questions need to be answered:

- What type of support will you offer?
- How will you deliver the support mechanisms?
- If they are to be system- or paper-based, who will develop and produce them?
- If they are to be delivered by people, are they available and will they require training and development?
- What resources need to be developed and produced?
- What will it cost?
- How will the support process be introduced to the learners?
- How will the support process be monitored and evaluated?

Developing the programme

This involves taking the proposed programme and producing all the relevant learning activities, learning resources and documentation, and providing management and administrative support. Blended learning also normally requires particular emphasis to be placed on setting up a specialist website or virtual learning environment and establishing the necessary technical support systems.

If possible, it is worthwhile piloting the blended learning programme with a small group of learners. This will help to identify any problems in the programme and will also enable the identification and correction of any errors or problems. Having a trial run on exercises and activities also enables the developers to obtain a sense of the learning experience and whether or not it is manageable, e.g. in terms of time, resources, type of activity. It is often not possible to run a pilot programme and in such cases it is worthwhile asking colleagues, particularly those who have not been involved in the design process, to give their feedback on the programme. Again, this feedback will enable the developers to improve the programme.

Developing a blended learning experience

A popular approach to designing teaching and training programmes is to divide the content into chunks. Figure 4.3 shows a commonly used approach to doing this. It involves dividing the programme into a hierarchy, e.g. programme, module, unit and activity. Different organizations will use different terms for the different levels within a programme. Each level of the hierarchy typically will have its own list of aims and indicative learning outcomes; at the programme level these are very general, while at the activity level they are very specific. A key point in planning programmes is to use the simplest structure possible.

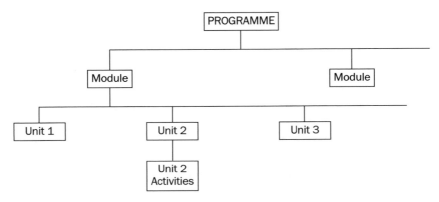

Figure 4.3 Producing an overall programme structure

This type of hierarchical structure may be used with blended learning programmes, and the integration of face-to-face and e-learning will take place at every level, i.e. programme, module, unit and activity. The learning programme may be documented using the structures presented in this chapter (see Example 4.1 on page 76, and Tables 4.3–4.5) and activities in Chapter 5, Figure 5.1 (page 100).

There are different approaches to managing this integration. Two commonly used methods are alternating modes of delivery and 100% integration. Blended learning programmes that alternate modes of delivery may have the types of structure indicated in Figure 4.4.

start					end
e-learning	F2F	e-learning	F2F	e-learning	F2F

F2F	e-learning	F2F	e-learning	e-learning	F2F

Figure 4.4 Alternating modes of delivery

The developing consensus among blended learning practitioners is that, if possible, it is best to start and end with face-to-face activities, as this will help to speed up the start of the learning process and to facilitate a clear and focused end of the programme. However, it is not always possible to start with face-to-face activities and, in this case, it is important to spend time on developing rapport and enabling the learners to engage with the learning process. This concept is explored in more detail in Chapter 6 with reference to Gilly Salmon's model of e-learning. Many blended learning programmes completely integrate face-to-face and blended learning activities. This is indicated in Table 4.2, which provides an example of a blended learning mentoring training programme.

Table 4.2 Example blended learning mentoring training programme

Schedule	Face-to-face activities	E-learning activities
Week 1 Induction	2-hour workshop Introduction to e-mentoring project	Introduction to e-mentoring system. Ice breaker activity.
Week 2 Skills for e-mentoring		Complete mentoring skills inventory. Read and discuss brief guide to mentoring. Identify and agree skills to be covered in next F2F workshop.
Week 3 Skills for e-mentoring	2-hour workshop Skills for e-mentoring	Reflection and review of Week 3 F2F workshop.
Week 4 Developing professional practice		Dealing with tricky situations. Small group work based on case studies.
Week 5 Developing professional practice	2-hour workshop Review of dealing with tricky situations Ethical issues Support for e-mentors Evaluation of training process	Reflection and review of Week 5 F2F workshop.
Week 6 E-mentoring		Start of e-mentoring. Online support provided to e-mentors by trainers.

One technique that is sometimes used to develop integrated blended learning programmes is to use a storyboard. A storyboard is rather like a comic strip that presents a box-by-box or screen-by-screen outline of the learning and teaching process from the perspective of the people involved in the programme. It provides an outline of the learning process with an indication of the activities that individual learners, the whole learning group and tutors will be doing at any stage in the programme. This is presented along a time line. Using storyboards is valuable because it enables programme developers to gain a sense of the learners' experiences, and this may be used to inform and improve the development process.

Chapter 3 presented approaches to learning and teaching such as problem-based learning (PBL). The very nature of many student-centred approaches means that the students or practitioners may carry out parallel or iterative series of learning activities and tasks. This is illustrated in Figure 4.5, where each of the five over-lapping shapes indicates different aspects of the learning process. This diagram doesn't indicate the range of online tools such as e-mails, discussion groups, chat rooms or the social-networking tools such as weblogs that may be used in PBL.

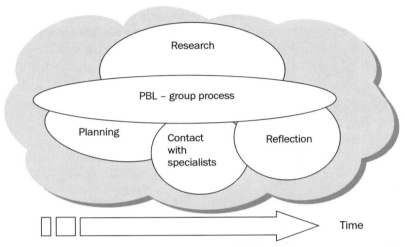

Figure 4.5 A representation of a possible learning process in PBL

Learning objects

Weller, Pegler and Mason (2005) define a learning object as 'a digital piece of learn-ing material that addresses a clearly identifiable topic or learning outcome and has the potential to be reused in different contexts'. An electronic guide to logging in to a database system that includes a clear aim, learning outcome and learning activ-ity with supporting materials is an example of a learning object. Such a guide may be incorporated into a number of different blended learning programmes devel-oped for different end-users. Other examples of learning objects include online articles, PowerPoint slides, digital images or podcasts.

The advantages of developing reusable learning objects is that, as their name sug-gests, they may be used in a wide range of blended programmes and so, in theory, provide a cost-effective means of programme development and delivery. In addi-tion, they provide a means of providing alternative approaches to achieving a particular learning outcome and this may be useful in supporting the needs of stu-dents or end-users with disabilities. The disadvantages of this approach are that the blended learning programme is broken down into small chunks and this may mean that there is an over-simplification of the learning process as a whole, resulting in a programme that is rather sterile.

Documentation

An important aspect of any blended learning programme is the development of appropriate documentation that provides an outline of all the levels of the programme, as indicated in Figure 4.3. The outline structure presented in Example 4.1 (page 76) may be used to document the blended learning programme at the programme and module levels.

At the unit level, which may equate to one to four weeks of a learning experience, the structure presented in Table 4.3 may be used. This shows a ten-day blended learning programme that involves online learning supported by telephone coaching with the tutor. This structure identifies the aims and learning outcomes; the duration of each activity; the topic, tutor and student activities; an estimate of the amount of time a student will take for each activity; informal assessment activities; and the resources. Another example of a detailed structure is given in Table 4.4 and relates to a blended learning process that focuses on plagiarism and referencing. It takes place over a five-day period and involves a range of online and face-to-face (lecture and tutorial) activities. A third example of a detailed plan is given in Table 4.5 and relates to a face-to-face workshop that includes an activity located in a library plus online activities. The degree of detail that is provided at this level of planning should be sufficient to enable an experienced colleague to pick up the plan and run the session for you. Finally, a structure for documenting individual or group activities is presented in Chapter 5, Figure 5.1.

It is important that the blended learning programme is presented using a consistent house style, which makes the whole programme look very professional and means that learners aren't distracted or confused by a number of different styles. The majority of organizations have their own house style for use in electronic and printed communications, and it is important to identify and use in-house guidelines that cover issues such as typeface, font size, choice, size and use of logos. Practical problems may arise, e.g. if the organization's house style is inappropriate for a blended learning programme. This may call for negotiations by the project leader with the appropriate staff, e.g. marketing people.

The help of a graphic designer is invaluable to ensure that the blended learning programme is presented in an accessible way. Although this will add to the cost of the overall project, in the author's experience it is well worthwhile, as the professional skills of a designer with appropriate ICT skills can enhance the blended learning programme and make it highly attractive to the student or end-user. It is also worthwhile involving an overall editor who will check that:

- the content, activities and resources all meet the overall aim and learning outcomes
- the materials all demonstrate the required level and language
- house style has been applied consistently to all elements of the programme
- the learning materials 'hang together' as a coherent whole
- there is 100% consistency between the face-to-face and e-learning sessions.

Table 4.3	Outline structure for the detailed design of a particular aspect, e.g. unit, of a blended learning programme

Title of unit	Introduction to e-learning
Aim of unit	As a result of completing this unit, students will be able to use the Blackboard system.
Indicative learning outcomes	By the end of this unit, students will be able to: • access and find their way around the Blackboard system • take part in an online discussion group and also a chat room session using netiquette • begin to use the online learning resources.

Days	Topic	Type of activity	Tutor activity	Student activity	Student time	Informal assessment activities	Resources
1	Induction Welcome activity	Online	Send introductory e-mail with instructions to students. Facilitate activity.	Receive e-mail. Log into system. Follow online welcome activity. Read guide. Post an e-mail to tutor from Blackboard. Introduce self to other students in discussion group area.	1 hour	Receipt of e-mail by tutor	Text for welcome activity; guide to e-learning
1–7	Help	Online Phone	Available for e-mail, chat room and/or phone help sessions.	Use help as and when required.	30 mins	Not applicable	Guide to e-learning; FAQ list
1–5	Online socialization	Online	Post activity in discussion group area. Facilitate activity.	Read and respond to other students' introductions. Agree ground rules for working online.	2 hours	Evidence of postings	Text for activity; guide to e-learning
5–7	Use of a chat room	Online	Post activity in discussion group area. Facilitate activity.	Agree the time for a chat room session with another student. Talk to each other for up to 15 minutes in a chat room following guidance in activity instructions.	30 mins (includes prep-aration time)	Evidence of postings + chat room transcript	Text for activity; guide to e-learning
8–10	Reflection	Online	Post activity in discussion group area. Facilitate activity.	Post messages in discussion group area identifying learning to date, any concerns and reflection on experience. Read and comment on other students' messages.	60 mins	Evidence of postings	Text for activity

Table 4.4 Example blended learning programme on plagiarism

Title of unit	Introduction to plagiarism					
Aim of unit	As a result of completing this unit, students will be able to reference their work using the Harvard system.					
Indicative learning outcomes	By the end of this unit, students will be able to: • explain why referencing is important in academic work • reference their work using the Harvard system.					
Days	Topic	Type of activity	Tutor activity	Student activity	Student time	Informal assessment activities	Resources
1	Awareness raising	Online	Send introductory e-mail to all students.	Receive e-mail advising them of importance of lecture and the number of students who are caught plagiarizing each year.	5 mins	None	Text for e-mail; plagiarism statistics
2	Introduction to plagiarism and referencing	Lecture	Lecture.	Listen to lecture. Take part in plagiarism quiz activity.	50 mins	Results of quiz	Lecture notes; quiz; handout
2	The students' experience	Online	E-mail audiofile with interview on plagiarism to all students.	Listen to audio file. Contribute to online discussion.	2 hours	Evidence of postings	Text of activity; transcript of podcast for students with hearing impairments
3–5	Correct referencing	Solo	Send e-mail asking students to bring draft assignment to tutorial.	Prepare and bring draft assignment to tutorial.	2 hours	Will bring to tutorial	Text for activity
3–5	Correct referencing	Small group tutorial	Facilitate tutorial.	Assess each others' use of referencing.	50 mins	Give feedback to each other	Handout
1 onwards	Help	Online	Remind students of availability for help – e-mail, phone.	Use tutor help facility.	Various	Evidence of postings or e-mail	Text for activity; handout

Table 4.5 Example blended learning induction programme

Title of unit	Introduction to the layout of the City Public Library for new library assistants
Aim of unit	As a result of completing this event, new colleagues will be able to find their way around the library.
Indicative learning outcomes	By the end of unit, colleagues will be able to: • find their way around the physical and virtual public library • guide readers to relevant departments or sections within the library.

Time	Topic	Type of activity	Tutor activity	Student activity	Student time	Informal assessment activities	Resources
10.00	Introduction	Class-room	Introduction and welcome. Give out folder. Aims and outcomes.	Collect folder. Listen.	10 mins	None	Folder
10.10 – 11.10	Finding your way around the library – quiz	Pairs – library-based	Introduce activity.	In pairs, work through quiz by walking around library and answering questions.	60 mins	Results of quiz	Floor plan; handout
Refreshment break							
11.25 – 11.40	Debriefing activity	Class-room	Facilitate debriefing session. Answer questions.	Listen, question and answer. Contribute to discussion.	15 mins	Evidence of postings	Answer sheet
11.40 – 12.10	Website	Pairs – online	Introduce activity.	In pairs, work through quiz by searching through website.	30 mins	Results of quiz	
12.10 – 12.20	Debriefing activity	Class-room	Facilitate debriefing session. Answer questions.	Listen, question and answer. Contribute to discussion.	10 mins	Questions and answers	Answer sheet
12.20 – 12.30	Question and answer session; Summary	Class-room	Facilitate debriefing session. Answer questions.	Listen, question and answer. Contribute to discussion.	10 mins	Questions and answers	
1 day later	Follow-up 'extension' quiz	Online	E-mail new colleagues with a new quiz.	Complete quiz.	30 mins	Results of quiz	Text for activity; quiz
Follow-ing day	Close session	Online	E-mail colleagues with answers and thank them for their participation.	Read e-mail.	2–3 mins	Not applicable	Text plus answers

Technical issues

A range of technical issues needs to be considered at the design and development stage. Enthusiastic technical people sometimes want to develop learning environments that demonstrate currently available and developing technical features. While these can be impressive they can also put up huge barriers to learners, who may be accessing the system from a relatively old PC using a land line. The following guidelines can be used to develop learning environments that are accessible to everyone:

- Ensure that the programme
  - runs on all supported brands and versions of browsers and browser add-ons, such as plug-ins
  - runs on all supported types of computer at the minimum supported specification
  - is free of software bugs and broken links.
- Minimize the time taken to load pages or files. If the delay is more than ten seconds, then give an estimate of the time to download and reasons why the download will be helpful. Provide alternatives where possible, e.g. script of an audio file.
- Ensure that videos display without breaking-up.
- Ensure that audio clips are free from hisses and other extraneous noises.
- Ensure that page refresh is quick so that the learners' attention is held throughout the process.

A useful source of standards for developing and maintaining e-learning materials is the Institute of IT Training (www.iitt.org.uk/). These have informed the development of this section.

Another issue to consider is that of ensuring that all aspects of the blended learning programme are accessible. Useful information sources are available at Web Accessibility Initiative (www.w3.org/WAI).

Copyright and other intellectual property issues

Copyright is a complex issue and it is very important that programme developers don't accidentally or intentionally infringe copyright legislation. There are very good guides to copyright legislation available, such as on the JISC website www.jisc.ac.uk and that written by Pedley (2007).

Some basic rules in the development of blended learning materials and programmes include the importance of clearly labelling, dating and identifying all learning materials. It is important to obtain written permission if you are using other people's intellectual property, e.g. images, text, sound, animation, list of URLs. Key points to cover when writing for permission include:

- a bibliographic reference for the required material
- a list of the pages, screens and frames
- details of material in preparation: outline materials; audience, size of audience; frequency of use, e.g. three times per year; anticipated life span; proposed use, e.g. educational, not-for-profit, commercial
- details of the organization, e.g. public, private or third sector.

Delivery

The moment of truth! Delivering a new blended learning programme can be exciting and challenging. Once the programme starts, the programme leader or e-tutor is likely to become involved in a number of distinct activities including:

- monitoring the virtual learning environment, learners' and tutor's activities
- monitoring the use of the support systems, e.g. technical support
- informing the programme team of developments
- networking with ILS key staff, e.g. senior managers, to keep them updated on the programme.

Evaluation

This section is concerned with evaluating the blended learning programme to ensure that it has met its stated aims and learning outcomes, and also the changing needs of the information and library service. Evaluation involves gathering information about the blended learning programme and then using this information to measure the value of the programme. What should be evaluated? Evaluation of a blended learning programme is likely to focus on three main issues:

- learning and its impact on the ILS
- the learning environment and learning materials
- the learning process.

Bee and Bee (2007) present a useful and detailed guide to learning evaluation.

Learning and its impact on the ILS

A very popular and simple evaluation model is that used by Kirkpatrick (1994), which evaluates learning programmes and events at four different levels:

- reaction
- learning

- changes in behaviour
- impact on information and library service.

The reaction to the blended learning programme is how learners feel at the end of a unit, workshop or whole programme. This is their immediate response without time for detailed reflection on the event or to apply their learning in another context. The next level of evaluation is concerned with the knowledge or skills someone has gained as a result of the programme. What impact has the programme had on the learner's behaviour in the workplace? Third is the effect of the blended learning programme on the learner's behaviour. The final level of evaluation is the impact on the information and library service – whether the programme is helping it to achieve its business objectives.

Different people may be involved in the evaluation process, e.g. learners and their co-learners, e-tutors, workplace colleagues, team leaders and managers. Involving a number of different people obviously improves the quality of the evaluation, but it also increases the cost (in time and other resources).

An important decision is whether to include the evaluation process as an integral part of the blended learning programme, e.g. all evaluation activities to be carried out as learners work through the programme, or to carry out the evaluation using other means such as e-mail, paper-based tools or face-to-face sessions. In the early stages of running a programme it can be really useful to include face-to-face evaluation sessions as they often produce rich information. Issues that had not previously been considered can then be picked up and explored in more detail.

Blended learning programmes are typically evaluated using a wide range of tools. These are summarized in Table 4.6, which has been adapted and updated from work by Penny Hackett (1997).

Learning environment and materials

Evaluating the learning environment and materials typically involves answering the following questions.

Physical learning environment

- Are the learning spaces (study areas, group areas, teaching rooms, workshops) easy to access and available at the required times?
- Are the learning spaces physically attractive and comfortable to use?
  Is it possible to carry out different types of learning activities, e.g. quiet or noisy activities, in these spaces?
- Do the learning spaces provide access to appropriate technologies?
- Is there easy access to help and support?
- Is there access to refreshments?

Table 4.6 Tools for evaluation

Tools	Level of evaluation			
	Reactions	Learning	Behaviour	Impact on ILS
Software tracking tools	▓		▓	
Online or paper-based questionnaires or reports	▓	▓	▓	▓
Team leader questionnaires or reports	▓	▓	▓	▓
Online assessment activities		▓	▓	
Customer survey			▓	▓
Employer survey			▓	▓
Interviews	▓	▓	▓	▓
Focus group	▓	▓	▓	
Performance appraisal		▓	▓	▓
Observation		▓	▓	▓
Team/unit performance indicators				▓
ILS performance indicators				▓
Senior management opinion	▓	▓	▓	▓

Virtual learning environment

- Is the learning environment easy to access?
- Do security systems work without being too cumbersome?
- Is the structure and layout of the learning environment intuitive?
- Is the design of the environment attractive and visually pleasing?
- Is it possible to take different routes through the learning environment?
- Do all facilities, e.g. links, quizzes, surveys, work?
- Is it up-to-date?

Learning materials

- Are they easy to access and quick to download?
- Is there a clear statement of aims, learning outcomes or objectives?
- Do they arouse the learner's interest?
- Do they use clear language?
- Is the content organized into manageable chunks?
- Is the content relevant?
- Do they provide a variety of routes through the materials?
- Do they use supporting images and diagrams?

- Do they give opportunities for learners to practise, e.g. activities and quizzes?
- Do they give personalized feedback?
- Are they up-to-date?

Learning process

Evaluating the learning process may involve exploring aspects of the blended learning programme such as:

- development of virtual communication skills
- development of learning to learn skills, e.g. time management
- use made of learning materials
- use made of virtual communication tools, e.g. e-mail, discussion groups, chat rooms
- balance of independent, collaborative or co-operative working
- specific learning activities and processes, e.g. group activity, individual activity, guest speaker
- peer support and e-tutor support
- other support processes, e.g. technical help desks, mentor support.

Results of evaluation

The findings of the evaluation may have a number of different outcomes:

- The blended learning programme is abandoned.
- The blended learning programme is redesigned, e.g. has new learning objectives, new structure, new content, new methods, new tutors.
- The preparation work is redesigned, e.g. has new briefing material, new pre-programme work.
- The virtual learning environment is redesigned, e.g. has a new virtual learning environment, reorganized site, change in navigation, change in design.
- The face-to-face and/or e-learning process is changed, e.g. has new activities, fewer activities, new timing.
- No change.

Summary

The design cycle involves a needs analysis, and design, development, delivery and evaluation. There is no simple solution or prescription for designing effective blended learning programmes. Success depends on researching and responding to the parent organizations and individual learners' needs. This should be followed up by establishing realistic aims and learning outcomes and then deciding on the appropriate blend of face-to-face and e-learning activities within the blended learning programme. It also involves incorporating key design principles into the programme and deciding on the appropriate use of technology and ensuring that the programme is accessible. Once the programme has been implemented it then needs to be evaluated and the feedback used to improve it.

References

Allan, B. (2002) *E-learning and Teaching in Library and Information Services*, London, Facet Publishing.

Bee, R. and Bee, F. (2007) *Learning Evaluation*, 2nd edn, London, Chartered Institute of Personnel and Development.

Disabilities Rights Commission (2006) *Disability Discrimination Act, Part 4, Learning and Teaching Good Practice Guide*, www.drc.org.uk/publicationsandreports/pubseducation.asp [accessed 12 May 2007].

Hackett, P. (1997) *Introduction to Training Essentials*, London, Chartered Institute of Personnel and Development.

Kirkpatrick, D. L. (1994) *Evaluating Training Programmes*, San Francisco CA, Berrett-Koehler.

Pedley, P. (2007) *Digital Copyright*, 2nd edn, London, Facet Publishing.

Seale, J. (2006) *Learning and Disability in Higher Education: accessibility research and practice*, Seale, Routledge.

Weller, M., Pegler, C. A. and Mason, R. D. (2005) Students' Experiences of Component Versus Integrated Virtual Learning Environments, *Journal of Computer Assisted Learning*, **21** (4), 239–315.

5 Planning and designing learning activities

Introduction

The aim of this chapter is to provide guidance on the design and use of different learning activities and technologies. Blended learning programmes are likely to include a diverse mixture of activities that together enable individual learners to achieve their learning goals and outcomes. This chapter provides a range of activities that may be used both online and offline, in the workplace and in the training room, and by individuals or small groups. Chapter 6 considers working with learning groups in more detail.

This chapter considers two main topics: general design principles behind developing and using different learning activities; and an alphabetical list of activities and their application in blended learning programmes. Chapter 6 considers group activities such as team-building, problem-based learning and project-based learning. It also considers the group processes involved in some learning activities and looks at how to manage large groups and diverse groups.

Design principles

For both individual e-learning and face-to-face activities, the design process involves answering the following questions:

1 What are the aims and indicative learning outcomes?
2 How will you enable the learner to achieve these outcomes?
3 Consider the learning process – is it an individual, small group or large group activity?
4 Consider the interaction structure – what are the levels and types of collaboration required in the activity?
5 How much time will be required by the learners to complete the activity?
6 What learning resources do you need to prepare or use for this activity?
7 What (if any) technologies will be involved in the activity?
8 How long is the activity likely to take?
9 How will you assess learning?
10 How will you evaluate the activity?

Once you have answered these questions it is worthwhile carrying out the research necessary to provide you with up-to-date information concerning the topic that the activity will focus on. An important stage in the design process is to produce an outline structure that provides all the information required to complete the activity (Figure 5.1).

Title of activity
Aims
Indicative learning outcomes
Start and end date of activity
Background to the activity
Rationale or benefits of completing the activity
Explanation of what the learner(s) should do
Estimate of time required to complete activity
Resources required for activity
Help and support
Outline of the next stage, e.g. debriefing, assessment
Follow-up work

Figure 5.1 Outline structure of a learning activity

This general structure may be adjusted to suit the needs of a particular activity, e.g. the following outline was used in an IT training activity:

Introduction to activity
Aims and learning outcomes
Advantages of using the tool
Outline explanation
List of instructions
Example screenshots
Assessment activity
Trouble-shooting.

Learning activities

Effective learning activities are those that mobilize, engage and enable learners to develop their knowledge and skills. This involves generating interest, enthusiasm and motivation to take part in the activity. Once learners are mobilized they can engage with the learning process. This will 'involve cognitive processes such as creating, problem-solving, reasoning, decision-making and evaluation. In addition, students are intrinsically motivated to learn due to the meaningful nature of the learning environment and activities' (Kearsley and Schneiderman, 1998). Effective learning activities, whether they take place in a classroom, in the workplace or online, are those that enable individuals or groups to work on authentic tasks or situations. All learners need to know that the learning activities are relevant and this means that they should be focused on a current issue or need rather than an abstract task. Gilly Salmon (2002) provides a helpful overview of e-learning activities, which she calls e-tivities. Table 5.1 summarizes commonly used learning activities and highlights their advantages and potential problem areas. The examples included in this section cover learning activities currently used in library and information blended learning programmes. They are organized in alphabetical order.

Table 5.1 Example learning activities

Activity	Characteristics	Reasons for use	Advantages	Potential problems	Applications
Action planning	Individuals produce a written SMART action plan.	To help transfer learning from a course into the workplace or practice.	Quick and simple method.	Individuals don't follow rules of action planning and make too general plans without a time frame.	**F2F** – can be carried out using Post-it Notes. **E-learning** – can be carried out individually and then individuals can share their plans with another learner.
Audiovisual presentations	The tutor gives an audiovisual presentation either in a classroom or via an online environment. Audiovisual presentations may be used as a stimulus for discussion and other activities.	To motivate learners. To illustrate or clarify concepts and ideas.	Accepted method of training. Materials may be reused for other courses. Wide range of tools and technologies available (see Table 5.2).	Can be very time-consuming to develop. Need appropriate equipment. Many off-the-shelf presentations are aimed at a general audience and may not appeal to ILS staff or customers. Individual learners may not engage with the presentation.	Work well in both **F2F** and **e-learning** situations.
Brainstorming or wordstorming	Individuals pool ideas and generate new ideas or options.	Enables ideas and new perspectives to be identified. Useful for focusing learners on a new topic.	Quick and simple method.	Can be very time-consuming to develop. Individual learners may not engage with the activity.	**F2F** – can be carried out using flipchart paper. **E-learning** – a 'quick' activity and therefore probably best carried out in a chat or conference room.

Continued on next page

Table 5.1 Continued

Activity	Characteristics	Reasons for use	Advantages	Potential problems	Applications
Case studies	Learners are presented with a particular situation and are typically asked to explore it and develop 'solutions'.	Enable individuals to explore different situations from a range of perspectives. Enable learners to share ideas and experiences, and construct their knowledge.	Case studies can be closely related to workplace situations. Can be used to prepare learners for future situations.	Can be very time-consuming to develop. May not be perceived as 'real' and therefore not valued. Individual learners may not engage with the activity.	**F2F** – paper-based case studies work well. **E-learning** – documentation may be uploaded into an online environment. Case study may be augmented by podcasts.
Debates	Structured or unstructured discussion based on two or more different perspectives.	Enable learners to explore issues or ideas. Enable learners to share ideas and experiences, and construct their knowledge.	The best debates are lively, based on real-life issues and concerns. Involve all learners.	Debate becomes a slanging match. Use of abusive language. A few participants dominate. Quieter group members may feel intimidated.	Work well in both **F2F** and **e-learning** situations.
Demo-nstrations	The trainer demonstrates a particular skill or product, e.g. website.	Enable learners to gain an overview. Often used when there is limited access to technology.	Provide an interesting and stimulating overview. Motivate learners to do it themselves.	Some demonstrations are over-long and boring (10–15 minutes is normally sufficient). Learners become bored because they are passive.	Work well in both **F2F** and **e-learning** situations.
Discussion groups	Structured or unstructured discussions. May be based on a specific issue or set of ideas.	Enable learners to explore issues or ideas. Enable learners to share ideas and experiences, and construct their knowledge.	The best discussions are lively, based on real life issues and concerns. Involve all learners.	Discussion peters out or is unfocused. Learners don't participate or hijack discussion. Individuals dominate. Not inclusive.	Work well in both **F2F** and **e-learning** situations. In e-learning situations may take place over an extended period of time, e.g. 2+ weeks.
Exercises	Typically a tutor sets up and facilitates exercises that involve pairs, trios or larger groups of e-learners working together on a specific task, e.g. produce a set of guidelines, review a website.	Enable learners to work in a focused way and benefit from sharing experience, ideas and support.	Can be highly motivating and satisfying experiences. Individuals learn from each other. Products may be of higher quality than if produced by individuals.	Time needs to be spent on working out how to work together. Individuals may opt out.	Work well in both **F2F** and **e-learning** situations.

Continued on next page

Table 5.1 *Continued*

Activity	Characteristics	Reasons for use	Advantages	Potential problems	Applications
Icebreakers	Relatively short activities that enable learners to get to know each other, become familiar with the technology and environment, and start the learning process.	To 'break the ice' at start of a new e-learning programme. Enable learners to start to develop their online voice.	Give individuals an opportunity to become familiar with each other. In e-learning individuals can join in as they access the technology (making it easier for late arrivals to get going).	People don't join in. A few participants dominate. Quieter group members may feel intimidated. Some people may find it frustrating, i.e. they want to get started with the content of the course.	Work well in both **F2F** and **e-learning** situations.
Problem-based learning	Learners work on a real live problem that doesn't have a simple right solution.	Enables students to learn from real life problems. To encourage deep learning.	Enables individual learners to apply their knowledge and skills to complex problems. A preparation for learning in the workplace.	Lack of engagement with the activity. May be time-consuming. May be difficult to anticipate the learning outcomes of this type of activity.	Work well in both **F2F** and **e-learning** situations.
Project groups	In co-operative groups individuals work on their own task, share ideas and, feedback, and give each other support. In collaborative groups the group works on a whole-group project.	Can be based on workplace projects. Enable multi-disciplinary or multi-professional teams to work together. Help to develop team-working and virtual communication skills. To encourage sharing of experience, ideas and support.	Can be highly motivating and satisfying experiences. Individuals learn from each other. Products may be of higher quality than if produced by individuals.	Time needs to be spent on working out how to work together. Individuals may opt out.	Work well in both **F2F** and **e-learning** situations. In e-learning situations may take place over an extended period of time, e.g. 2+ weeks.
Quizzes	Individuals, small groups or a whole group work through a series of questions.	May be used as an assessment activity, e.g. diagnostic tool, on-course or post-course activity. May be used to generate energy and excitement. May be used to validate learning to date.	Familiar tool. Can be highly motivating. Can be used to add interest and excitement to a programme. Provide useful feedback to the tutor.	Time-consuming to develop. The level of the questions must be appropriate, otherwise the quizzes may be too easy or too hard and can reduce motivation.	Work in both **F2F** and **e-learning** situations. May be used in a variety of formats.

Continued on next page

Table 5.1 *Continued*

Activity	Characteristics	Reasons for use	Advantages	Potential problems	Applications
Reflective practice	Individuals or small groups reflect on their learning experiences.	May be used as an assessment activity, e.g. through the use of a learning journal or learning log.	Particularly useful as a means of improving performance and motivation.	Students need to be introduced to this approach to learning. Works best if the reflective process is structured by the tutor. May be time-consuming.	Works in both **F2F** and **e-learning** situations. May be used in a variety of formats.
Role play (see under 'Simulations', page 121)	Individuals take on a specific role in either an F2F workshop or a virtual environment (see virtual worlds in Chapter 2). They then explore the role and the consequences of selected kinds of action. Needs to be facilitated by an expert.	Enables individuals to explore different situations from a range of perspectives.	Provides practical experience in handling particular situations. Time to reflect and learn from experiences.	Many people dislike role play and the use of this phrase may turn them off the whole training session. Individuals don't engage with the role play. Individuals engage too closely with it – this is potentially dangerous particularly if individual learners have mental health issues.	Works in both **F2F** and **e-learning** situations.
Simulations	A group follows a set of rules or a situation that simulates a real life situation. May be facilitated by a tutor or group member(s).	Enable individuals to experience a 'real life' situation. May provide experiences that are hard to work on in real life.	Provide practical experience in handling particular situations. Time to reflect and learn from experiences.	Can be very time-consuming to develop. May not be perceived as 'real' and therefore not valued. May be difficult to relate experiences to workplace.	Work well in both **F2F** and **e-learning** situations.
Team-building activities	A group takes part in an activity that involves everyone (the classroom or online equivalent to outward-bound training). The discussion and reflection on the activity is more important than the actual activity.	Enable e-learners to experience and become familiar with online group work.	Learners can learn about themselves and how they work in or lead a team. Learners can develop online netiquette skills and experience good practice in an online learning environment.	Individuals don't engage with activity and may perceive it as a waste of time. Learners don't participate or individuals dominate.	Work well in both **F2F** and **e-learning** situations. In e-learning situations may take place over an extended period of time, e.g. 2+ weeks.

Continued on next page

Table 5.1 *Continued*

Activity	Characteristics	Reasons for use	Advantages	Potential problems	Applications
Virtual visitor or guest speaker	Typically a tutor invites an experienced practitioner or someone with specialist expertise to visit the group either in a classroom context or as a virtual visitor. A virtual visitor may visit the online group either synchronously or asynchronously for a set period of time.	Introduces specialist knowledge. Opportunity to explore different perspectives. May be used to emphasize particular perspective.	'Breath of fresh air'. Provides 'excitement' and 'difference'. Provides additional ideas, experiences, perspectives. Guest speaker can be recorded and recording presented as an embedded audiofile or podcast so that the students can listen to the talk again and it can be reused on other courses.	Time involved in organizing the guest speaker. Technical issues, e.g. problems with access to site. Guest speaker doesn't prepare for visit and misreads culture or tone of group. Guest speaker 'highjacks' session and leads it into unwanted arenas. Guest speaker or visitor usurps tutor's role. E-learners don't accept virtual visitor. Unrealistic expectations (tutor, virtual visitor or learners).	Work well in both **F2F** and **e-learning** situations. Virtual visitors help to overcome the time and travel requirements of F2F guest speakers.
Visits	A group of learners may visit another organization or group (F2F or online) and share their experiences either F2F or in an online environment.	Opportunity to explore different perspectives.	'Breath of fresh air'. Provide 'excitement'. and 'difference'. Provide additional ideas, experiences, perspectives.	Time needed to set up and organize visit. Technical issues, e.g. problems with access to site. Problems with different groups of learners developing rapport. Visit becomes a social rather than a learning experience. Unrealistic expectations (tutor, virtual visitor or learners).	Work well in both **F2F** and **e-learning** situations. Physical tours may be embedded in a blended learning programme by including pre-visit and post-visit online activities. Virtual tours may be developed using online tools such as weblogs, e.g. www.blogger.com, or webtrails, e.g. http://trailfire.com, as well as 3D virtual tours and fly-throughs, e.g. www.icreate3d.com.

Continued on next page

Table 5.1 *Continued*

Activity	Characteristics	Reasons for use	Advantages	Potential problems	Applications
Work-based project	A real life work problem is used as a vehicle for learning.	The learning that takes place is located within the needs of the workplace.	Can be extremely motivating as the learning experience is focused on the needs of the workplace and real-life problems. The learning that takes place as part of the learning programme is entirely embedded in the needs of the workplace.	The real workplace problems may not provide a suitable vehicle for learning. There may be problems in obtaining permission to use a workplace project. There may be issues of data protection and confidentiality.	Work well in both **F2F** and **e-learning** situations.

Action planning

Action plans are frequently used as a means of encouraging learners to identify what they are going to do either during or after the blended learning programme. The process of writing an action plan and then sharing it with peers, tutors or work colleagues can be extremely motivating. The key to a good action plan is that it should be SMART:

- **S**pecific, i.e. have an identifiable action
- **M**easurable, i.e. include something to see or hear that will show that the action has taken place
- **A**chievable, i.e. be manageable within the context of the blended learning programme and the working environment of the ILS
- **R**elevant, i.e. so learners will immediately understand its relevance to them
- **T**ime bound, i.e. have a deadline set or time allocated on a regular basis.

An example action-planning activity is given in Example 5.1, with an associated action plan form presented in Example 5.2.

Example 5.1 An example action-planning activity

Introduction

The purpose of this activity is to encourage you to apply your new internet skills when researching your next assignment. As a result of completing this activity you will have an action plan to help you to use your new research skills. This activity will help you to transfer the skills that you have learnt for evaluating websites to your academic studies. Hopefully this will help you to improve your grades!

What you should do

Complete the action-planning pro-forma (see Example 5.2).

E-learning version – e-mail the completed pro-forma to your workshop buddy and give each other feedback via e-mail about the proposed action plans. Remember to be a supportive, critical friend. Amend your action plan in response to the feedback. Agree a date to review your completed action plan with your buddy.

F2F version – share your action plan with a colleague attending the workshop and give each other feedback about the proposed action plans. Remember to be a supportive, critical friend. Amend your action plan in response to the feedback. Agree a date to review your completed action plan with your colleague. This review can be carried out by telephone, e-mail or F2F.

Further work

You may like to visit the following websites for additional information about evaluating websites:

-
-
-

Example 5.2 Action plan pro-forma

What are you going to do as a result of the workshop?

1 What do you want to do? Choose a particular task or activity.

2 When will you do it?

3 Where will you do it?

Continued on next page

Example 5.2 *Continued*

4 Will you be working by yourself or with someone else? If you are working with someone else, then have you obtained his or her agreement?

5 What will you see, hear and feel when you have achieved your goal?

6 Is there anything that will stop you from doing it? How can you prevent this happening?

7 How will you reward yourself when you have completed your task or activity?

Audiovisual aids

Audiovisual aids are used to motivate, and to illustrate or clarify concepts and ideas. They may be used in both face-to-face and e-learning environments. Table 5.2 provides a summary of a wide range of audiovisual methods that may be incorporated into a blended learning programme.

Table 5.2 Using different audiovisual aids

AV aids	F2F or e-learning	Advantages	Disadvantages
CD or DVDs	F2F and e-learning	Convenient, flexible and low-cost. Portable. Useful for portraying real life situations. Stimulates participants to ask questions and to test out new approaches in the workplace. Provides a high-impact, high-interest learning experience. Learners can stop and review Wide choice available.	Expensive to update. Off-the-shelf DVDs may not be entirely relevant. Realism may be lacking. Passive medium. Quickly become out-of-date. Need access to appropriate equipment. Equipment may break down.
Embedded audio files	F2F and e-learning	Easy to use. Easy to distribute. Flexible – easy to stop and start. Relatively cheap. Low-cost equipment.	Learners can be reluctant to listen. Not very interactive. Sophisticated recordings need to be produced professionally, which can be expensive.

Continued on next page

Table 5.2 *Continued*

AV aids	F2F or E-learning	Advantages	Disadvantages
Flipcharts	F2F	Can be prepared in advance. Can be used to record information elicited from audience, e.g. in a brainstorming exercise. Can write 'secret' notes (in pencil for tutor's eyes only). Can use colour, symbols, pictures. Can mark place using Post-it Notes. Can be torn off pad and displayed on wall. Useful to record findings from group exercises with groups presenting their own flipchart. Can be seen in normal room light.	Effective only with groups of up to about 20. Breaks eye contact with group when you write. Some tutors may be concerned about their handwriting or spelling.
Interactive video	E-learning. May be incorporated into an F2F workshop.	Learner-paced. Learner is fully involved. Cost-effective (especially if large numbers need to be trained). Flexible and easy to use. Training can be individualized. Motivating and fast moving. Learner receives rapid feedback. Monitors and records learner's progress. Training packages can be used many times. Wide choice of off-the-shelf packages. Some packages can be customized. CDs and DVDs are portable and easy to install and store.	Few programmes available relevant to ILS world or using ILS examples. Development and production can be lengthy and costs high. Problems with compatibility and formatting. Quickly becomes out of date.
Interactive whiteboard	F2F and e-learning	Can be pre-prepared. Learners and tutor may interact via board. May integrate text and images. May be used for brainstorming and other idea-generating methods.	Learning activity may focus on technology rather than content.
Microphones	F2F	Allow you to be heard without raising voice.	Feedback and distortion may be irritating to audience. Can break down. Easy to forget you have got turned on, so you must switch off as soon as you stop presenting.
Podcasts	E-learning and F2F	Useful method of presenting interviews or short video clips. Reusable. Learner may access them a number of times.	Need appropriate equipment to prepare them.
PowerPoint presentations	F2F and e-learning	Look very professional. Simple to edit, change sequence, etc. Can use animation. Can use colour, symbols, pictures.	Need access to appropriate software – not all e-learners may have this. Equipment may fail. Need low lights to view them F2F.

Continued on next page

Table 5.2 *Continued*

AV aids	F2F or E-learning	Advantages	Disadvantages
Text-based materials	F2F and e-learning	Cost effective. Flexible and portable. Relatively cheap to produce and update. Easy to use.	Need to look professional. Not as interactive as computer-based materials.
Videoconferencing	F2F and e-learning	Access to multiple locations worldwide. Face-to-face support and contact with fellow learners and tutors.	May get visual distortions. Equipment must work. Sometimes time is wasted in sorting out technical problems.
Web-based training	E-learning. May be incorporated into an F2F workshop.	Learner-paced. Flexible and easy to use. Cost-effective. Convenient. Consistent approach to training for each learner. Relatively cheap. Wide choice of packages. Can be used in many different locations.	Lacks personal touch. Needs PCs to run it. Equipment can break down. Lacks personal contact if delivered 100% via e-learning.
Whiteboard	F2F and e-learning	Can be used to record information elicited from audience, e.g. in a brainstorming exercise. Can use colour, symbols, pictures. Can wipe off and reuse.	Only effective with a small group.

Brainstorming

Brainstorming is a problem-solving technique that involves quickly generating and sharing ideas without censoring them. It is often used in face-to-face sessions as a means of focusing on a particular issue, generating a wide range of options and/or raising the energy in a group. In face-to-face sessions it is often carried out over a very short time span, e.g. a few minutes.

Brainstorming in an e-learning environment involves group members working in a chat or conference room and typing in ideas very quickly. They don't respond or comment on other people's ideas during the process. It enables people to generate ideas freely and to build on other people's ideas as one idea triggers another. It also allows simultaneous contributions. Specialist software, e.g. FacilitatePro (http://facilitate.com) and MindJet (www.mindjet.com), may be used to support online brainstorming activities.

Carol Glover (2002) suggests that individuals become anxious when brainstorming in a group and that this can limit the effectiveness of the technique. One way around this problem is to give people advance warning about the use of this technique. This enables them to start brainstorming alone before bringing their ideas to the group.

Case studies

Case studies are a useful method of enabling learners to focus on a particular situation, explore it and develop 'solutions'. They take some time to prepare as the tutor needs to collect appropriate materials and examples, work out an appropriate case study, and then mentally 'walk through' it and the likely processes that the learners will engage in as they work on the materials. The best case studies are those based on real situations that are closely linked with the learners' experiences.

Debates

Debates are a useful means of engaging students in an active discussion and allow them to explore opposing sides of an argument. For example, a group of students may be asked to discuss the issue of plagiarism from the points of view of two groups: students and authors. The group is divided into two and each sub-group is then given either the student or author perspective to research. The actual debate may take place face-to-face or online.

Demonstrations

A useful approach to getting your point over is to demonstrate it. On ILS training events demonstrations are frequently used as part of an information skills programme, e.g. demonstrating a database or search strategy, and they may be used as part of a skills development programme, e.g. assertiveness skills, management skills, health and safety training. Tutors need to be able to:

- perform the demonstration themselves
- plan the demonstration carefully
- keep it simple
- provide supporting materials, e.g. handouts
- carry out the demonstration and instruct at the same time
- provide participants with the opportunity to practise afterwards.

Demonstrations that work well attract and hold people's attention; they are easy to understand and convincing. However, their usefulness may be limited if the pace is too slow or quick for some learners. They can go wrong and many tutors are likely to have had the experience of testing a computer-based demonstration before the start of a workshop, only to find that it doesn't work when the time comes to carry out the demonstration. Another disadvantage is that some participants may feel overwhelmed by the skill of the tutor and think that they will never achieve that level of competence.

Preparing for a demonstration

- Prepare your demonstration.
- Run through the presentation.
- Provide back-up demonstrations, e.g. using screenshots or special software such as SnagIT (see Chapter 2).
- Pilot the demonstration to colleagues.
- Adjust the demonstration in response to feedback from colleagues.
- Produce the relevant documentation.

During the demonstration:

- If you are using a volunteer then thank them for volunteering and explain to them that you will be talking to the whole group at certain times.
- Describe your objectives and procedures clearly.
- Describe each step.
- Summarize key points.
- If you are being supported by a training assistant they can write the key points on a flipchart as you work through the demonstration.

After the demonstration

- Thank the volunteer(s).
- Raise questions to clarify points.
- Link the demonstration to work situations.
- Link the practice to theory.
- Give everyone the opportunity to practise the skill or technique.

Points to be aware of

- If you are using equipment, prepare a contingency plan.
- If you are carrying out a demonstration with the help of a volunteer from the audience, be careful whom you choose. Often people who are very quick to volunteer are sometimes not the most helpful volunteers. Choose the person whom you will feel most comfortable working with and who you think will provide the simplest and clearest demonstration material.

Discussion groups

Discussions are usually focused around a specific activity or current theme and the tutor's role is normally to start off the discussion and, if necessary, provide background learning resources. Once the discussion has started the tutor will facilitate it using skills described in detail in Chapter 7. Discussion may involve the whole group or small groups who may then feed back to the whole group.

Example 5.3 Message: referencing sources

Hello everyone,

Neil has asked me to help you learn how to reference your work. The aim of this activity is to help you get high marks in your first assignment.

For most of your assignments you will need to research and consider other people's ideas. When you use these ideas in your own written work, you must credit the sources within the main body of your assignment and also provide detailed information about the source in a bibliography. This is called information citation and is an essential part of academic practice.

If you are unsure of what referencing involves, then look at the example article (hotlink provided) – in particular notice the list of references at the end and also the way there is a connection between the ideas mentioned in the article and the reference, e.g. on page 3 (final paragraph) Dewar quotes Virginia Griffin (1988) and this will lead you to a reference listed in alphabetical order at the end of the paper. Spending ten minutes examining the way this paper uses references will really help you to get it right in your assignment.

There are two key questions we will explore in this discussion:

* Why is it important to reference work?
* How do you reference work?

So does anyone want to get the ball rolling? Why is it important to reference work? How do you reference work?

Best wishes,
Alison

This message started off a discussion involving the following:

* Students sharing horror stories (examples of plagiarism that resulted in students failing their course).
* Experienced students pointing new students to library guides on referencing and providing their own examples of how to do it.
* Students sharing other resources on plagiarism, e.g. an online test.

Continued on next page

Example 5.3 *Continued*

- Someone preparing a list of reasons why it is important to reference work:
  - a moral issue about cheating and intellectual honesty
  - a netiquette issue about giving credit to other people's work where it is due
  - a learning issue: the need to identify and separate your own and other people's work; you will then be able to reflect on and learn about their learning experience.
  - an academic issue: by referencing someone else's work, your reader will then be able to look up the source.
- Someone sharing a metaphor relating plagiarism to driving and speeding:
  'Many people speed, some accidentally and some deliberately, but no one wants to be caught speeding. If detected the penalty varies from a small fine to loss of licence depending on the particular situation. These penalties occur whether or not we meant to speed. To make sure we do not break the law we need to know what the posted limit is and concentrate on keeping within it. This is particularly true if driving abroad, when you may not know the local rules. Increasingly tutors are using detection equipment similar to speed cameras and can detect plagiarism, both minor and major. Educational institutions and examination awarding bodies have the power of the court to deduct marks or expel the student.'

An important difference between face-to-face and online discussions is that the latter may take place over several weeks and individuals may return to the discussion after it has been officially ended and the programme has moved on to another theme. Example 5.3 shows an example message posted by an academic librarian as part of an information skills module (Neil is the tutor).

Exercises

A wide range of activities and exercises can be used to enable learners to develop their knowledge and skills, and to learn from each other. Activities may be carried out individually or in groups. Individual or paired learning activities include the following:

- Complete a pro-forma or question set.
- Investigate a website and provide feedback.
- Read and respond to an article or report.
- Evaluate a website, service or learning environment.
- Produce a product or report, e.g. website, set of guidelines.

Icebreakers

Icebreakers are useful in both face-to-face and online situations. They help a new group to 'break the ice' and start to get to know each other. In a blended learning programme it is worthwhile making sure that icebreakers occur at the start of the first face-to-face and in the first online meeting or activity. This is because individuals need to orientate themselves and get to know the other people on the course. In an online environment they also give people the opportunity to become familiar with the technology and to develop their online voice.

An important point about all icebreakers is that the activity should be acceptable to the group, who should be able to see its relevance to their learning programme. Here are two example icebreakers 5.4 and 5.5:

Example 5.4 Icebreaker from a blended programme called 'Developing your management skills'

Face-to-face meeting

On the first day the participants met together and after a welcome and general housekeeping announcement they were asked to carry out the following activity:

'We are going to be working together both face-to-face and in an online environment for the next three months. To start off the learning process and to help us to get to know each other I'd like you to split up into groups of four. Make sure that you are with people that you do not know. In your groups introduce yourselves to each other and state your name, your job role and what you want to get out of the management programme. I'll give you ten minutes for this activity and then I'll ask you to introduce yourselves to the whole group.'

During the introductions to the whole group the trainer wrote everyone's name and aim on a flipchart pad. After this activity the programme moved on to a skills assessment activity.

After the face-to-face meeting on the first day of the workshop the participants were asked to go online and read the welcome message in their discussion group area. This is the message that they read:

'Welcome to your online discussion area. This is a private area that is only accessible to your group. The first activity is to become comfortable in working in this online environment and to reflect on the first face-to-face workshop. To help start off this process you may like to respond to the following questions:

1 Briefly introduce yourself – how will others remember you from meeting you face-to-face?
2 What did you learn from the face-to-face workshop?
3 Have you any unanswered questions relating to the programme as a whole?
4 Any other comments?

This activity starts on 14 February and will conclude on 21 February when I will post up the next online activity. Do contact me if you have any queries.

Regards,
Barbara

Example 5.5 Icebreaker from a blended e-learning module aimed at ILS and academic staff

Hello everyone,

It was good to meet you all at the face-to-face induction workshop. What we are going to do now is start the online work. To help us get going please would you send a message in which you introduce yourself by identifying:

- your main learning point from the induction workshop
- your expectations about working online
- any concerns you have about working online
- when you think you'll be coming online, e.g. lunchtime, early evening, etc.

Please would you respond to each other's messages and use this as an opportunity to find out more about each other.

The next activity will be posted on 20 September.

Best wishes,
Jane and David

Sample icebreakers

1   Meeting someone new. Work in pairs. Choose someone you don't know. Find out: who they are; why they are here; what they want from the session. Introduce your partner to the whole group (10–20 mins). **F2F or possibly in chat rooms**.

2   Snowball hello. Work in pairs. Choose someone you don't know. Find out: who they are; why they are here; what they want from the session. Each pair then joins up with another pair. Introduce your partner to the foursome. Then join another pair and repeat the exercise until everyone has been introduced (10–30 mins). **F2F.**

3   Name game 1. Ask everyone to sit in a circle. Ask one person to start the process and call out a name with an associated activity, e.g. 'I am Barbara and I like bananas'. The next person repeats the first person's name and follows it with their own, e.g. 'I am John and I like jelly'. Once the list has got to six to eight names (depending on the confidence of the group) start a new list. This process is repeated until everyone has had a go (10–15 mins). **F2F.**

4   Name game 2. Participants sit in a circle and there is a round where everyone says their name. It may be worthwhile asking people not to go too quickly. The

trainer throws a ball (or bean bag) into the circle and asks one (named) person to pass it to someone else while calling out the name of the person who receives the ball. This is repeated from person to person. It is important to keep the ball moving and to make sure that everyone is included in the activity. Continue until everyone is familiar with everybody's name (5–10 mins). **F2F**.

5   Name game 3. This can be used with a group of up to about 25 people. The first person introduces themself. The next person says 'This is X (the person who has just introduced themself) and my name is . . . . The next person repeats the first and second person's name and then introduces themself. This process continues and is likely to end in laughter. It is a good icebreaker and can be used to introduce humour very early in the course (10–15 mins). **F2F**.

6   Finding out about each other. This is a simple exercise which involves everyone meeting other members of the group and obtaining answers to six questions. The questions could be at a fairly trivial level, e.g. do you like dogs, or they could be questions relevant to the content of the learning programme. The trainer has to prepare the questions in advance and display them during the activity (10–15 mins). **F2F or in a chat room**.

7   Ask everyone to introduce themself by saying their name and what they want from the learning session (5–10 mins). **F2F or in a chat room**.

Problem-based learning

See Chapters 3 and 6.

Project-based learning

See Chapters 3 and 6.

Quizzes

Quizzes are relatively simple to set up and may be run in either face-to-face or virtual learning environments. Everyone is familiar with the idea of a quiz. Using a quiz provides an easy and fun way of reviewing the content of a course, integrating learning and identifying gaps in learning. In a face-to-face environment quizzes can be set up in a number of ways. TV game shows provide a wide range of familiar formats – use one of these or create your own.

If you have access to an audience response system (see Chapter 2), this can provide a motivating and exciting game. If you don't have access to such a system then think about how individuals or groups will respond to questions; a simple red/green card can be used to elicit responses; people may shout out answers or write them down. The following list provides guidance on developing a quiz (see also Examples 5.6 and 5.7).

Questions

- The tutor can prepare a list of questions.
- The participants can prepare a list of questions.
- Start off with easy questions.
- Stack the questions for success (this is a game, not an exam!).
- Questions can be serious and may also include some joke questions.

Question master

- This may be the tutor(s) or a participant.
- Alternatively, the participants can ask the tutors the questions!

Teams

- You may want to work with pairs or small groups.
- Think about how you will set up the teams.

Adding fun

- It is up to the tutor to create the learning environment.
- Party hats, beepers, bells and whistles are all very effective!
- Including joke questions, tasks, etc. can enliven the atmosphere.

Scoring

- May be serious or semi-serious.

Example 5.6 Quiz used as part of an induction programme

As part of an induction programme for six new ILS staff there was a quiz. The new staff were asked to work in pairs and find out the answers to 30 questions by walking around the library and identifying the key features.

Example questions:

- Where are the toilets on the 1st floor?
- What is kept on the 4th floor?
- Whose office is near the back stairs on the 2nd floor?
- Where are the newspapers kept?
- Whose office door is covered with pictures of Scotland?
- Where is the fire exit on the 1st floor?

Continued on next page

Example 5.6 *Continued*

- Where is the entrance for people in wheelchairs?
- Where are the trolleys kept on the 1st floor?
- How many computer terminals are there in public areas?
- Where is the video library?
- Where are the patents?
- Where is the staff rest room? When you have found it go and have a cup of tea or coffee. The trainer will meet you there (final question).

In an e-learning context many virtual learning environments such as Blackboard and WebCT provide quiz or testing facilities that may be used to deliver a quiz. Alternatively, software such as SurveyMonkey can be used to generate a simple quiz. Another approach is to deliver a quiz via a chat room. In this situation the facilitator types in the first question and, once it is correctly answered, then moves on to the next question, and so on until the end of the quiz. The advantages of this method of delivering a quiz are that everyone gets an opportunity to respond, they can check their answers before sending them in, and there is a transcript of the session. The disadvantages are that a few people may dominate the session and it can appear rather slow. My own experience is that a limit of ten questions works well for chat room quizzes.

Example 5.7 Online quiz

As part of an in-house IT training programme staff were given a quiz at the end of the course. They were asked to work in pairs in an online environment and complete the quiz of 30 questions within the next ten days. They were asked to post their results in the general discussion group forum. They were allowed to ask the trainer questions during this time. The quiz helped to integrate the staff's learning about IT and it also helped to transfer their new knowledge and skills into the workplace. The trainer generated a lot of enthusiasm about the quiz and, as a result, staff who were not on the training course asked if they could join in too.

Reflective practice

Chapter 3 introduced the concept of reflection and reflective practice. This section provides an overview of practical approaches to reflective practice. Learning journals (or logs) are commonly used as a tool to enable individual learners to chart their progress, problems and challenges, thinking and development, and knowledge construction, and can include their changes of mind, uncertainties, feelings and other experiences during the learning process (Moon, 1999). A learning journal is often used as an assessment tool and, in this situation, the learner may be asked to submit either their learning journal or a statement that summarizes their learning processes and outcomes. Keeping a learning journal enables individual learners to:

- record their development
- reflect on the links between theory and practice
- recognize and trace how their experiences affect their employability and/or professional practice
- develop their knowledge and skills
- develop their ability to engage in reflective practice
- develop their self-awareness and become empowered to be effective learners.

There are many different ways of keeping a learning journal, including: keeping notes in a book; using a weblog; sending e-mails to yourself; or printing out and reflecting on discussion group messages or conference room transcripts. It is important that learners are advised to find the method that suits them and to:

- write about what is important to them
- be open and honest
- go back to earlier entries and reflect further on them; they can add comments on these earlier entries
- remember to date all entries
- be flexible in the way they keep their journal
- select critical experiences and write about them.

One of the challenges of maintaining a learning journal is to find time to develop the habit of writing it. Consequently, it is important for course developers and tutors to build in time for reflection and to encourage their students to reflect at regular intervals. There are a number of different methods of helping students to get started on reflection and the following question sets provide useful starting points:

Four basic questions to encourage reflection

1 What went well?
2 What didn't go so well?
3 What have you learnt?
4 What will you do differently as the result of this learning?

Critical incidents

1 Select a critical incident.
2 Briefly describe it.
3 What contributed to this situation?
4 What was your role in creating the situation?

5 What do you need to do differently in future?

Personal responses

1 How do you feel about this task/activity/group/module?
2 What are you enjoying?
3 What do you dislike?
4 What do you need to do differently?

Finally, it is worth remembering that for many people it takes some time to get into the habit and become comfortable with the process of reflecting as part of a blended learning programme. It is important that the tutor supports learners during this development process.

Simulations

Learning simulations simulate a real-life situation so that students gain an experience that is as close to the real one as possible and can learn about the situation and develop their knowledge and/or skills. There are two main types of simulations: computer-based and using role play. Computer-based simulations are created using computer animation or graphics. They are expensive to develop and are typically used to simulate situations that are very difficult or extremely expensive to replicate in practice. A typical example is the flight simulators used to train pilots to deal with emergency situations. In contrast, role play involves students, tutors or actors who act out a particular situation that can then be used as a source of discussion. One of the disadvantages of role play is that many people have very strong negative feelings about this type of learning activity and will switch off from the learning process as soon as they know that it involves role play.

Team building activities

See Chapter 6.

Virtual visitors or guest speakers

Information workers with particular experiences or expertise, e.g. an information officer with experience of using a particular system; customers who are willing to share their perspectives on the service; or individuals who can share a particular perspective, such as the experience of using a library service as a hearing impaired customer, may be invited as special guests on blended learning programmes or to enhance special events.

The invitation of guest speakers for either a face-to-face or virtual visit involves a fair amount of preparation as not only do the logistics of the event need to be

organized but the guest needs to be fully briefed about the blended learning programme and their contribution. In particular the organization of online access for
virtual visitors needs to be managed and, ideally, the virtual visitor should be given
an opportunity to practise with the technology before the visit.

Guidelines for tutors

- Make contact with the virtual visitor or guest speaker several weeks before
  the visit.
- Negotiate fees and expenses (if appropriate).
- Clarify aims, outcomes and expectations of the visit.
- Ensure that the visitor's contribution to the programme is timely.
- Provide the visitor with guidelines.
- Provide learners with background information about the visitor.
- Provide learners with the aims, outcomes and expectations of the activity.
- Integrate the visit with other learning activities – make it an integral part of
  the blended learning programme and, ideally, link it with assessment
  activities.
- Introduce the visitor to the group and then keep a low profile.
- Thank the visitor at the end of the session and also by private e-mail.

Visits

A visit to another library or information service, e.g. to look at a particular service or system, can be a very good way of enlivening a blended learning programme
and providing ideas for discussion. Physical visits to other organizations take some
organizing and it is important to consider the requirements of participants
with special needs. A risk assessment should be carried out for all visits and most
organizations will provide guidance on what is required. If in doubt, contact your
health and safety officer. An example completed risk assessment is presented
in Example 5.8.

Sometimes it is impossible to organize a physical visit to another service and in
this case it is worth considering a virtual tour or safari. This requires some research
but one can be set up by providing a schedule of the virtual tour and a list of sites
to visit, with questions to be answered at each site. Many ILS provide a virtual tour
to their facilities and this can be incorporated into your tour. The virtual tour may
be managed by an online site, e.g. a weblog which gives individuals the opportunity to comment on their visits and ask questions. If possible, asking library and
information workers from the ILS that are visited to come online and answer questions can really add a buzz to the virtual tour. If the tour is explicitly linked to an
assessment activity this adds to its credibility and the level of discussion that is
achieved during and after the tour.

Example 5.8 Risk assessment

Library and information managers' programme visit
Thursday 8 March 2007

Purpose of trip
To take the LIM students on a visit to two libraries as part of the LIM blended learning experience.

Institutions to be visited
The event is to be hosted at:

- ACITY Public Library
- AVOLUNTARY Organization information service

Group leader
Jane Smith, Programme Leader

Group members
16 part-time LIM students. All students are above 21 years of age.
1 additional member of staff – Wendy French.

Medication/Health
All group members have been asked to notify the LIM student co-ordinator (Janet Craig) or director (Jane Smith) of any health problems and/or medication they are currently taking for health problems.

Two students have identified health issues.

- One student has MS – she has been given a detailed breakdown of arrangements. She is satisfied with the arrangements for the trip and has notified us that she will need to sit down if she becomes tired.
- One student is in a wheelchair – both organizations visited are aware of this and are wheelchair accessible. The bus used for the trip has wheelchair facilities and the driver has had training in assisting passengers in wheelchairs.

Continued on next page

Example 5.8 *Continued*

Medical emergencies

As the trip is to an office building in an urban area covered by medical services no special medical contingency arrangements will be required. The group leader will carry a mobile phone.

AVOLUNTARY Organization is a medical humanitarian aid charity and is staffed by doctors who will be on-site during our visit.

Travel arrangements

The journey between the university and the two organizations is by a coach hired by the university through an approved supplier.

The coach leaves the university at 10.30 a.m. and returns by 2.30 p.m. (at the latest).

The group will stay together during the trip and the bus will be parked on the organizations' sites.

Activity

Library tours and presentations will be together in one venue. No special clothing or equipment are required. Both organizations have their own induction programme on arrival and their own health and safety, fire regulations and disability access regulations.

Location

As noted, the group will travel together to the two locations (see above) for the duration of the event.

Review date

This assessment will be reviewed should a similar event take place.

Copies

Copies of this assessment are lodged with the LIM office, the Master's Office, and the University's Health and Safety Office.

Signed and dated
Jane Smith
Monday, 5 March 2007

Work-based learning

See Chapter 6.

Summary

This chapter has provided guidance on the use of a range of learning activities that can enhance students' learning and enjoyment when participating in a blended learning programme. The most effective programmes are those that provide a carefully balanced mixture of learning activities that enable individuals to explore new ideas and develop their knowledge and skills in a safe environment. This chapter has indicated that many activities may be adapted for use in either a face-to-face or an online context. The next chapter covers the important topic of group activities and group learning processes.

References

Glover, C. (2002) Storm in a Tea Cup: brainstorming – the process of generating new ideas, *People Management*, **8** (7), 44–5.

Kearsley, G. and Schneiderman, B. (1998) Engagement Theory, *Educational Technology*, **38** (3), http://home.sprynet.com/gkearsley/engage.htm.

Moon, J. (1999) *Learning Journals*, London, Kogan Page.

Salmon, G. (2002) *E-activities*, London, Kogan Page.

6   Working with groups

Introduction

The aim of this chapter is to provide guidance on facilitating group work. Blended learning programmes offer many flexible approaches to group work and this may involve individuals meeting face-to-face and/or in a virtual environment. Online group work provides new opportunities for individuals to learn and work together as it means they can collaborate across traditional time and space boundaries.

The chapter starts by considering a number of specialist group learning activities, including team building and inquiry-based learning. This is followed by a general overview of group processes, including the group development process and team roles. Next there is a section that looks at online group learning processes and this includes an adaptation of Gilly Salmon's model of e-learning. This is followed by a discussion about working with diverse learning groups. Individual ILS tutors are likely to work with groups of varying sizes, from four to 400 people, and the section on working with large groups focuses on mass lectures and on managing large groups in an e-learning environment. Finally, there is a section on working with challenging learners.

Group learning activities

This section considers learning activities that are commonly designed around group work, and it is worth noting that many of the activities described in Chapter 5 may be used as either individual or small group activities, e.g. quizzes, exercises and simulations. This section considers team-building activities and examples of inquiry-based learning, including problem-based learning, project-based learning and work-based learning

Team-building activities

While icebreakers are a useful technique for helping learners to get to know each other it is sometimes worth spending additional time getting to know each other and becoming confident about working together. Examples of group building activities that may be used in a face-to-face context include those involving children's toys such as Lego™ or Duplo™, or asking a group to build the highest tower possible that supports a fresh egg at its highest point, using ten sheets of paper and ten paperclips (the tower should support an egg for one minute). I have used the following 'desert exercise' (source unknown) in both face-to-face and online contexts during the early stages of a number of blended learning programmes for library and information workers. Example 6.1 is the script from the e-learning version.

Example 6.1 Desert exercise – introductory message

Hello everyone,

Here is the next group activity. You may find it helpful to print out these instructions for further reference. I hope you enjoy the activity.

The purpose of this activity is to enable you to:

- develop your skills in online group work
- develop online threads on particular discussion topics
- discover some of the advantages and disadvantages of online group working.

The exercise

Your group was attempting to cross the Sahara Desert and your mini-bus has broken down. You are able to obtain five items from the following list:

- torch (4 battery size)
- jack-knife
- sectional air map of crash area
- plastic raincoat
- magnetic compass
- bandage kit with gauze
- 45 calibre pistol
- parachute (red and white)
- bottle of salt tablets (1000)
- 1 quart of water per person
- book entitled *Edible Animals of the Desert*
- 2 pairs of sunglasses
- 2 quarts of 180° proof vodka
- 1 overcoat per person
- cosmetic mirror.

What you need to do

Individually, you need to identify your top five items and your reasons for selecting them. You need to share your thinking with the group.

Continued on next page

Example 6.1 *Continued*

Then working as a group you have to select the group's top five items. The selection should be based on consensus, i.e. be a group decision-making process. Consensus is difficult to reach. Therefore, not every ranking will meet with everyone's complete approval. Try, as a group, to make each ranking one with which all group members can at least partially agree. Here are some guides to use in reaching consensus:

- Avoid arguing for your own individual judgements.
- Approach the task on the basis of logic.
- Avoid changing your mind only in order to reach agreement and avoid conflict. Support only solutions with which you are able to agree somewhat, at least.
- Avoid 'conflict-reducing' techniques such as majority vote, averaging or trading in reaching decisions.
- View difference of opinion as helpful rather than as a hindrance in decision-making.
- View your initial agreement as suspect.

I will be popping in at regular intervals although I won't take part in the activity unless you want to ask me specific questions.

Once you have decided your top five group items, post a group message with the subject name 'Five items' by 27 April.

Best wishes,
Barbara

This activity enables individual learners to get involved in a group process and it is the type of activity that many people are familiar with in face-to-face training sessions. This kind of activity may take 7–14 days to complete online and it is important to allow enough time for everyone to take part and have a real discussion.

Example 6.2 Desert exercise – tutor's response at the end of the activity

Hello everyone,

Well done for succeeding with the task and delivering a list of five items by the deadline. I was very impressed with the way you worked, and noted the following really good practice:

- acknowledging each other's messages
- backing your ideas up with brief explanations

Continued on next page

Example 6.2 *Continued*

- keeping your messages relatively short
- asking for ideas, asking for agreement
- using other information sources, e.g. experience, TV programmes, internet
- appropriate use of humour
- a volunteer producing summaries of findings
- completing the task on time
- creative ways of using materials present, e.g. mirrors.

This is an excellent start to the e-learning course. Well done. You will find that the skills you have developed here will be very useful in your first assignment.

If you have been quiet during this exercise (and I am aware that there are many reasons for this, e.g. half-term holiday, pressures of day job, teething problems with the technology) then my suggestion is that you get more involved in the next activity. This is important as you will need to use some of your messages in your assignment. Do contact me if you have any queries or concerns.

The definitive list

So, what is the definitive list? Here are the top five items from the 'experts':

1 Mirror – for signalling purposes
2 Overcoat – to keep warm
3 Water – to drink
4 Torch – for signalling purposes
5 Parachute – to signal and keep warm.

What to do next?

You may like to think about what you have learnt from this activity. Also, what helped the exercise to work well and how could it be improved? You could share your thoughts in this general discussion area.

The next activity will be posted on 10 May.

Finally

Well done. You have got off to a brilliant start to the course.

Barbara

This message in Example 6.2 praises the learners' work, identifies good practice, addresses individuals who have been 'quiet' and it gives the recommended answer. It also points the learners to a general discussion area and explains when the next activity will be posted. This 'desert exercise' may be referred to later on in the same course, e.g. as an example in discussions about netiquette, group working or using a diverse range of sources.

Inquiry-based learning

The pedagogy of inquiry-based learning (IBL) is outlined in Chapter 3, where three different approaches to IBL are described: problem-based learning, project-based learning and work-based learning. Developing IBL activities involves considering:

- the development of the IBL activity
- the processes involved in setting up the groups
- the management and support of the learning groups.

The starting point for the IBL activity is a real-life problem or issue and this may be generated by the tutor, the student or another person, e.g. a manager or colleague in the workplace. As a tutor developing an IBL activity it is worthwhile carrying out some basic research on the topic and issue. This will enable you to determine the size of the problem or issue, its boundaries, relevant information resources, specialist knowledge or skills required to tackle the activity, and likely problems or challenge. This information may then be used to facilitate the learning activity.

A number of practical issues and questions arise in the running of IBL. The first of these is to think about the size of the group, which may vary from four to five students up to nine or ten. The second question to be addressed is who decides on how the groups are made up. There is a variety of approaches: students allocated to groups as a means of ensuring the groups are mixed, with no choice or movement between groups allowed; chance allocation mechanisms (such as the use of playing cards); self-organizing groups. The third question is: how are IBL topics determined? For example, there might be a list of topics from which groups choose on a 'first come, first served' basis, or students might negotiate their own topic within the group and then with the tutor.

The next issue concerns the actual management of the IBL group process. In some disciplines where the whole curriculum is underpinned by IBL, e.g. medicine, the learning process may be facilitated by specially trained facilitators. Frequently, IBL is facilitated by tutors who have developed their own knowledge and skills in this area, e.g. by attending short courses. You need to consider how you will manage and support the IBL process. In general, this approach to learning is considered to be student-centred and involves the tutor moving from a leadership role to one of guiding from the side. Consequently, the tutor needs to be available to support the student groups, e.g. by e-mail, but should step back from the learning process and let the students engage in it and learn from their successes and mistakes.

Group learning processes

Some knowledge of group learning processes is valuable for tutors involved in IBL, and common ideas about group development and group roles are useful, as they provide potential tools for managing the group process. It is common knowledge that groups go through a development cycle that is made up of five stages:

* forming
* storming
* norming
* performing
* adjourning.

Jaques (2000) offers a variation of this model and proposes an additional stage, 'informing', that comes between performing and adjourning. This is particularly relevant to group learning activities as the group is often asked to disseminate and discuss its results to the whole learning group.

At each of these stages a group is likely to go through a set of experiences and if you, as tutor, are aware of these stages you will be less likely to be surprised by what happens with the group and you will be able to use some standard intervention techniques to help the group progress. It is worth noting that groups may spend different amounts of time within each stage and that they may get stuck at a particular stage. If a group does appear to be stuck at one of these stages then Table 6.1 provides some ideas of ways to move them forward.

Table 6.1 Stages in group development

Stage	Characteristics	Facilitation techniques
Forming	Individuals are starting to get to know each other. Some people may be shy and quiet. Others may be over-participative. People may 'cling on' to people they already know. There may be confusion about the purpose of the blended learning programme and how it will work.	Use icebreakers and small group activities. Give people time to get to know each other. Encourage and enable people to talk to those people they don't yet know. Follow up absent members and ensure that they have a full briefing.
Storming	Individuals may challenge the tutor or other group members. They may also challenge the concept of the blended learning programme and its learning activities. There may be personality clashes and differences of opinion about how to carry out the work.	Provide time for people to 'let off steam'. Ensure that the intended working practices are fully discussed and agreed by everyone. Be clear about what is negotiable and what isn't. If there are some people in the group who appear to be very disruptive, then see them alone (ideally face-to-face or by phone) and sort out their issues. Occasionally you may need to make a decision about whether or not you keep someone in the group or ask them to leave.
Norming	At this stage, people begin to settle down and get on with the task. The unwritten rules or 'norms' of the group develop. The group establishes set ways or 'norms' of carrying out its work. Everyone knows what to expect and how events such as meetings will be run.	Highlight and clarify working practices. Agree standards of work. Ensure that the norms that are set are useful ones, e.g. everyone arrives on time for meetings. Provide time to discuss working practices and their effectiveness.

Continued on next page

Table 6.1 *Continued*

Stage	Characteristics	Facilitation techniques
Performing	There is a high level of trust within the group. Individuals accept each other and their strengths and weaknesses. There is a strong commitment to achieving the group goals. People work flexibly to achieve the group goals. This stage is often accompanied by increased use of humour, 'in-jokes' or stories.	At this stage the tutor takes a relatively low profile. The group is working well. Your role is to support and facilitate the group. You may be asked to intervene with respect to specific problems.
Informing	This is the dissemination stage and the tutor needs to facilitate each group sharing its work, findings and ideas.	This needs to be structured in some way and common methods include using posters (on the wall or in the virtual environment), and verbal (face-to-face) or text-based (online) dissemination and feedback.
Adjourning	The programme is coming to an end and the group is about to disband. This stage is characterized by 'goodbye' rituals – celebratory party, exchange of personal information and ideas for meeting in the future, exchange of stories about the project and what has been achieved.	Organize some kind of closing event. This may range from special cakes at a meeting to a party. In a virtual environment it may involve an online party with virtual refreshments! Give time at the final session or online activity to evaluate the programme and the learners' achievements. Make sure that you thank everyone for their work on the programme.

Another approach to thinking about team work is to consider the team roles that individuals adopt when they are working in a team. One of the most popular approaches to exploring team roles is based on the work of Meredith Belbin (1993), who identified nine team roles (Table 6.2). Belbin suggests that the most successful teams are those that include individuals with a preference for different team roles, so that, as a whole, the team contains the full set of roles. In reality

Table 6.2 Belbin's team roles

Role and description	Team role contribution	Allowable weaknesses
Plant		
Creative, imaginative, unorthodox.	Solves difficult problems.	Ignores details. Builds 'castles in the air'.
Resource investigator		
Extrovert, enthusiastic, communicative.	Explores opportunities. Develops contacts.	Over-optimistic. Loses interest once initial enthusiasm has passed.
Co-ordinator		
Mature, confident, a good chairperson.	Clarifies goals, promotes decision making, delegates well.	Can be seen as manipulative. Delegates personal work.
Shaper		
Challenging, dynamic, thrives on pressure.	Has the drive and courage to overcome obstacles.	Can provoke others. Hurts people's feelings.
Monitor, evaluator		
Sober, strategic and discerning.	Sees all options. Judges accurately.	Lacks drive and ability to inspire others. Overly critical.

Continued on next page

Table 6.2 *Continued*

Role and description	Team role contribution	Allowable weaknesses
Team worker		
Co-operative, supportive, empathetic and diplomatic.	Listens, builds, averts friction, calms the waters.	May be indecisive. Can be easily influenced.
Implementer		
Disciplined, reliable, conservative and efficient.	Turns ideas into practical actions.	Somewhat inflexible. Slow to respond to new possibilities.
Completer		
Painstaking, focuses on detail and deadlines, conscientious.	Searches out errors and omissions. Delivers on time.	Inclined to worry unduly. Reluctant to delegate.
Specialist		
Single-minded, self-starting, dedicated, focused on a particular topic or issue.	Provides knowledge and skills in rare supply. Contributes on only a narrow front.	Dwells on technicalities. Overlooks the 'big picture'.

and in small teams it may not be possible to select people who together demonstrate the full range of role types. However, most people are versatile and are capable of filling a number of different roles. It is possible to identify Belbin role types among team members by using self-perception questionnaires or by observing IBL activities and team work. Further information is available at www.belbin.com.

These concepts of a development cycle and of different roles are useful ideas to introduce to learning groups because they offer a framework for exploring and reflecting on the group experience. This is illustrated in the following example, which comes from a blended management development programme. Following a face-to-face workshop in which the group worked together on a series of team development activities and then worked with the Belbin inventory, they completed the online activity described in Example 6.3.

Example 6.3   Online activity

Aim: The purpose of this activity is to help you to develop your knowledge and skills in team work.

Outcome: A 100-word reflective commentary

Hello everyone,

This activity will help you to link theoretical ideas and practice in regard to team work. You may use examples from your current life situation, past work or other experiences, or even from TV programmes such as *The Apprentice*!

Continued on next page

Example 6.3 *Continued*

What you should do

1) Read the paper with the filename 'Managing teams' – it is attached to this message.
2) If you want to follow up these ideas in more depth then carry out a Google Scholar search.
3) What do you think of the **model of team development** (forming, storming, etc.)? Have you ever experienced this type of process in real life, e.g. in the workplace, on a course, or in sports or social activities? Does the theory match the practice? Be critical of the theory – do you think teams really go through this process? What evidence from your own experiences do you have to support or challenge this model? Write about 50 words on your ideas.
4) What do you think of the **model of team roles** (Belbin's model)? What do you think are your preferred roles? Have you ever worked in a team where you could identify people with these team roles? Does the theory match the practice? Be critical of the theory – do you think people match these categories? What evidence from your own experiences do you have to support or challenge this model? Write about 50 words on your ideas.
5) Finally, read and comment on other students' ideas about team work. This will help you to develop your understanding of team roles and see it from a number of different perspectives.

Do post a message if you have any queries about this activity.

Thanks,
Barbara

Online groups

One common strategy for circumventing geographic and time constraints is to work in virtual groups using online communication tools such as e-mail, discussion or bulletin boards, and conference or chat rooms. These tools are explored in Chapter 2. The ideas about group learning processes outlined above all apply to online groups. However, there are some additional special considerations that need to be taken into account with online groups.

Although working in virtual groups gives individual members the opportunity to access the blended learning programme from their desktops at a time and place that suits them, it also raises some challenges to group work. How do you develop trust and confidence in the group and its members if you have never met them or only met them once or twice during a face-to-face workshop?

Working together in face-to-face groups gives individuals the opportunity to size each other up, get to know each other's work styles, habits and preferences, and build relationships. In particular, sitting around a meeting table means that you gain very quick feedback through someone's replies (or silences) and also their body language. In contrast, virtual group working involves communicating with other group members through text (in the case of e-mail, discussion groups or conference rooms), sometimes with the support of video-streamed images, e.g. in the case of video-conferencing. Individuals need to get to know each other and develop trust in their tutor and group members

In virtual groups, the role of the tutor includes managing technical, individual learning, group work and social aspects of the communication process. This will include managing:

- Technical points
    — ensuring an appropriate virtual communication platform
    — ensuring appropriate technical support
    — ensuring that the administrative arrangements, e.g. user IDs and passwords, are in place
- Individual learning
    — scaffolding the learning process
    — encouraging independence in learning
    — encouraging growth and development
    — answering questions
    — providing feedback
    — encouraging reflection
- Group work
    — overall management of group work
    — monitoring and controlling tasks and activities
    — providing feedback and support to individuals and group(s)
    — offering advice and support to those with problems
- Social aspects of learning
    — developing an appropriate online working environment
    — developing friendly informal communications.

The five-step model based on the work of Gilly Salmon (2000) provides a helpful outline of the key stages in virtual group work. This model integrates many of the theoretical ideas mentioned earlier in Chapter 3, e.g. learning as a social activity, and knowledge construction. Salmon's model is adapted here by the inclusion of an additional stage, the informing stage, based on the work of Jaques (2000). This model is presented in Table 6.3 and explored below.

Table 6.3 Model of virtual group work		
Stage	**Group member activities**	**Tutor activities**
Stage 1 Access and motivation	Accessing the system Finding their way around	Welcome and encouragement Guidance on where to find technical support
Stage 2 Online socialization	Sending and receiving messages Getting to know each other Starting to develop a group culture	Introductions Icebreakers Ground rules Netiquette
Stage 3 Information exchange	Exploring roles, responsibilities, project tasks Carrying out activities Reporting and discussing findings	Facilitating structured activities Assigning roles and responsibilities Encouraging discussions Summarizing findings and/or outcomes
Stage 4 Project or learning activities	Completing project tasks or learning activities Giving and receiving feedback Problem solving	Facilitating online activities Monitoring process within overall programme Facilitating the process Asking questions Encouraging reflection
Stage 5 Informing	Disseminating findings Giving and receiving feedback Reflecting on outcomes and learning process	Facilitating the process Asking questions Encouraging reflection
Stage 6 Closure	Completing all tasks and activities Completing review and evaluation processes Goodbyes	Leading review and evaluation process Ensuring loose ends are completed Leading closure
Adapted from the work of Gilly Salmon (2000)		

In order to encourage an effective virtual learning group here are some examples of the types of activity that e-tutors are likely to be involved in during the six stages:

Stage 1 Access and motivation
- Ensure that the online group is set up with a welcome message.
- Ensure group members know how to access the online group.
- Open and close the discussion group.

Stage 2 Online socialization
- Lead a round of introductions with, perhaps, an online icebreaker.
- Welcome new group members or late arrivals.
- Provide a structure for getting started, e.g. agreement of group rules, netiquette.

- If individuals break the agreed group netiquette then address the issue (either privately or through the discussion group).
- Wherever possible avoid playing 'ping pong' with individual group members and ask other people for their opinions and ideas.
- Encourage quieter group members to join in.
- Provide summaries of online discussions. This is called weaving, and involves summarizing and synthesizing the content of multiple responses in a virtual group.

Stage 3 Information exchange
- Provide highly structured activities at the start of the group's life.
- Encourage participation.
- Ask questions.
- Encourage group members to post short messages.
- Allocate online roles to individual members, e.g. to provide a summary of a particular thread of discussion.
- Close threads as and when appropriate.
- Encourage the online group to develop its own life and history. Welcome shared language, metaphors, rituals and jokes.

Stage 4 Group learning activity or project work
- Facilitate online activities.
- Monitor the process with respect to the project plan.
- Facilitate the process.
- Ask questions.
- Encourage reflection.

Stage 5 Informing
- Facilitate an online (or face-to-face) dissemination activity.
- Give feedback.
- Ask questions.
- Encourage reflection.

Stage 6 Closure
- Ensure 'loose ends' are completed.
- Highlight group achievements.
- Encourage (structured) reflection and evaluation on the group process.
- Thank group members for their contributions and work.
- Formally close the activity (or programme).

Working with diverse learning groups

Kandola and Fullerton (1994, 8) introduce the idea of managing diversity as follows:

> The basic concept of managing diversity accepts that the workforce consists of a diverse population of people. The diversity consists of visible and non-visible differences which will include factors such as sex, age, background, race, disability and work style. It is founded on the premise that harnessing these differences will create a productive environment in which everyone feels valued, where their talents are being fully utilised and their organisational goals are met.

Managing group work frequently involves working with people from a range of cultures and faiths, different countries and perhaps generations. In addition, people will come to the group with different educational and work experiences as well as individual needs, e.g. as a result of disability. In the UK, the Disability Discrimination Act has resulted in a heightened awareness of the importance of disability issues and the need to make an appropriate adjustment in order to meet an individual's needs. If this doesn't happen the tutor and their organization may end up in an expensive and time-consuming legal contest. Students will vary in their home situations too, e.g. some people may have childcare or other responsibilities which limit the amount of time that they can commit to the programme, and there may be differences in the amount of access students have to information technology. This means that the tutor or facilitator needs to be aware of the diversity of their group members and encourage a learning environment in which individuals are respected and their needs are accommodated.

One way of recognizing diversity is to provide an environment in which individuals can inform the tutor (either in private or in the presence of the rest of the group) or the programme administrator of their needs. This can be achieved in a number of ways. Educational institutions normally have very clear policies and procedures for managing diversity, and this is likely to involve tutors being informed of particular requirements. An awareness of the different needs, e.g. as a result of faith festivals, of different cultural, religious and national groups is important because it enables programmes to be scheduled to accommodate the various requirements. For ILS that provide blended learning programmes to the public, it is a good idea to ask participants to identify any special needs when they book onto a course. As tutor, it is useful to include this in the introductory stage of the course. For example, at the start of online group work it is useful to discuss and agree on expectations as to the frequency of participation in online activities. This enables individual group members to recognize each other's availability to participate in the online activities.

Unexpected individual or group needs may arise during the life of the blended learning programme. For example, a student may recognize that they have a learning need such as dyslexia and the results of a specialist assessment may advise that their learning materials be provided in a particular format. A student may have a temporary disability, e.g. as the result of an accident, and need access to a special chair for the duration of a workshop. An end-user may have limited access to an online system, e.g. while working overseas, and adaptations to the scheduling of the programme may need to be made to accommodate this. It is important that the tutor is aware that specific issues may arise during the course of a blended learning programme and of the need to respond to them in an appropriate manner. If they are unsure of the appropriate way to manage a particular situation then they need to obtain advice, e.g. from a disability service or a human resources department.

Staff development programmes such as diversity awareness workshops are extremely useful in raising awareness of this important issue and indicating local sources of information and support.

Working with large groups

Many library and information workers, particularly those working in the education sector, are frequently involved in working with large groups. This may occur as part of an induction programme or it may be part of an information or academic skills programme. In blended learning programmes working with large groups may involve giving a lecture to between 100 and 1000 students and then managing an e-learning follow-up process. This section provides some insights into the challenges of and approaches to managing large groups.

The most important aspect of working with a large group is forward planning. The more care and attention that goes into the planning of the blended learning programme and individual learning activities, the less likely there are to be errors or problems arising when you deliver the programme. If you provide an e-learning activity for a group of 12 students and half of them e-mail you with general queries about the activity this takes up much less time than if you receive 200 e-mails when dealing with a large group. This means that it is important to provide extremely clear and accurate information, and to anticipate any problems. There are ways of streamlining the communication processes with large groups and these are considered later in this section. At the planning stage it is worthwhile considering the following questions:

1 For face-to-face activities – is there a choice of room? Most library and information workers in post-16 educational settings find that there is a limited choice of rooms for working with large groups. This can mean that you need to develop the session with the specific room that you are using and its limitations or advantages in mind.
2 For e-learning activities – do you have access to a virtual learning environment?
3 How do you engage with a large audience – face-to-face and online?

4 How do individuals participate – face-to-face and online?

5 How do you control the group – face-to-face and online?

6 How do you respond to the needs of a diverse group of people – face-to-face and online?

7 How do you get your message across – face-to-face and online?

It is worth spending a few moments thinking about the psychology of large groups before going into any detail about managing them. Individuals behave in a different way when they are in large groups than when they are in small ones. When people are part of a crowd they often behave differently from if they were by themselves. Crowds often act overly frantically or fearfully. In crowds individuals feel anonymous and there is diffused responsibility, which means it can be difficult to obtain responses from individuals in a large group, particularly if it requires them to stand out from the crowd. At the same time, it is possible to use the powers of suggestion and contagious behaviour to help instigate the types of behaviour that are helpful to the learning process.

Mass lectures

Many library and information workers deliver lectures to large groups of people. Typically, a mass lecture will be delivered using one or more tools such as Power-Point, live ICT demonstrations, interactive whiteboard or video clips (see Chapter 2). During a lecture (and other learning activities) concentration and retention of information is not constant. Typically, it drops off over time, and introducing activities will help to improve concentration and recall of information. Consequently, it is a good idea to include one or more activities during a lecture. They will also help to improve motivation and student participation. Common advice given to new lecturers is to provide some kind of change, e.g. an activity, after 20 minutes as students' concentration typically starts to fade then.

Activities need to be carefully managed, otherwise they can either take up too much time or fizzle out like a damp squib. Managing activities involves providing very clear instructions, given both verbally and visually, using PowerPoint, and making it clear when you want the students to start and end their activity. In mass lectures you need to use very clear commands such as 'start the activity NOW' and 'please END the activity NOW'. I find it helpful to flash or lower the lights in the lecture room, e.g. to give a five-minute warning of the approaching end of an activity and then to flash or lower the lights again at the end of the activity. This use of non-verbal stimuli helps to make it clear that you are moving on to the next part of the activity or lecture.

A wide range of activities (outlined in Chapter 5) may be used within a lecture and examples include:

• quizzes

- case studies or other activities
- interviews
- mini discussions
- question and answer sessions
- action planning.

Quizzes may be used in a variety of ways within a lecture, as shown by the following examples:

- A paper-based diagnostic quiz can be placed on each chair and as the students arrive they are asked to complete the quiz. As tutor you may then ask for answers using a show of hands. This is a useful starting activity because it can be used to identify the levels of knowledge within the group and so inform the rest of the lecture. However, this type of activity does need careful handling so that it doesn't become too long and drawn out.
- Quizzes involving simple multiple-choice or true and false questions may be included in the lecture. Answers can be generated in a number of ways: a show of hands; use of different coloured cards; or through an audience response system.
- A paper-based quiz can be used part way through the lecture, the audience being asked to mark each others' answers as the tutor works through the correct answers.

Finally, the lecture may be followed up by a paper-based, online (in a virtual environment) or e-mail quiz, with a prize offered for the first five correct sets of answers that are chosen at random. If you use this type of activity, remember to allow sufficient time for people with special needs to complete it.

Examples of mini case studies or other activities include:

- An example of a mini case study that could be presented, either as part of a PowerPoint presentation or on paper, is a search strategy of a student looking for information relevant to their dissertation. Ask the students to critique the search strategy using both their general information-searching skills and those covered in the mass lecture. Ask them to work with a neighbour and then share their findings with the pair sitting in front of or behind them. You can debrief the activity by asking for feedback from the audience or by going through a model search strategy yourself.
- An example activity that I have used in teaching students to evaluate information sources involves a simple listing process. I have asked management students to list the following in terms of academic credibility:
  — a newspaper article (*The Times*)
  — a textbook
  — a journal article (refereed)

— a journal article (not refereed)

— a conference paper (American Academy of Management)

— a government report.

I then ask them to show the list to their next door neighbour and discuss differences in their order. I then present the 'correct' answer and this always leads to a heated discussion about the credibility of different sources.

- I often use anagrams (or word puzzles, as I have learnt to call them in international groups). I introduce the activity with the following instructions:

  — Copy down the following word puzzles or anagrams – there will be ten presented during the lecture. These will appear in different places on different slides.

  — Work out the words or phrases (after the lecture).

  — Write an explanation of each word.

  — Hand in your answers on a sheet of paper with your name and student ID to the post box outside my office by 4 p.m. tomorrow.

  — Next week there will be a PRIZE draw and the five correct answer sets drawn from the box will each receive a book token for £15.

  I produce the anagrams using internet-based tools such as Hot Potatoes (http://hotpot.uvic.ca/). I often use this activity in a session on referencing and plagiarism and it works well. The students are motivated by the activity and it helps them to focus on and read the slides, and they frequently then show their neighbours the location of the anagram. Asking students to write an explanation means that they have to understand the concepts. Giving them about 24 hours to complete the activity means that students for whom English isn't their first language and those with disabilities, such as dyslexia, have time to work on the activity. Finally, the book token acts as a great motivator to complete the activity!

Interviewing guests can provide a welcome change during a lecture. My own experience is that many people don't like speaking in front of very large groups, so to facilitate this I often suggest that I interview them as part of the lecture or I ask a couple of students to interview them. This works well, as it offers a different type of activity within the lecture and the guest speaker may feel more comfortable being interviewed rather than speaking to the whole group. I often ask students who did the course the previous year to come along and be interviewed. This can be very valuable as they put over important messages about academic skills in a way that has great credibility. Whenever possible I record the interviews using a digital recorder and load up the files in the virtual learning environment or e-mail them to students.

Mini discussions can be used during lectures, e.g. asking students to discuss specific ideas in twos or threes and then sharing their findings and thoughts with another group. One way of facilitating this activity is to provide every student with a Post-it™ Note (it may be stuck under their seat before they arrive), and ask them to write down one thought that they have on the subject and then to swap notes three times so that each has one whose writer they don't know. Then ask specific students to read out the thought on their note and use this to generate discussion.

Question and answer sessions are traditionally held at the end of a lecture, though it is often useful to include opportunities for questions at the end of each theme. If you are introducing a question and answer session, remember that you control the question time. It is useful at the start of a lecture to say when and how you will handle questions. If you do ask whether there are any questions, then give students time. I often silently count to ten to give people time to think of their questions. A number of techniques can be used to generate questions. A popular one is to ask students to talk to their neighbours and then give them three or four minutes to identify any outstanding questions or points that require clarification. You may then ask them to write their questions on pre-circulated Post-it™ Notes or cards. Collect the questions and answer them. If there are any questions that you can't answer, say that you will post the question and answer online.

Case study 6.1 Teaching information skills

A colleague teaches information skills to nursing students. She found that the group tended to be quiet and unresponsive in their first session. Consequently, she identified six questions commonly asked by students and wrote each one on a numbered piece of card. She then handed out the cards to students as they came into the lecture. At set times during the session she would ask one of the students to read out their question and she then answered it. This process helped to introduce questions into her session and also helped the students to develop the habit of asking questions.

A useful activity at the end of a lecture is to ask everyone to identify and write down one thing that they will do differently as a result of the lecture. Ask them to set a SMART outcome (see Chapter 5). You may want to provide prompt action plans via a PowerPoint presentation and include examples such as: use advance search facilities when next searching academic databases; explore the use of citation indexing tools; or read the relevant chapter in an appropriate textbook. Once they have written down their action point, ask them to share it with a neighbour. This type of activity only takes a few minutes but helps the students to put into practice their learning from the session.

Managing the lecture process involves managing the group, making good use of your material and looking after yourself. In a perfect lecture, students will arrive in good time, be ready at the start of the lecture with their pens and notepads poised for action, and attentively listen to your every word. In reality, it can sometimes seem like a struggle. Some common issues with groups are:

- Students arriving late. If you are presenting a lecture to 300 or 400 students then some may arrive late. Before the start of the lecture think about how to handle this situation. Some educational institutions have rules about late-comers which can make life easier. Others leave it up to individuals to handle on a one-to-one basis. My own approach is to ignore late arrivals and not to adapt my lecture to take into account their needs, because if I stop and start for ten latecomers the whole session begins to lose its flow and energy. It's worth noting that I take a very different approach if someone arrives late when part of a small group.
- Students talking to each other during your lecture. There are a number of approaches to dealing with this issue, e.g. you stop speaking and don't start again until there is silence, or ask the chatterers if they have any questions or are having a problem understanding the content of the lecture.
- Students texting their friends during the lecture. I tend to ignore this practice as it does not disturb others.
- One person attempting to dominate the session, e.g. by asking continual questions. I tend to praise their enthusiasm and then ask them to give other people an opportunity to ask questions, or ask them to see me later.

Making good use of your material involves being well prepared with contingency plans to cover possible technical failures. If you find that you have too little material, e.g. because you have spoken faster than normal or an exercise has taken half the allocated time, include 'nice to know' topics or use more examples or detail. However, be conscious that packing your session with material that your audience doesn't consider highly relevant may reduce its impact. Sometimes it is worthwhile finishing early, as most students welcome a slightly longer break before their next session. If you find that you have too much material, limit your session to 'must know' topics and skim over less crucial topics. However, it is really important NEVER to overrun your time.

Many people find it stressful managing large groups, and if you are asked to present a mass lecture it is worthwhile thinking about how you can minimize your stress levels. Obvious points include being well prepared with a good-quality lecture that you have rehearsed; and checking out the room and equipment before the session so that you are confident that you know the layout and how everything works. Other ways of helping yourself include asking a colleague to come along and run part of the session, e.g. if I am carrying out an online demonstration then I ask a colleague to run the demonstration and I can then focus on explaining to the audience what is happening. This means that I can focus my attention on the audience and keep them under control while my colleague focuses on the technology.

Case study 6.2 Distributing handouts

Circulating handouts in a mass lecture can be very time-consuming and one mistake I made a number of years ago was to attempt to hand out a paper-based quiz to 500 students halfway through a lecture. I discovered it took almost ten minutes and I had lost the audience's attention by the time everyone had received their handout. This meant that I then had to work harder to refocus the students.

What I learnt from that experience was that it is worthwhile handing out materials before the start of a lecture, and I often ask a colleague to help me to do this as it speeds up the whole process. I also find that colour coding materials is helpful so that during the lecture you can refer to specific handouts by their colour. This helps to smooth the whole process of students moving into an activity.

Managing large groups online

As well as managing large groups in a lecture, many library and information workers facilitate learning through online learning environments such as Blackboard and WebCT (see Chapter 2). Managing large groups online involves being well organized and having a well-planned learning environment. Traditionally these are divided into sections such as announcements, learning materials, learning activities, web links and assessment activities. The site may be organized by theme, topic or time, e.g. Week 1, Week 2, etc. Presenting a consistent and repetitive structure seems to help many learners work through their e-learning activities.

I find it helpful to put up a weekly announcement and to send a weekly e-mail to students to remind them of what is expected on a week-by-week basis. I also have a frequently asked question (FAQ) thread in the discussion group area and any non-personal individual e-mails that I receive from students are answered in this section (without revealing their source). This means that if I receive a series of e-mails on one issue I can respond to them by asking students to look in the FAQ section. This saves my time and I find that after a while students begin to look there for answers themselves.

Case study 6.3 Academic and professional skills module

I have been involved in delivering an academic and professional skills module to between 300 and 450 undergraduate business and management students for a number of years. This is a first-year module which covers key academic skills such as information searching, referencing, ICT skills, quantitative methods and group-working skills. The structure of the module involves a blended mixture of:

- weekly lectures
- weekly ICT tutorials
- online activities, e.g. plagiarism quiz, quantitative methods, diagnostic test
- online or face-to-face group work supported by face-to-face group tutorials
- open clinic every fortnight.

The whole module is managed via a Blackboard site and every activity that the students complete, including those that take place during lectures, forms part of the assessment of the module.

The whole module is complex and involves 20 tutors, including study-advice staff, information-skills tutors, ICT tutors and lecturers. In addition, the assessment activities are linked into another first-year module, so there has to be detailed co-operation between staff working on both modules. Consequently, not only the students but also the staff receive a weekly e-mail reminding them of current activities.

In addition, we use the student tracking system in Blackboard and attendance at tutorials to identify students who are not engaged with the module activities, and then carry out follow-up activities to identify and rectify any issues.

It took three years to develop the current structure of this module and each year we find areas for improvement and new ways of delivering aspects of the module. Overall, it works well and students report that they find it useful.

Working with challenging learners

There are no difficult learners only inflexible tutors

Anon.

All tutors encounter challenging participants and groups at some stage or other. This may be the result of the participant(s):

- not wanting to attend the course
- having low expectations about the course
- feeling uncomfortable with the tutor
- feeling uncomfortable with one or more participants
- feeling uncomfortable with the environment (face-to-face and/or online environment)
- being distracted by factors in the workplace (e.g. forthcoming disciplinary meeting, forthcoming merger, restructuring of department)
- being distracted by factors outside the workplace (e.g. argument with partner, family health problems, debt problems).

Many of these factors have nothing to do with the tutor but, if she does not manage the situation, these learners can adversely affect the whole learning process and programme. Common difficulties affecting the whole group may include:

- one or more participants take over learning activities
- one or more participants will not join in
- participants have side conversations
- individuals are excluded by the group

- disagreement, leading to confrontation
- one or more individuals attempt to sabotage the activity or programme.

In most groups a few participants are willing to talk and become involved in discussions, and this may result in others not contributing to the activity. Possible ways of handling these participants include:

- setting up appropriate ground rules at the start of the programme, session or activity
- acknowledging their contribution and asking for someone else to contribute
- acknowledging their contribution and pointing out that everyone needs an opportunity to speak
- structuring discussions and feedback sessions so that everyone has an equal opportunity to speak
- giving them a task, e.g. observe and report back, so that they focus on this during a discussion
- letting the group handle it.

The problem is sometimes associated with the formation of cliques, i.e. small groups that form and become exclusive. This can have a very detrimental effect on the whole course because other participants may feel like 'outsiders'. A key strategy is to structure exercises and activities so that the clique members can't work together.

Sometimes one or more people will not participate in the course, e.g. as a result of more senior staff being present, because they feel that they have nothing to contribute, or because they need more time to think. Possible ways of handling this situation include:

- giving them more time
- setting up small-group work and ensuring that everyone has an opportunity to give feedback
- asking these students for their views.

There are two main types of side conversations: those that are about the course content and take place through the participants' interest and enthusiasm; and those that have nothing to do with the course and are, perhaps, a sign of boredom. Possible ways of handling this include:

- setting appropriate ground rules at the start of the session
- stopping talking and waiting for them to be quiet
- asking them to share their conversation with the whole group
- asking them a direct question.

The final common type of challenging situation is when there is a major disagreement between one or more participants and the rest of the group. This can be handled in a number of ways:

- Take control immediately.
- Never take sides.
- Interrupt the discussion with a direct question and refocus them on the training materials.
- Bring another participant into the discussions.
- Summarize the differences, state that everyone is entitled to their own opinion and then move on to a new topic.
- Ask everyone to summarize their position, with the evidence to support it, and then ask them to 'agree to disagree' (this has the added value of them actually agreeing about something!).
- Change the subject.
- Speak to the people concerned in private, e.g. outside the training room, or by phone if it relates to an online element of the programme.

Summary

Managing learning groups involves understanding group development processes and using team-building and other activities. Online learning groups follow a similar process to face-to-face groups and Gilly Salmon's model of e-learning provides a useful structure for organizing the learning process in a virtual environment. Tutors need to recognize and respect the diverse needs of their learners. Managing large groups, e.g. in mass lectures and in an e-learning environment, involves detailed planning and preparation. Finally, tutors need to identify and address challenging situations, otherwise they may lead to disruption of the whole learning process.

References

Belbin, R. M. (1993) *Management Teams: why they succeed or fail*, London, Heinemann.

Jaques, D. (2000) *Learning in Groups: a handbook for improving group work*, London, Kogan Page.

Kandola, R. and Fullerton, J. (1994) *Managing the Mosaic: diversity in action*, London, Chartered Institute of Personnel and Development.

Salmon, G. (2000) *E-moderating*, London, Kogan Page.

7 Working as a tutor

Introduction

The purpose of this chapter is to explore issues associated with working as a tutor in a blended learning programme. Reading this chapter will enable library and information workers who are involved in the design and delivery of blended learning programmes to have an understanding of their role and responsibilities.

Library and information staff may deliver or support teaching and learning in a blended learning programme in a number of different ways:

- Lead and facilitate all learning and teaching activities, including face-to-face and/or online provision.
- Co-facilitate a variety of face-to-face and/or e-learning activities as part of a blended learning programme delivered by a multi-professional team.
- Provide face-to-face or online support to learners who are accessing online learning opportunities using ICT in the library or e-learning centre.
- Provide additional support to a programme facilitated by another tutor, e.g. face-to-face on a help desk, or via telephone, e-mail or a virtual learning environment.

Information workers who are involved in facilitating and supporting blended learning programmes need to develop and use a range of teaching and training skills. Although working in a virtual environment requires many of the same skills and techniques that are used in a face-to-face environment, it also requires the development of new approaches to communicating with learners. This chapter will consider the following topics: principles of tutoring; e-tutoring; presentations; working with a co-tutor; and student helpers.

Principles of tutoring

In recent years the landscape of education and training has become more complex as models of teaching and learning have shifted from a didactic tutor-centred model of learning to one that is more student-centred. There has also been a shift from face-to-face or e-learning programmes to blended learning programmes. In addition, individual library and information workers may be working in a context where they are required to work collaboratively in teams that may be designing learning programmes based on different underlying pedagogies. Consequently, this means that tutors must be extremely flexible and adept in working with a range of pedagogies and different approaches to teaching and learning. Figure 7.1 illustrates two extreme approaches to teaching and learning (from Goodyear, 2000), and in today's world tutors need to be able to span both of these extremes.

Tutor-centred programmes ←——→	Learner-centred programmes
Tutor as 'sage on the side'	Tutor as 'guide on the side'
Tutor as expert	Tutor as facilitator of learning
Lecturer	Consultant, guide and resource provider
Provider of answers	Expert questioner
Provider of content	Designer of learning experiences
Sole worker	Member of multi-professional learning team
Controls teaching environment	Shared control with the learner who is a co-constructor of knowledge
Total power over teaching experience	Shared power with the learner

Figure 7.1 The flexible tutor

Tutors take on a number of different roles associated with the design and delivery of blended learning programmes, and this will be in addition to their other ILS roles. In terms of the overall blended learning process, every tutor is likely to undertake some of the following activities and a few ILS tutors may undertake all of them:

- planning and designing a blended learning programme
- developing learning resources or learning activities
- delivering or facilitating learning programmes, including assessing learning
- evaluating the blended learning programme
- providing learning support and advice
- providing feedback to managers and team leaders.

This means that the traditional skills set of library and information workers is extended to include learning and teaching in a variety of contexts. The following sections consider the range of skills required by tutors.

E-tutoring

Increasingly all library and information workers are taking a part in e-tutoring, whether it is responding to queries by e-mail or taking part in a blended learning programme. The role of an online e-tutor is to facilitate learning within the online environment, and early research by Collins and Berge (1996) identified four main types of e-tutor activities: pedagogical, social, managerial and technical.

Pedagogical activities involve enabling learners to learn in an online environment, develop their subject knowledge and also develop their effective learning and thinking skills. This involves a number of different activities: modelling appropriate online behaviours, and supporting and developing subject learning by introducing ideas and insights, questioning and probing learners' responses, and focusing discussions, e.g. on critical concepts, principles and skills.

E-tutors also need to engage in and encourage **social activities** with their learners. This includes creating a friendly and informal environment, a necessity for successful online learning. It includes acknowledging learners' contributions and helping individuals to work together. It can also mean sharing experiences outside the e-learning programme, e.g. holiday experiences, outside interests, jokes. Online socialization is the second stage in Gilly Salmon's model of e-learning described in Chapter 6 and it appears to be an essential prerequisite for effective learning. It provides the 'glue' that helps individuals to work together as an e-learning group.

As with face-to-face groups, e-tutors need to **manage** the agenda for the discussion or conference, starting the learning group; introducing the outcomes; setting the pace; introducing and setting tasks; focusing and refocusing the discussion or conference; managing the time; summarizing the outcomes; and closing the discussion or conference. The learning group may be led by an e-tutor whose style is directive or by someone with a 'light touch'.

The online e-tutor must be competent with the **technology** and enable learners to develop their competence in the particular technical environment. This means that new e-tutors need to spend some time getting to grips with the technology and they also need access to technical back-up from either their own organization or their supplier.

In addition to these functional roles, effective e-tutors need to have certain characteristics, which were identified by Hislop (2000) and based on experiences of e-tutoring an online Masters degree in Information Systems at Drexel University. These are presented in Table 7.1.

Working as an e-tutor

Online learning and teaching involve e-tutors (and also learners) developing new skills. The practical realities of learning online include the need to:

- distribute time

- deal with overload
- develop skills in reading and following threads
- develop an online voice
- develop skills in knowledge construction.

Table 7.1 Characteristics of effective e-tutors (adapted from Hislop (2000))

Motivated	Motivated e-tutors have a strong interest in working to make their online class successful. They are willing to make the effort to deal with technology and a new teaching and learning environment.
Approachable	Approachable e-tutors encourage learners to interact with them. Being approachable reduces barriers to interaction in the online environment.
Visible	Visible e-tutors make their presence felt frequently in the online environment. This helps add substance to the online experience and to provide glue to hold the community of learners together.
Explicit	Explicit e-tutors provide timely, detailed directions about what the learners need to do and how the class will operate. They are also explicit in addressing course content. This helps to ameliorate the limitations of the restricted communication channels in the online environment.
Pro-active	Pro-active e-tutors make an extra effort to reach out to learners in ways beyond what would be necessary or typical in a traditional environment. For example, a pro-active instructor might put extra effort into contacting an inactive learner in an online class.
Discreet	Discreet e-tutors manage a class without dominating it. They facilitate online discussions while encouraging learners to provide most of the comments. They also know when to comment publicly and when to switch to private communication with a learner or learners.
Collaborative	Collaborative e-tutors are willing to work with staff and other e-tutors engaged in online education. They are also comfortable working with learners in a coaching role rather than a more hierarchical style.
Technically capable	Technically capable e-tutors have sufficient technical knowledge and adeptness to be comfortable with the online environment. Online e-tutors do not need to be technical experts but they need basic technical skills to get started. They also need to be able to deal with the inevitable technical glitches and technology changes (with technical support help).
Credible	Learners accept credible e-tutors as experts in the subject of the course. Past research has shown the importance of credibility, particularly in technical fields, including information systems. For online classes this may be even more important since the learner's connection to the university is embodied largely in interactions with the instructor.

E-tutors who are involved in facilitating online activities need to access their virtual learning environment and interact with their learners frequently, e.g. two or three times a week. This is quite different from traditional training or user education practice, where contact normally takes place during scheduled events, and it may involve some changes in time management. Managing their own time and learners' expectations of online access to their e-tutor is an important part of the initial stages in e-tutoring. My own research into e-learning and time (Allan, 2007) identified three distinct approaches to time management: planned, where individuals use tools such as diaries to schedule and limit their time online; opportunistic, where the e-tutor goes online as and when they are able to throughout the day (and sometimes night); and a mixed approach of some pre-scheduled sessions and others that arise opportunistically.

There is concern about information and work overload of e-tutors. It can be quite a challenge to return to work after a weekend and discover 60 to 100 new messages in the e-learning site in addition to your own e-mails. It is really important that new e-tutors are clear about the demands and expectations that arise as a result of their role. The following strategies are useful for managing time in a virtual environment:

- Set very clear boundaries around time online.
- Let learners know how often you are likely to be online, e.g. three or four times a week.
- Ask learners to phone or to send private e-mails for urgent actions.
- Set up a frequently asked questions (FAQ) list.

The e-tutor (and learner) also needs to be able to read a large number of messages and become 'comfortable in trying to make sense of jigsaws of text' (Cooper and Smith, 2000). This skills are, in many respects, a standard part of the library and information worker's toolkit, i.e. analysing large amounts of information, synthesizing the different ideas or threads (this particular skill is called weaving), managing potential uncertainties about this jigsaw of ideas, and then having the confidence and time to post comments and responses.

Lewis and Allan (2005) describe the online skill of weaving, which involves moving into and out of online discussions and helping to move them forward. E-tutors need to bring together the messages on a particular topic or thread and present them in a structured way. If you imagine a party with ten different conversations all taking place at the same time and people moving from conversation to conversation, then the task of weaving involves creating a summary from the key points of these multi-stranded conversations. In some respects it is like a plenary session at a conference. The following list identifies some of the activities an e-tutor may be involved in as they weave a discussion.

Weaving an online discussion
Typical activities involved by e-tutors:

- Using open-ended comments
- Leaving 'handles' for future threads
- Linking responses and threads
- Using names in linked comments
- Standing back
- Having a 'weave day'
- Seeking similarities across threads

- Affirming and moving discussion on
- Contrasting views
- Referencing back to more than just the previous comment
- Sharing the flow and encouraging learners to weave themselves by modeling good practices.

(Cox et al., 2000)

How do you engage students or end-users in online activities? In general, individuals will participate in online activities if they feel that they are of benefit to them and that they are accepted as part of the learning group. For example, using relevant and authentic materials, e.g. real-life case studies or problems based on the learners' own situations, will help to make the online activity and learning process 'real' and one that generates enthusiasm and means that individuals want to learn more about the topic and each other's perspectives. The recent rise in interest in inquiry-based learning and specific approaches such as problem-based learning, project-based learning and work-based learning is, in part, because these approaches to teaching and learning help to engage students' interest (Chapter 6). If an online process is flagging, then, as with face-to-face sessions, it is important to bring in a new stimulus, e.g. a virtual visitor or a relevant podcast. Figure 7.2 illustrates the increase in messages posted to an online discussion group as a result of a visit to another organization by the participants, a learning group of 19 students. Figure 7.3 shows a similar effect as the result of an online guest speaker presenting a rather controversial session to a group of 16 students. Together, Figures 7.2 and 7.3 illustrate the impact on a blended learning programme of different activities.

One important online facilitation tool used in conferences and discussion groups (and also face-to-face meetings) is meta-comments.

Meta-comments can help repair matters if the conference is suffering because of insufficient clarity of response, irrelevant contributions, information overload.

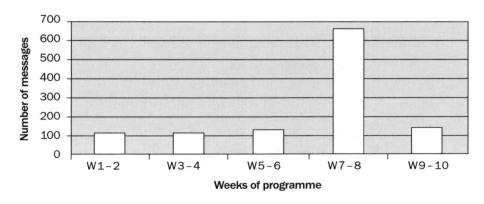

Figure 7.2 Impact of a visit in Weeks 7–8

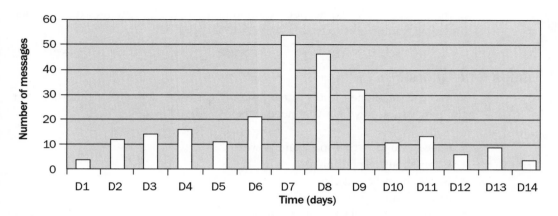

Figure 7.3 Impact of a controversial guest speaker on Day 7

Meta-comments are comments at a 'higher level' than the individual contributions to the substantive discussion in a conference. They are more general and probably don't refer directly to any one person or any one contribution. A timely comment like 'One of the difficulties with conferences like this is if people put in very lengthy contributions then newcomers may be put off participating' can have a marked effect on contribution styles, without needing to 'point the finger' at anyone in particular. Unobtrusively managing the flow and direction of the conference discussion without stifling the participants is a sine qua non of successful conference facilitation.

(Collins and Berge, 1996)

E-tutors and learners need to be able to create and project their online voice and this involves developing a writing style that is appropriate to the online environment as well as confidence in posting messages. Alexander (1999) provides guidance on this topic and he identifies the following key principles in online communications:

• Go for consensus.
• Thank, acknowledge and support people freely.
• Acknowledge before differing.
• Speak from own perspective.
• Follow netiquette principles.

E-tutors also need to develop skills in knowledge construction, and interventions by e-tutors are likely to include appropriate questioning; acknowledging and challenging learners' ideas and perspectives; presenting alternative perspectives; encouraging independent thinking; and encouraging learners to take a lead in their learning processes. The concept of 'scaffolding' is often used with regard to e-tutors, providing frameworks to enable learners to learn.

Issues for e-tutors

Working as an online e-tutor brings not only new roles and working methods but also new issues. Key ones that need to be considered include:

- issues around virtual space and power
- issues about responsiblility
- issues about boundaries
- issues about computer misuse
- issues about intellectual property rights.

In a traditional teaching room the tutor normally leads from the front and the physical layout of the room identifies their central position. In an online environment the e-tutor takes up the virtual space in the same way as learners. At first glance, apart from names there is very little to differentiate e-tutors and learners. However, unlike the learners, the e-tutor may well be the only person in the group who has the technical rights to set up and organize the virtual learning environment. Some e-learners may have relatively little experience of virtual communications and this is likely to be in contrast to the e-tutor, who may be the person with the most experience of online teaching and learning. This power over the micro-learning environment and higher knowledge and skills level can immediately raise issues of power and control. In the context of an e-tutor working with a community of learners, e.g. a developing community of practice (see Chapter 8), it makes it harder for the e-tutor to be an equal member of the community.

There are issues about responsibility for online groups and their discussions. Informal conversations with some e-tutors suggest that there are two main approaches: some e-tutors will say that if all the learners are adults, then the e-tutor doesn't have any special responsibility for facilitating discussions or managing behaviour in an online environment; in contrast, other e-tutors believe that their responsibilities are similar to those of a tutor in a classroom, i.e. they need to accept responsibility for facilitating the group discussions so that they stay on track and group harmony is maintained. These e-tutors also suggest that they are responsible for contributing specialist knowledge and weaving together different discussion threads. My own approach is that I believe the responsibilities of an e-tutor are similar to those of someone working with a group in a classroom. This brings with it a need to monitor and reflect on group activities and processes, and to decide whether or not I need to intervene in an activity.

Example 7.1 shows conflict that arose in an assessed online group activity. The source of the conflict was an inappropriate file name and the students resolved the issue for themselves (all names have been changed to maintain students' confidentiality). Bushra was the student who was offended by the file name and Brenda helped to resolve the issue. The e-tutors observed this interchange and didn't intervene as the students appeared to be handling it themselves.

Example 7.1 Discussion group messages showing conflict resolution

Bushra

In my opinion our report is still far from ready. I had anticipated it being ready, well typed and just about to be handed in. As it is now I can see different fonts in the typing. I don't understand where this report is going. At this point, we are supposed to be dotting the I's and crossing the T's, ways to go about it are cropping up. We have been instructed to produce a report with a specific word count of 2000.

Bushra

I'd pls like to know who sent me a copy of the report titled B*** S*** doc. coz I found that really offensive. Is that to say my effort was wasted? Was that deliberate? And wasn't good enough? Is someone mocking?

Amy

Hi,
Even I was worried about the filename.

Brenda

I don't think it was meant to be offensive . . . I know that personally I have so many variations of the report that I re-name each one to keep track . . . I wouldn't have chosen that name, but maybe it's just to separate it from the rest! I doubt it was meant as an attack . . .I think everyone is getting edgy as we near the end. I know they don't mean to be . . .

Amy

Great. Happy to see the report. Good team work. :-)

Bushra

Well done Brenda! you've done a good job . . .

Brenda

Hi All,
I've left the report in Theresa's hands . . . she'll get hold of Bushra's resources and post in GROUP section for us . . . I'm at a library computer now as my sister's one didn't want to open documents . . . 3 computers in one day . . . glad it's over and DONE.
Thankx all for your contributions. Good team effort! C U all tomorrow.

The e-tutor may be faced with a range of dilemmas about boundaries. The first of these relates to the boundaries between their main ILS role and their e-tutor role. Some ILS staff find themselves under pressure because of the competing demands of these different roles and the time and other pressures that arise with them. If the e-tutor is working as part of a team, then there may be issues about roles and responsibilities, i.e. who does what? This needs to be sorted out at the planning stage of the programme, and later in this chapter the possibility of co-tutoring is explored. Another issue that sometimes arises about boundaries is concerned with learners' access to the tutor. The development of a 24/7 society and increased expectations of instant access via mobile phones, instant messaging and e-mail mean that some learners may expect that their e-tutor is available to them at all times. The boundary between work and private time may become blurred and this sometimes causes tensions.

Another issue that sometimes arises with e-learning (and other ICT-based programmes) is that of computer misuse, e.g. through hacking, viruses or access to unacceptable materials. It is really important that e-tutors understand their organization's policies on computer misuse. These need to be brought to the attention of e-learners at the start of the e-learning programme. If individuals do break these policies (either inadvertently or deliberately) then it is important to deal with them in an appropriate manner. If in doubt, ask the head of ICT service, or human resources or personnel staff for guidance.

Copyright issues are considered in Chapter 4 and, as with computer misuse, it is important to know and understand the principles of copyright with respect to e-learning programmes. If in doubt, then obtain advice and support from library and information professional bodies such as ALA, ALIA or CILIP. Another intellectual property issue is that of plagiarism and it is of particular concern in many educational organizations where students may pass off other people's intellectual property as their own. It is very easy for students to access documents on the internet and then cut and paste whole or part documents and attempt to pass them off as their own work or to take work from other students and present it as their own. Universities and colleges generally have clear policies and procedures for dealing with allegations of plagiarism and other cases of unfair practice. Library and information workers in educational institutions frequently play a central role in educating students and staff on the issue of plagiarism and the need to reference information sources correctly. Some useful websites on this topic include:

- Copyright
  — American Library Association (ALA)
    www.ala.org/ala/washoff/woissues/copyrightb/
  — Australian Library and Information Association (ALIA)
    http://alia.org.au/advocacy/copyright/
  — Chartered Institute for Library and Information Professionals (CILIP)
    www.cilip.org.uk/professionalguidance/copyright/

- Plagiarism
  — Joint Information Systems Committee (JISC) Plagiarism Advisory Service www.jiscpas.ac.uk
  — Netskills Project www.netskills.ac.uk/content/projects/eduserv-info-lit/schplagreport.pdf
  — Example software package is Turnitin www.Turnitin.com.

As in face-to-face learning situations, e-tutors are likely to experience challenging situations. It is worthwhile being prepared for them and developing a range of strategies for handling them. Examples of situations that arise include:

- flaming (the online equivalent of road rage)
- quiet students or non-participants (sometimes called 'browsers')
- dominant students
- online work fizzling out.

Challenging situations

Here are some examples of challenging situations that new or potential e-tutors may like to consider and identify strategies for handling. There is no 'right' answer for any of these situations. However, time spent thinking about your response may help you to be prepared for similar situations in real life!

Situation 1 Irate student

Example e-mail

Grrrr. It has taken me 4 hours to get online. I have had little or no help from the college. Now that I'm online I am finding the level of discussion inane. I have come on this course to learn about project management NOT to have a meaningful relationship with other students. (I am happily married though my wife is sick of the amount of time I am spending on the course.) Don't expect me to contribute.

Situation 2 Over-enthusiastic learner

Week 3 of the course. You are managing a discussion group involving six information workers. They are working together on a mentoring programme. One participant (John) responds to everyone else's contribution and has taken to sending long responses with quotes from the books that he is reading. You notice that contributions from others are getting shorter.

Situation 3 Quiet student/browser

Week 3 of the course. You are managing a discussion group involving 12 library and information workers from different organizations. Eight of them contribute regularly while two of them have not made any contributions.

Situation 4 Challenging student

Example e-mail

I am increasingly getting fed up with this course. I am expected to read up all the materials for myself and some of them are more than 3 years old. I wish we had traditional lectures and seminars. That way the tutor works too! I don't think library staff should be tutoring us – their job is to issue books! The fees are expensive and I don't think I'm getting value for money.

Situation 5 Sexist comment

Example e-mail

Has anyone read the project management book by Stevens? I think it provides the best introduction to the subject. I was surprised as it is written by a woman. Bob

Situation 6 Using discussion group as a bulletin board

In your information skills discussion group a number of students (3 out of 12) have started to use the group for buying/selling books, finding homes for kittens, and selling tickets to a rave.

When faced with challenging situations e-tutors need to consider:

* Whether or not to intervene.
* When to intervene.
* How to intervene – what organizational policies and procedures need to be taken into account?
* How to intervene – in group or in private? If in private, then is it best to use e-mail, phone or to speak to the learner face-to-face?
* What are the likely short- and long-term implications of the intervention – for the individuals, the whole group, the e-tutor?
* Whether or not to get help or support, e.g. from a colleague or specialist such as a disabilities officer.

Presentation skills

The majority of blended learning programmes involve the need to make presentations, e.g. to advertise the programme to colleagues; as part of the blended learning programme; or to report on the outcome of the programmes to managers or at a professional conference. Successful presentations are important, as they enable you to communicate clearly with your audience. There are a number of areas to consider when embarking on a presentation: planning and preparation; the use of visual aids; rehearsal and delivery; working with a co-presenter; and dealing with questions.

Planning and preparation

Though invisible to an audience, planning and preparation are essential components of any good presentation. You need to begin by thinking about the overall purpose and the specific objectives of your presentation. How does it fit into the blended learning programme? What is the main message that you want someone to take away from your presentation? Once this is clear, it will help you to structure and organize your presentation.

If you are making a presentation that is part of a blended learning programme, then it is likely that many of the following questions will have been considered at the planning stages (see Chapter 3). However, it is still worth revisiting these questions when you plan a specific presentation:

- What is the purpose of the presentation? How does it fit into the blended programme?
- Who are your audience, what are their expectations from the presentation and what is their current knowledge of the topic?
- How will the presentation be delivered? Will the audience be in the room with you or will it be delivered live online or recorded and made available via a podcast?
- What length of time is available for the presentation? How can you make best use of it?
- What is your main message?
- What other information do you need to convey to meet your objectives?
- What approach(es) could you use to present the topic and material in a clear, interesting and involving way?
- How formal or informal should your delivery of the material be?
- Is it appropriate to involve your audience in activities?
- How will you use technology within the presentation? What equipment will you have access to? What handouts, visual, audio or audiovisual aids could reinforce the content? When and how should they be used?
- How will you gain audience feedback? By inviting questions? When? Where – face-to-face or online?

Preparing the presentation involves identifying the structure and the main points that you need to get over to your audience. A standard structure for a presentation includes an introduction, a middle section or main body, and a conclusion.

Introduction

This normally takes up no more than 10% of the available time. In the introduction you need to:

- Introduce yourself.
- Clearly outline the main purpose of your presentation, its subject and its overall structure.
- Motivate the audience to listen by pointing out what they will gain from the presentation.
- Include any housekeeping announcements, e.g. health and safety notices (for face-to-face presentations).
- Capture the attention of the audience (for example, through a story, a quotation, a question).

Main section

This typically forms about 80% of the presentation and in it you should:

- Outline your subject and present it in three to five main chunks.
- Lead the audience from the known to the unknown.
- Make sure that your information is up-to-date and correct.
- Use examples and anecdotes.
- Use images, graphs and photographs.

Common errors that are made in presentations include: providing too much detail; attempting to cover too many topics; and using examples that are not of interest or relevance to the audience.

The conclusion

This should take about 10% of the time and should:

- Summarize the key ideas.
- End on a positive note.
- Thank the audience.
- Provide appropriate contact information, e.g. your e-mail address.

If you have decided to involve the audience actively, then you will need to decide what form the involvement will take and how it will fit into the presentation's structure. Example activities include: asking the audience members to discuss a topic with their neighbour; asking them to complete some kind of questionnaire or take part in a quiz using an audience response system (see Chapter 2); and inviting questions from the audience. You will need to think about how much time to spend on the activity and how you will intervene if the activity does not work.

Visual aids

Good visual aids support or reinforce the presentation and they should add interest, variety and impact. Any visual aids you use should:

- be relevant
- complement and enhance the presentation
- help the audience understand the topic
- be professional in appearance and presentation.

Chapter 2 covers a wide range of visual aids that may be used to enhance a presentation. Do remember to bring a copy, e.g. printout of your presentation, so that you can keep track of your progress during the presentation.

Whatever aids you choose, you need to check before the presentation that the venue is suitable for their use and that the necessary equipment is available and working. Even then, it is prudent to have contingency plans ready in case of equipment failure! If you are using PowerPoint, it is worthwhile having copies on a disk, memory stick and CD. If you are using audio or video clips and making a presentation on unfamiliar equipment, it is worthwhile bringing along two copies of your presentation: one copy that contains all images, audio clips and videos, and a stripped-down version that will work even if the ICT facility is fairly basic. Run through the presentation on the equipment that you will be using on the day. Expect equipment to fail and have a contingency plan.

Rehearsal and delivery

If you are not experienced as a presenter, it is a good idea to rehearse your presentation, e.g. to trusted colleagues or at home to family, friends or even the dog or cat. Practise delivering the presentation aloud rather than silently. Use a tape recorder or a video to record yourself and then think about how you could improve the presentation. Rehearsal is essential to check the timing of your presentation, to enable you to become familiar with presenting your information orally, to enable you to develop fluent use of the presentation aids, and to reinforce your confidence in both materials and delivery. Practice really does make perfect and the more you rehearse, the better the end result is likely to be.

Effective presentations are those that have been well prepared and are delivered with confidence and enthusiasm. Key points for effective delivery include:

- Dress appropriately – smartness instils confidence in both audience and speaker. If in doubt about the dress code, dress formally in a suit or with a smart jacket rather than in more informal clothes.

- Arrive in time to make any checks and to organize your materials and equipment without haste or confusion.
- Have a printout of your presentation.
- Aim for a natural, confident and relaxed posture and delivery.
- Avoid distracting mannerisms.
- Use eye contact to draw all parts of the audience into the presentation.
- Show interest and enthusiasm in your tone and manner throughout.
- Speak more slowly and carefully than you would in normal conversation. Pace is important. You are familiar with your material; the audience are not.
- Project and pitch your voice so that everyone can hear you easily, and vary your expression appropriately.
- Stand clear of visuals when referring to them to ensure that everyone can see them.
- Face the audience when talking about a visual aid – don't turn your back on them and talk to the screen.
- If you make mistakes, correct those relating to accuracy of content. Ignore those that are unlikely to be noticed and simply carry on.

Points to avoid

- A word-for-word script – if you take one, you will read from it!
- A monotonous delivery tone.
- Humour (unless you are certain it is appropriate and will be well received).

Dealing with questions

General techniques for dealing with questions are the same whether you are in a lecture theatre or teaching online, e.g. working in a chat room or a telephony conference using a system such as Skype. Handling difficult questions is made easier by realizing that you are in control. It is up to you to decide when you will accept questions, e.g. during or at the end of a presentation. Inexperienced presenters often find it easier to take questions at the end of the presentation so as not to break their flow. The following general tips will help you answer any type of question:

- Listen carefully to the question. You need to listen to the actual words and also the emotions behind the question. Often the body language of the questioner will give you some useful information.
- If you are not sure about the meaning of the question, ask for clarification.
- Repeat the question in your own words. This will allow the whole audience to hear the question and it also allows you to check that you have fully understood it.
- Answer the question to the best of your ability.

- If you don't know the answer, be honest and say that you don't know the answer. You may then want to ask if anyone in the audience can answer it or you may offer to e-mail the answer.
- Signal how many questions you will take, e.g. at the end of your presentation say that there is time for three or four questions.
- When you want to close the session, say that there is time for one more question and that after that question you must move on.

Sometimes tricky situations arise in question time and Table 7.2 provides examples of situations and makes suggestions as to how they can be tackled.

Table 7.2 Handling tricky situations during question time

Situation	Strategy
You ask if there are any questions and you are met with a wall of silence.	• Count up to ten in your head. This will give people a chance to think through and articulate their questions. • Accept that there are no questions and invite people to contact you later if they have any questions later on. Move on to the closure of your presentation. • Ask people to talk to their neighbour (or a designated person if they are in a chat room) and to identify any questions that they have. Give them a few minutes for discussion and then ask for questions again.
Someone asks a question that has nothing to do with your presentation.	• Thank them for the question. Say that it is beyond the scope of your presentation and advise them how they can get their question answered. For example, 'That is an interesting question but we are not covering that topic today. Perhaps we could talk about it after the session or in the coffee break.' • Alternatively, ask them to post the question in an online discussion group where it can be explored at leisure.
Someone asks a bizarre question.	• Thank them for the question. Say that it is an interesting/unusual viewpoint. If you can't comment on it, then say so.
Someone asks a question that is insulting, e.g. it is sexist, racist or offensive to a particular group of people.	• Say that the question is likely to offend people and that this unacceptable. You may want to add that you personally feel extremely uncomfortable with the language used in the question. Move on to the next question or start to end your presentation. • If you are working in an online environment, remove the question from the public arena as soon as possible.
Someone asks a challenging question, e.g. criticizes your library, project or service.	• Thank them for raising the issue, then suggest that this isn't the right forum for raising it. Suggest that they talk to you in private after the event and you will help them to progress their issue, e.g. through the complaints procedure.
Two or more people in the audience disagree with each other. A public argument starts to take place.	• Interrupt their discussion. Say that there are clearly different points of view in the audience and that there is insufficient time to explore the issue in more depth. Move on to the next question or start to end your presentation. For example, 'It's clear that there are a number of different points of view here. We can't discuss them in any more detail but perhaps individuals would like to follow them up after the session or in the coffee break.'

Working with a co-tutor

If you are working with another tutor or tutors, you will need to work out individual roles and responsibilities within the blended learning programme and how you will work together in public, e.g. giving a joint presentation or working together online. There are two main approaches to working together: taking turns; or shared delivery.

Taking turns is probably the simplest way of co-tutoring with a colleague and it means that each tutor is able to play to their strengths by presenting and facilitating their own areas of expertise; observing the group and learning process when they are not involved in delivering material; and having breaks from training. If you are making a joint presentation, it is worth thinking about:

- who will present which part of the content and its relation to the presentation overall
- when you will each speak and how you will pass over to each other
- where you will both stand or sit.

Each presenter needs to make a conscious effort to give unity and continuity to their presentation. For example, you need to devise appropriate 'handovers' from one person to the next, and to decide how and when questions will be dealt with. If you are presenting with another person, it is important to be in agreement with what you are going to say and how you are going to say it. Don't interrupt or disagree with each other during the presentation. Keep any disagreements off stage!

Case study 7.1 Working with a co-presenter

Law librarians Jane and John were asked to make a presentation at a conference on their experiences of lecturing to large groups of students in their university. They spent some time planning the presentation and how they were going to deliver it. They produced the presentation plan presented in Table 7.3. Their plan shows that the same person starts and concludes the presentation. They take turns in presenting different aspects of the subject but in the advantages and disadvantages section they work together. In this section, their PowerPoint presentation had advantages on the left and disadvantages on the right. The two presenters stood on the left (John) or right (Jane) of the room to repeat and emphasize this pattern. This is illustrated in Figure 7.4. This helped to give a very professional and 'slick' look to their performance.

Table 7.3 Presentation plan

Timing	Topic	Presenter
5 mins	Introduction to presenters. Introduction to topic. Reasons for being asked to deliver presentation.	Jane
5 mins	Background to their work as information skills trainers. Outline of their work in lecturing to large groups.	John
10 mins	Advantages and disadvantages of lecturing to large groups.	John (advantages) Jane (disadvantages)
10 mins	Use of technology.	Jane
10 mins	Use of activities.	John
5 mins	Any questions.	John (lead) Jane
5 mins	Summary and closure.	Jane

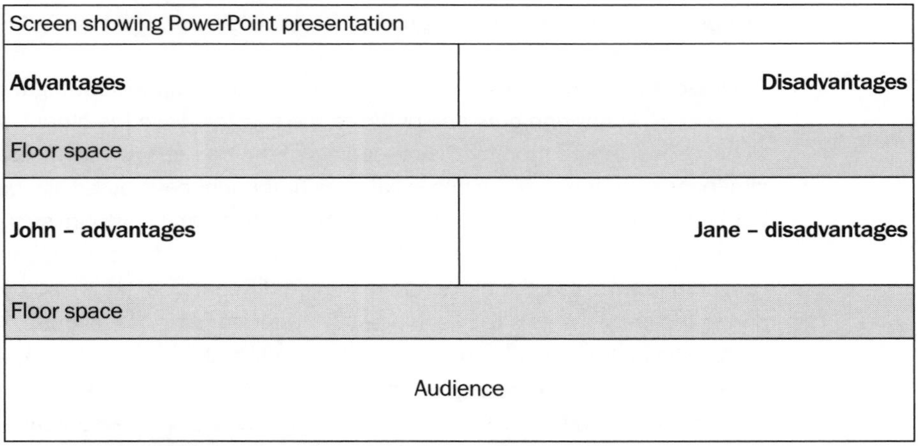

Screen showing PowerPoint presentation	
Advantages	**Disadvantages**
Floor space	
John – advantages	**Jane – disadvantages**
Floor space	
Audience	

Figure 7.4 Effective use of space by co-presenters

The second approach to co-tutoring, where both tutors deliver the whole programme, is clearly described in Case Study 7.2, prepared by a colleague, Dina Lewis, who was involved in delivering a series of team-building workshops.

Case study 7.2 Working with a co-tutor

The effectiveness of this collaboration was immediately apparent as we started to plan the first workshop. In the past the planning stage has been a lengthy and laborious process. I have formulated aims and learning outcomes slowly and painfully. This time, however, our combined approach quickly generated clear aims and objectives, new ideas for warm-ups and group exercises, and a fluent and coherent structure to the session. Instead of the planning stage feeling like a trip to the dentist's it felt like fun: quick, stimulating and enjoyable.

The shared approach also encouraged a new readiness to take risks and try out new ideas. We both found the previous experience and repertoire of our co-trainer a great source of inspiration. Using each other's knowledge we extended our own resource bank of good ideas and practice. . . . Supported and encouraged by each other, we shared our experience and generated new ideas to produce a programme that was much more varied than either of us could have achieved individually. . . .

We also found that a rapport developed between us that enabled us to take control and hand over control during a session. Instinctively, we made the most of our own particular strengths and weaknesses. At any one time, quite naturally, we seemed to sense which of us was best suited to the task in hand. Our communication skills and styles seemed to complement each others'. Trainees commented on the success of our contrasting presentation styles. One trainee in particular said how annoying he had found co-trainers who behave as a double act. He congratulated us on avoiding that pitfall and said how unobtrusively we handled our changeovers.

One of the greatest benefits of co-training was the opportunity it gave us to talk things over. At any one time one of us led the session while the other was free to closely observe and monitor the responses of the trainees. On many occasions the observing trainer picked up on verbal cues that might have otherwise been missed. It was fascinating to share insights and observations and compare strategies for dealing with tricky situations and the individual needs of the participants. Our conversations revealed that we had observed different reactions and behaviours during the sessions: this led us to a better understanding of the group.

Co-training these workshops proved to be an invaluable learning experience for us both. Although it could be argued that co-training is not cost-effective (why use two trainers when one trainer will do?), I would argue that it is an economic and effective means of delivering staff development within an organization. I have acquired many new skills, I find myself taking more risks and adapting more flexibly to the differing needs of different groups. My presentation skills and communication skills have developed, not least because of my improved confidence.

The third approach to co-tutoring involves a mixture of taking turns and shared delivery. This offers the opportunity to work together in areas where both trainers feel comfortable with the training material and to present their own particular sections too.

The major potential problem area with co-training is the situation where the two tutors do not share the same values and beliefs about learning and teaching, and a power struggle ensues. This is damaging to the whole educational experience, for both the tutors and the participants, as the focus shifts onto the tutors rather than the learning processes. Any differences of opinion need to be sorted out outside the classroom or online learning environment.

Student helpers

Student helpers, either paid or volunteers, are increasingly used in ILS as a means of providing additional help and support to students or end-users. For example, an increasing number of library and information services that operate new 'learning spaces' (see Chapters 1 and 3) also provide new forms of support using student helpers.

This strategy fits into current thinking about the value of peer learning and support, as evidenced by the rise of approaches such as inquiry-based learning. It means that students will receive help and advice from their peers, who are likely to have recently undergone the same or similar experiences and so find it easy to relate to each other. It also means that ILS have the potential to provide a wider range of services, as the cost of employing students is cheaper than involving professionally qualified staff and it provides a flexible work force, e.g. student helpers may be more willing to work anti-social hours than the established staff. One of the disadvantages of using student helpers is that the whole process must be carefully managed, and this can be time consuming. The student helpers need to be recruited following appropriate recruitment and selection policies and procedures, and once recruited they need to be carefully trained to ensure that the advice they give to their peers is accurate and correct. They will also need to be supervised and managed as they contribute to the learning process.

The benefits for the student helpers are that they gain employment and can use the skills developed during their programme of study to support other students. In addition, they gain valuable work experience and something to add to their curriculum vitae. The following quotation is from a PhD student, Devaki, who worked as a paid helper on the information desk in an academic library one evening each week:

> Overall, I enjoyed my work on the help desk. I worked with another student and I got on with her well. I dealt with the computing queries and she did the library ones. If need be, then we swapped. I found it really helpful working in the library. I got to know its resources much better and I made some friends. The money was handy too. I want to become a lecturer and I feel it will improve my CV. The only disadvantage is that if I'm in the Business School, then some of the undergraduates assume that they can come and ask me library or computing queries, but that doesn't happen very often.

Student helpers may be used on some blended learning programmes, e.g. to offer support for using an e-learning system or to work as coaches or mentors. Some tutors will ask a student who has successfully completed the programme to come back to talk to a current cohort of students as either a guest speaker or a virtual visitor.

Summary

Nowadays library and information workers need a range of teaching and training skills so that they can deliver and support a wide variety of learning programmes. The shift to a student-centred pedagogy means that they need to be able to facilitate learning in both face-to-face and e-learning environments. E-tutoring involves working in new ways and this brings new challenges. Presentation skills are still important, and this includes the ability to answer and manage questions. Finally, working with a co-tutor or student helpers provides new opportunities for developing and delivering blended learning programmes.

References

Alexander, J. O. (1999) *Collaborative Design, Constructivist Learning, Information-Technology Immersion and Electronic Communities*, www.emoderators.com/ipct-j/1999/n1-2/alexander.html [accessed 23 June 2005].

Allan, B. (2007) Time to Learn? E-learners' experiences of time in virtual learning communities, *Management Learning*, **38** (5), (December).

Collins, M. and Berge, Z. (1996) *Facilitating Interactions in Computer Mediated On-line Courses*, http://star.ucc.nau.edu/~mauri/moderate/flcc.html.

Cooper, T. and Smith, B. (2000) *Reflecting and Learning from Experience of Online Tuition: implications for staff development and quality assurance processes to support learner learning in this medium*, Open University Millennium Conference proceedings.

Cox, S. et al. (2000) How to Herd Cats in Piccadilly, *Times Higher Education Supplement*, (14 April), 36–7.

Goodyear, P. (2000) *Effective Networked Learning in Higher Education: notes and guidelines*, Networked Learning in Higher Education (JISC/CALT). Copies available from http://csalt.lancs.ac.uk/jisc.

Hislop, G. (2000) *Working Professionals as Part-time On-line Learners*, www.aln.org/alnweb/journal/Vol4_issue2/le/hislop/LE-hislop.htm.

Lewis, D. and Allan, B. (2005) *Virtual Learning Communities*, Maidenhead, Open University Press.

8 Communities of practice

Introduction

Librarians and information workers have a long history of working together and anyone reading the professional literature will soon realize that there are many professional groups and organizations that promote networking and collaborative working. Membership of these groups often provides access to information, help and support as well as informal mentoring and professional development. For many library and information workers, membership of these groups or communities is an important aspect of their development as professional practitioners. They provide opportunities for support, coaching and mentoring, as well as a group of like-minded individuals willing to work together on shared problems and issues. Communities of practice provide a means of enabling groups to come together and learn from and with each other. Many professional groups and organizations now support communities of practice and these are frequently mediated by a website hosting virtual communication tools.

The purpose of this chapter is to introduce the concept of communities of practice, and these are distinguished from communities of interest. This is followed by an outline of the characteristics of communities of practice, which are illustrated with a number of practical examples of library and information communities of practice. An extensive case study exploring the long-term impact of a multi-professional blended learning community is presented in this section. This is followed by an outline of the processes involved in establishing a work-based community of practice. The final part of the chapter considers the topic of mentoring, as this process is often located within a community of practice.

Communities of practice and communities of interest

There is a large and developing academic literature on communities of practice and Andrew Cox (2005) provides a helpful comparison and summary of four seminal works on this subject: Lave and Wenger (1991); Brown and Duguid (1991); Wenger (2003); and Wenger, McDermott and Snyder (2002). Ideas presented in this chapter focus on those developed by Wenger, McDermott and Snyder (2002), as they have developed the concept of communities of practice by linking it with professional or work-based communities.

Wenger coined the phrase 'communities of practice', which he defined as:

> groups of people who share a concern, a set of problems, or a passion about a topic, and who deepen their knowledge and expertise in this area by interacting on an ongoing basis.
>
> (Wenger, 2003, 4)

This definition is a helpful one because it enables us to distinguish between communities of practice and communities of interest. Communities of practice may develop spontaneously but they are often established by individuals who communicate with each other on a regular basis and are working together on a specific problem or issue.

Anyone reading the literature on communities of practice is likely to come across the term 'communities of interest'. These are large groups or networks, perhaps involving hundreds of people, and they support the dissemination and exchange of information but do not necessarily support collaborative learning processes. They develop when people come together to exchange news or information about a specific topic. Examples include groups that cluster together around their interests in hobbies, technology, education, research fields and specialist work-related practices. E-mail discussion lists are a good example of communities of interest and sometimes a sub-group of such a community may develop into a learning community. An example of a community of interest within the library and information world is the Freepint community accessible at www.freepint.com. Examples of other communities of interest can be found in discussion lists which may have several thousand subscribers (see Chapter 2). Table 8.1 illustrates the differences between communities of interest and practice.

Table 8.1 Comparison of communities of interest and communities of practice (adapted from Lewis and Allan (2005))		
Characteristics	**Community of interest**	**Community of practice**
Purpose	To be informed.	To create, expand and share knowledge. To develop individual's professional practice.
Membership	People who become subscribers or members of a particular group, e.g. mail list, e-learning programme. Membership may be very large, e.g. up to 1000.	People who share a particular interest or passion in a topic. People who become subscribers or members of a particular group, e.g. mail list, e-learning programme. This may be by self-selection or by invitation. Membership is likely to be relatively small, e.g. 6–24.
What holds them together	Access to information and sense of community.	Interest, commitment, identity with group. Personal relationships within the group.
Examples in the library and information profession	Some discussion groups. Newsgroups.	Some groups involved in collaborative project work. Professional groups supported by professional organizations.

Characteristics of communities of practice

What are the features of communities of practice in the library and information profession? Communities of practice are normally focused around a particular group of information and library workers, such as law librarians or business information workers, or they may focus on specific workplace issues and problems, such as e-learning or training skills. Membership is normally open to individual practitioners whose interests and professional practice map those of the community, i.e. they share a common goal or purpose. Members may be at the same or at different stages in their professional lives and they develop their professional practice by sharing information and ideas, through shared learning and through knowledge construction. Learning is an integral part of the process of participation in a community and it cannot be separated from the social situation and interactions through which it occurs.

Individuals may be members of a number of different communities of practice, as shown in Case Study 8.1. Figure 8.1 illustrates the ways in which an individual information worker may be a member of different and overlapping communities of practice.

Case study 8.1 Membership of different communities of practice

Jane is a law librarian in a UK university. She is a member of a number of different communities of practice, including:

- the British and Irish Association of Law Librarians (BIALL)
- The Chartered Institute of Library and Information Professional (CILIP)
- the group of learning advisers within the university's library service
- the university's Blackboard user group
- the university's learning development group
- a group of librarians who previously worked together
- an online Facebook group of librarians interested in biking.

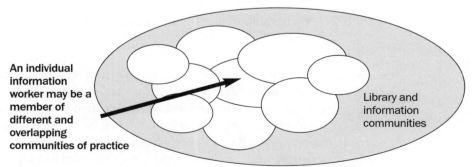

Figure 8.1 An individual information worker's membership of different and overlapping communities of practice

Wenger, McDermott and Snyder (2002) identify different levels of participation by individual members within a community of practice and this is represented in Figure 8.2. They are: peripheral members, who rarely participate but are on the sidelines observing discussions; active members, who join in with discussions when they feel they have something to say; and core members, who introduce new topics or projects, and help shape and lead the community. They suggest that there is a development route from being peripheral through to becoming an active or core member. Many information workers will be familiar with this model, even if they hadn't previously conceptualized it in these terms. It is a model that appears to operate in traditional face-to-face professional groups, e.g. special interest groups of ALIA, ALA or CILIP. In virtual groups, as in more traditional professional groups, the presence of a co-ordinator or facilitator may help to integrate new members into the community and this will enable them to become active or core members. Again, like the face-to-face support groups, in virtual environments the use of e-buddies or mentors can be a useful means of providing support and encouragement to new community members, and this topic is considered at the end of the chapter.

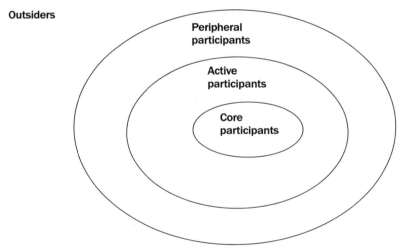

Figure 8.2 Membership of a community of practice

One method of identifying levels of participation within a virtual community is by counting the number of messages posted by individual members. The graph presented in Figure 8.3 illustrates different levels of participation in an online community established as part of an undergraduate inquiry-based information skills module. In this graph, students A and B may be considered 'outsiders' and don't contribute to community activities, while students C and D are peripheral participants and barely contribute. Students E to J are active participants, while students H to N are core members of the community. In reality, as this graph demonstrates, there is a continuum between community outsiders and core members. Individuals may change their levels of activity and roles within the community, e.g. as a result of workplace pressures or changes to the focus of activity of the community, or as the result of the support of a mentor. Another feature of communities of practice is that there is a lack of hierarchy and all members have the same status within the community. The community may be supported by an administrator or, if it is a facilitated community, leadership may be shared or rotated.

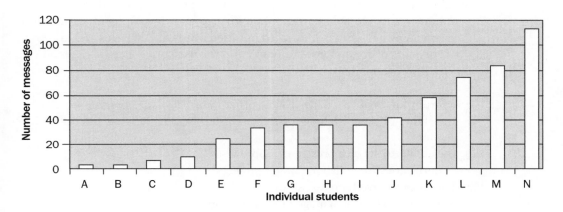

Figure 8.3 Levels of participation in an online community of practice

What are the benefits of establishing or participating in a community of practice? The benefits of membership can be divided into three groups: task-specific, social and career benefits. Some examples of these benefits are listed below:

- **Task-specific benefits**
  — access to information and expertise
  — wider perspective on problems and issues
  — opportunities for sharing resources
  — opportunity to find innovative solutions to complex problems
- **Social benefits**
  — access to like-minded individuals
  — support and friendship
  — sense of identity and group membership
  — opportunity to 'let off steam' in a safe environment
- **Career benefits**
  — confidence building
  — development of professional expertise
  — continuing professional development.

An increasing number of library and information services is supporting the development of communities of practice and they may be used as a means of supporting staff development, e.g. a university-based community established to enable members to develop their knowledge and understanding of e-learning (see later in this chapter). Using a community of practice rather than one-off workshops or staff development events means that the learning that takes place within the community is grounded in workplace practices and may be readily transferred into practice. One of the advantages of using a community of practice for staff development is that it also develops a group of people who work together as a community and are able to champion change and development within their department or unit (this is illustrated in Cased Study 8.3 on pages 182–5). Additional benefits of communities of practice in the workplace include the following service improvements:

- a forum for 'benchmarking' against other information or library units
- the ability to establish long-term relationships with colleagues and other ILS services
- the ability to act as a pressure group
- opportunities for collaboration on projects
- opportunities to share resources
- the ability to take advantage of emerging opportunities
- the emergence of unplanned capabilities and opportunities.

Evaluations of communities of practice demonstrate that they are particularly helpful for three groups (Lewis and Allan, 2005):

1 New entrants to a profession who are managing the challenges of establishing their own professional credibility and translating and applying academic theory into practice. Communities of practice can provide newly qualified professionals with ready access to established practitioners' knowledge and experience, offering a safe environment in which to model and observe professional practice.
2 Individuals who are moving into situations that are new to them, e.g. as a result of a change in employment, in which they want to quickly develop relevant knowledge and expertise.
3 Individuals who are working at the forefront of specialist knowledge and tackling new problems and unique situations. Communities of practice provide them with access to experienced colleagues with whom they can discuss and construct knowledge and develop new approaches to practice.

Lewis and Allan (2005) identify a range of specific characteristics that may be used to classify communities of practice according to whether they are spontaneous or managed; open or closed; face-to-face or virtual; or a mixture of face-to-face and virtual. Spontaneous communities spring up in response to a specific issue or perhaps as a result of an event such as a conference or training course that enables individuals to realize that working together will help them to improve their workplace practices or to solve a particular problem or issue. Wenger, McDermott and Snyder (2002) suggest that communities of practice are spontaneous, free-flowing and develop out of existing communities of interest and networks. Nowadays, the focus has shifted to managed communities of practice (e.g. Swan, Scarborough and Robertson, 2002; Lewis and Allan, 2005) where facilitators enable the community to work towards goals that match the organizational ones. Some of these are open to new members, and existing members may invite colleagues or friends to join the community. In contrast, many communities are closed and are established with a specific membership in mind. This may be reviewed at regular intervals.

Many communities of practice operate through face-to-face meetings and e-mail, and a typical example of this is a community established within an organization with a particular remit. In other instances, some communities spring up over the internet and enable library and information workers working in different regions or countries to work together. Virtual communities of practice provide an opportunity for individuals with a common purpose to come together across barriers in time and space. Many communities of practice operate using a mixture of face-to-face and virtual communications. Some of the benefits of membership of a virtual community of practice are expressed by Hyams and Mezey (2003, 36) who write:

> virtual communities offer much richer opportunities to share best practice and know-how in an active sense. They can stimulate the sharing of intelligence, and make it possible to harvest, organise and share 'knowledge' for preservation and re-use. They provide common ground for solving problems and sharing insights. . . . Communities offer much more than mere email discussion lists to members, too, because they can share access to resources (including multimedia and datasets), and communicate in real time using facilities such as live chat.

Virtual communities of practice use a variety of online communication tools to support their interactions and this means that busy professionals and individuals who are geographically isolated can access a community of peers at a time and place that suits them. Virtual communities may be mediated in a number of different ways (see Chapter 2):

- using a virtual learning environment such as Blackboard or WebCT (both available via www.webct.com)
- using collaborative communications software such as iCohere (see www.iCohere.com)
- using a website that provides access to communications tools such as discussion groups and chat software

- using Web 2.0 tools such as weblogs, wikis or social-networking software such as Facebook or MySpace.

Many virtual learning communities also involve face-to-face meetings. It is important to note that many such communities do not carry out all their activities using technology. Many communities combine a range of approaches including online, face-to-face, facilitator-led and resource-based activities. Taking advantage of a blended learning approach provides many communities with an effective environment for learning. Data gathered from research into learning communities has shown that the participants rate a blended learning approach more highly than 'pure' online communications (Lewis and Allan, 2005).

Examples of communities of practice

The library and information profession supports a huge number of communities of practice. Individuals may be members of a number of different communities representing their professional interests, the interests of their library or information service, and also their membership in professional associations. They may also be members of multi-professional communities involving individuals from other professions. In addition, library and information workers are likely to be involved in communities that match their private interests. In this section, a range of communities of practice is outlined as a means of illustrating their importance to the profession and to the development of individual practitioners.

Professional associations such as the Chartered Institute of Library and Information Practitioners (CILIP), the American Library Association (ALA) and the Australian Library and Information Association (ALIA) all support a wide range of communities of practice through their websites and face-to-face activities. These communities may be open to all members or to a specific group of members, e.g. those involved in a particular type of information service (such as school libraries), a particular issue (such as digitization) or a particular type of member (such as those working towards a particular qualification). The communities may be moderated or facilitated by members.

Another example of a national community of practice is the librarians' community supported by the Scottish Further Education Unit (www.sfeu.ac.uk/communities_of_practice/librarians), which was established in 1997 with the purpose of enabling members to:

Provide a platform for discussion and opportunity for networking
Keep members informed of current good practice
Promote the role of libraries and librarians within the sector
Provide a channel of communication between the network and other organizations
Organise events to facilitate these objectives
Support the LIAN [Library & Information Assistants Network] network.

This community provides a range of activities, including conferences and other events, and also a website. It is managed by a steering group whose remit includes having arrangements in place to help refresh the membership.

Some communities represent a particular group of librarians, e.g. the International Association of Music Librarians. These communities provide a wide range of activities and resources for members. They frequently offer training courses, which may be organised through the community and run at appropriate venues. One of the advantages of this approach to the design and delivery of training programmes is that it is firmly embedded in the needs of the librarians or information workers.

Communities may be established around a particular theme, as shown in the following example. One community established around a particular theme is the National Electronic Library for Communicable Diseases (NeLCD). This is one of the specialist libraries within the NHS in the UK and it is a digital library that brings together quality resources on the investigation, treatment, prevention and control of communicable diseases (see www.nelcd.co.uk). The NeLCD established a project to facilitate an online community of practice and this involved identifying a link person who represented a society involved in communicable diseases, e.g. Royal College of Pathologists. It described setting up the community as involving moving the users from being passive users of the NeLCD resources to becoming active participants in engaging with the NeCLD team and reviewing and assessing resources. The process is still ongoing and barriers to the development of the community include technical issues, the current political climate and conflicts of interest.

Traditional learning programmes, e.g. short courses or longer programmes, such as a Master's degree in Information Management, may lead to the development of a network or community of learners who continue to meet, discuss and work on professional issues after the end of a formal, taught programme.

Case study 8.2 Training the trainer

A few years ago I delivered a two-day 'train the trainer' workshop in an academic library. The 12 participants were extremely enthusiastic about the event and their newly developed skills. At the end of the workshop they decided to establish an online community of practice using their organization's virtual learning environment, WebCT. Two years later the community is still alive and well! Members exchange news and share resources via WebCT. They all meet face-to-face at least once a semester and value their community of practice. This is an example of a self-forming, closed and self-managed community of practice.

The Canadian Heritage Information Network (CHIN) established an online community of practice in December 2005 as a means of gaining worldwide input into the agenda for its annual digital Cultural Content Forum meeting. This community is of particular interest because it was established over a specific time period (three months) with a particular task; in addition, it was an open community.

Case study 8.3 Long-term impact of membership of a virtual community of practice

The case study is an edited version of a paper by Allan, Hunter and Lewis (2006) and concerns the long-term impact of membership of a blended learning community (LC) established in 2001 by a development unit within a UK university. The purpose of the community was to enable staff to develop knowledge and understanding of e-learning pedagogy and to equip them with the skills to support e-learning within their roles at the university. The programme was validated by the university at Master's level and also accredited by the Institute for Learning and Teaching (now the Higher Education Academy). There were 16 community members representing a multi-professional group of staff: academic, information and library, ICT support and administrative, and the community was facilitated by two external facilitators using an underlying pedagogic framework of socio-cultural theories of learning. The community members participated in a series of face-to-face workshops (induction, mid-life, end-of-community) and structured collaborative and co-operative online activities designed to develop their understanding of e-learning theories and constructs, and to highlight implementation issues from a learner's perspective. The participants were also encouraged to reflect on their learning experiences. The sponsoring UK university and original members of the learning community were revisited in 2005 in order to research the long-term impact on the individuals and their workplace.

This case study is based on data collected via the community discussion board messages and in-depth interviews (held four years after the inception of the community) with six participants, two facilitators and the manager of the development unit. Narrative analysis of both the discussion board messages and the interview transcripts was used to identify significant themes and issues.

Impact on individuals

The findings from the study suggest that the LC had a long-term impact on the work-based performance of many of the members and enabled some members to change and develop their professional identities. The analysis of the interviews indicated that, as would be expected, membership of the virtual learning community impacted differently on different members. An analysis of the findings suggests that the LC provided a continuing professional development programme for members to develop their knowledge and skills, and also their careers. Two members of the original LC went on to facilitate a future community. The role and skills of e-learning facilitators and the differences between the approaches of online facilitators and face-to-face tutors were explored in the community discussion groups and online activities. In particular, the importance of working in a supportive community was mentioned by all the interviewees. For some members, their experiences within the community had a transformational impact and led to them moving on to part-time study on a degree programme and/or promotion within the university. One member stated that she had changed her role within the university, had received a substantial salary increase and was now speaking at professional conferences. At professional conferences she directly attributed her newly adopted professional identity to the confidence she had developed as a result of her membership of the learning community.

Impact on workplace practices

The interviews also illuminated how the e-learning experience had an impact on the workplace practices of individuals. Specific examples showed that community members had developed in the following ways:

- gaining confidence to present papers at conferences
- having a new appreciation of students' experiences at the start of their university careers
- having an understanding of the importance of social aspects of the student learning experience and the need to develop learning communities within both full- and part-time student groups
- learning approaches to working with groups online
- developing e-learning facilitation skills
- developing innovative teaching and learning activities, materials and programmes.

The development of the LC provided opportunities for members to develop and change their workplace practices. Once members became established within the community and had overcome their initial anxieties, the community appeared to provide a 'comfort zone' from which they could develop and improve their workplace practices. The development of the comfort zone appeared dependent on individual members honestly acknowledging their feelings, both positive and negative, within the virtual environment. A visual image of the comfort zone and associated learning trajectories is presented in Figure 8.4. It appeared that, once a comfort zone had been established, members then used it as a launching pad, retreating to the security and comfort of being with like-minded professionals when the going was too tough. Members used the community comfort zone to gain the strength and confidence to initiate new learning trajectories, work practices, innovations and solutions outside the community in the 'real' world of their work and professional lives. These activities took them way beyond the secure boundaries of the community. This process of bursting out into innovation and improved performance and then returning to the community was a recurrent pattern for those individuals who were fully engaged with the life of the community. During their interviews, many members

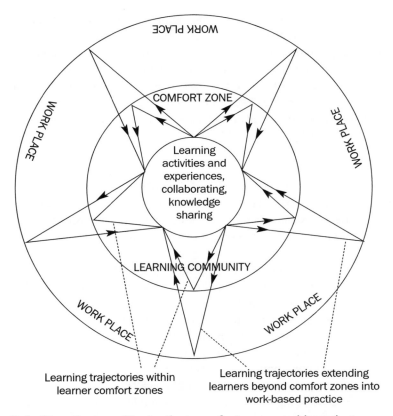

Figure 8.4 Star diagram illustrating comfort zone and learning trajectories

stated that they still felt part of the LC and were in regular contact with each other via e-mail, phone and face-to-face meetings. However, individuals who were less engaged or negative about their LC experiences did not appear to experience this process within the community.

Impact on the organization

The interview with the manager of the development unit highlighted that the LC was part of a wider change process that was concerned with developing and integrating e-learning into learning and teaching within the university. The use of a blended learning community provided an environment which supported change and innovation, and this appeared to be as effective as one that was established using only face-to-face meetings. The LC played a significant role in the university's broader change process because it addressed and changed people's perceptions of the uses of information technology in learning and teaching. It enabled a group of people to develop their understanding of what was required to change, and to facilitate the changes. In addition, community members networked with each other and key stakeholders within the university. An evaluation of the programme led to two approaches to e-learning development: a ten-credit module facilitated by the department for lifelong learning; and a number of short e-learning programmes which were delivered through the development unit.

Developing a community of practice

Trainers and staff developers, project managers and others who are interested in establishing a community of practice are likely to be involved in facilitating the community through a number of stages. Different researchers provide differing models for the stages in the development of a community of practice. The following model is based on the work of Lewis and Allan (2005) and involves six phases as illustrated in Figure 8.5:

- foundation
- induction
- incubation
- improving performance
- implementation
- closure or change.

This model has some similarities to Gilly Salmon's (2000) model of e-learning (see Chapter 6) but an important difference is the inclusion of the foundation stage and of a closure or change stage.

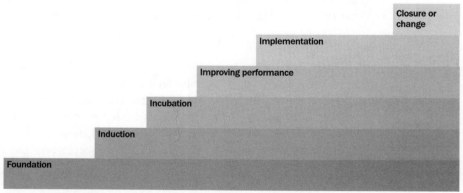

Figure 8.5 Stages in the life cycle of a managed community of practice

Phase 1 – Foundation

The community may be initiated for a number of different reasons and the starting point may be an individual, a group of practitioners or a sponsor or employing organization. The idea of forming a community of practice may emerge from a particular issue or problem, the need to enable practitioners to share good practice and exchange ideas, to help implement the organization's strategic plan, or the need to overcome issues of time and/or geography. Conversely, some communities evolve organically, e.g. from a group of colleagues working together on a new project, and some may be created as part of a professional or strategic workforce development activity. Sometimes communities of practice evolve out of communities of interest, conferences, training events or other professional activities.

Sometimes communities are sponsored, e.g. by an employer, professional association or other agency, and in these cases it is likely that there will be a 'formal' foundation phase. This is likely to involve the sponsor, facilitator(s) and library and information workers spending time planning and working out how the community will come together and interact. It means establishing the key components that will enable the community to achieve its goals, e.g. identify community participants and (if required) the facilitator(s), communication methods, administrative support and the technical infrastructure that will support the community. The following questions, based on the work of Lewis and Allan (2005), need to be addressed at this stage:

- What is the purpose of the community?
- What is the structure of the community?
- Who are the potential community members?
- How will members work and learn together?
- What ICT infrastructure is required?
- What administrative support is required?
- What type of design is required for the virtual learning environment?

Phase 2 – Induction

This is the stage when the community facilitator introduces members and enables them to get to grips with the technical infrastructure. In some respects this is rather like the process of taking part in icebreaking activities in a face-to-face workshop. Sometimes the process will take place in a workshop where members and facilitator(s) are in the same room. However, it will often take place online. The facilitator will be extremely active throughout this phase, reassuring participants and creating a safe and comfortable community environment. Much of the facilitator's work will be online, although it may also involve face-to-face sessions and telephone conversations with members. The following activities are helpful during the induction phase:

- personal introductions
- icebreakers
- technical introduction to the ICT infrastructure
- establishment of community ground rules
- surfacing and discussing hopes and fears of community members.

These activities can occur online or face-to-face, depending on the circumstances of the community and facilitator.

Personal introductions

Personal introductions by participants and facilitator(s) help the community to become established and enable members to begin to know each other and develop a sense of each other's identity and professional interests. Photographs also help participants and facilitators to get to know each other, and some collaborative software systems attach a photograph of the author of each message as it is posted in the community. However, some participants are reluctant to make their photograph available online. Examples 8.1 and 8.2 provide an insight into the style of a typical online introduction.

Example 8.1 Facilitator's introduction

Hello everyone,

I am really looking forward to the opportunity to work with you in this new *Information skills in higher education* community of practice.

A little about myself. I am the Information Skills librarian at Esk University and part of my brief is to enable the Business School students to develop their skills and move beyond Google! It means that I'm always busy.

In my spare time I enjoy the rigours of family life (we've two kids approaching independence), travel (without offspring) and walking in the Yorkshire Dales.

I'm excited about this new project and the chance to establish a community of practice. I know that many of us have worked together previously and also met at conferences. In addition, there are new members who have recently moved to the region. I'm sure that we will be able to work together in this way and develop new approaches to teaching information skills.

In addition to the VLE online community I can be contacted on: J.Smith@esk.ac.uk or phone 0123 456789.

I look forward to working with you.

All the best,
Jane

Example 8.2 Participant's introduction

Hi folks!

I'm Project Information Skills Development worker for the University of Ambridge Learning Development Unit. My previous experience has included working in a further education college library and I've also spent a few years in government libraries. I have been at Ambridge for just over three years and really enjoy my work. I currently support information skills teaching in two faculties: science and engineering, and health.

About me. I enjoy socializing, don't do any sport although I should, and LOVE food, any time/type/amount (I also love McDonalds!). I have two cats, one of which weighs 7.1 kilos and lost his first tooth recently, the other is neurotic and a pain in the butt! I am really enjoying being involved in this learning community and find it great to be learning again.

Finally, my biggest fear about being in this community is a worry about my technical skills. I'm not a technology person!!!

Cheers,

Sam

Icebreakers

Most facilitators and participants have mixed feelings about the value of online ice breakers or social games used to encourage the group to get to know each other. Chapter 6 describes the use of icebreakers. If you are considering using an icebreaker with your group it is worthwhile using the following list of questions to help ensure that it is an effective activity:

- Is this activity appropriate for my group?
- Is it work related?
- Will this activity encourage informal interactions and collaborative learning?
- Will my group enjoy this activity?
- Are the instructions clear and easy to follow?
- Will the group feel comfortable doing this activity?
- How can I encourage them to extend their comfort zones?

Technical induction

During the induction phase, it is important to provide a technical induction to the ICT facilities. If there is a face-face-induction session, it may be helpful to invite a technician or an IT trainer to deliver a short practical session on using the virtual communication site. Participants definitely benefit from a hands-on exploration of the functions and facilities of the ICT infrastructure. Sometimes one session is not enough and it may be necessary to arrange for a follow-up session within a week or two so that any technical difficulties that have arisen can be resolved quickly and effectively. However, this is not always possible and for those groups that are inducted online it is helpful to provide basic guidance and online interactive guides to software facilities. Having step-by-step instructions available in hard copy is also very useful.

Ground rules

Establishing ground rules is a useful way of enabling individual members to start to take ownership of the community, as they can explicitly identify and agree on expectations in terms of community behaviour. Ground rules also enable variations in expectations between individual members to be raised and explored, e.g. one member may anticipate accessing an online community once or twice a month while another member may expect interactions daily. Identifying and resolving these differences is important for successful community development.

Facilitators of communities of practice will find that spending some time to explore the ground rules of the community will help the induction process. There are generic topics that are relevant to most communities and the facilitator can offer helpful prompts on the following:

- confidentiality
- frequency of online participation
- respect for others.

Examples 8.3 and 8.4 illustrate the type of posting a facilitator may use to initiate a discussion and typical sets of ground rules.

Example 8.3 Facilitator's posting encouraging the community to agree ground rules

Hello everyone,

At the beginning of a new virtual learning community it is helpful to agree a set of ground rules for group participation. At this stage it is usually useful for members to make explicit and agree their expectations for online participation. Examples of ground rules that you may find helpful are:

a) For the group to agree a minimum frequency of participation. With a learning set such as this it is important that the group agrees to participate regularly.

b) Confidentiality – anything discussed within this area is confidential to the group.

Please make your own suggestions for ground rules for participation in this learning community and also comment on each other's suggestions.

Thanks very much.

Dina

Example 8.4 Ground rules for health professionals

We all agree to check out the Blackboard site at least twice a week and most of us will aim for three times a week. (Any less than this and you will be in danger of missing out on activities.)

Confidentiality is an agreed underpinning principle.

We will encourage succinct written contributions.

We will aim to be focused and avoid procrastination.

Speling is not an issue and we will not make judgements about typoss and speling errers.

We recognize and respect the differing levels of experience and technical competence within the group.

We will avoid gossip and encourage and support less confident and verbal members of the group.

All opinions will be valued equally; we aim to nurture tolerance.

Humour is to be encouraged; we want the experience to be enjoyable.

Members will be encouraged to ask for and offer help.

We want to encourage the whole community to grow and thrive; sub-communities should be discouraged.

Everyone agrees to contribute to every activity whenever possible.

If the behaviour of individual members later becomes a problem, participants can be reminded of the original ground rules agreed by members and this can help to restore standards of behaviour, e.g. regarding the use of inappropriate language or the need for all views to be accepted and considered. Example 8.4 shows a set of ground rules that was developed in a learning community for health care knowledge workers and trainers (Lewis and Allan, 2005).

Community expectations

During the induction phase it is helpful to encourage participants to surface their expectations of the community; this often involves them in voicing their hopes and fears. It is surprising how many 'fears' participants voice if given the opportunity. Common fears or concerns include:

- not being able to keep up with other members
- not having the same levels of expertise as other practitioners in the community
- technical skills letting them down
- being embarrassed by poor spelling or grammar.

Example 8.5 shows a list of hopes and fears that was generated by a virtual learning community whose members included health-sector knowledge workers and trainers.

Example 8.5 List of hopes and fears

This list was developed at the beginning of a facilitated learning community designed to introduce NHS knowledge workers and trainers to the potential of online learning communities (Lewis and Allan, 2005):

Hopes

To ensure that e-learning is a positive experience.

To be able to influence strategy for the NHS technical infrastructure in the region.

To ensure that support systems for us as learners on the programme will be effective.

To reach and engage non-traditional learners, in fact all potential users in our area.

To co-ordinate development of e-learning nationally, though initially regionally, including co-ordination of learning materials.

To co-ordinate the provision of e-learning on a huge geographical scale.

To sustain outcomes from this programme and develop a strategy that is sustainable.

To make accessible another training mode – 'blended approaches to learning'.

To develop the ability, skills, knowledge and understanding to set up our own learning communities.

To use e-learning to influence practice in the workplace and influence NHS strategy.

To be able to integrate learning from this programme into other training practices within the NHS.

Fears

Infrastructure – funding, concerns about support, additional workload.

Time commitment, that we won't be given time release to undertake the programme.

Sufficient time won't be allowed for us to implement the next phase of cascading the training.

Access to computers for learners in the NHS.

Not coping with the pressure of the programme – workload.

E-learning co-ordinators fear participants will drop out.

That the technology won't work.

Feelings of isolation of participants on programme.

ICT skills of staff that we will train in second phase.

The facilitator will need to encourage openness in discussing any issues that arise. A discussion around different types and levels of participation may be useful at this stage. It is useful to return to the original hopes and fears lists during the community closure phase, and discussion around the induction hopes and fears of the community can make a valuable contribution to the community evaluation process.

Fears associated with technical difficulties need to be addressed during the early stages of community formation. The need for technical support is discussed earlier in this chapter. It is helpful to provide a discussion thread or forum within the virtual discussion area specifically for technical queries. Facilitators will need to respond to technical queries very quickly in order to maintain ICT confidence within the group and sometimes it will be necessary to refer participants to other sources of technical help.

Phase 3 – Incubation

The incubation phase is an important phase in the life cycle of a learning community as the foundations of good practice are established and the conditions for healthy growth are embedded. During the incubation phase successful communities establish a safe and comfort-giving environment where honesty and trust are nurtured and co-operative and co-dependent ways of working are encouraged, a place where humour and fun are found. Lewis and Allan (2005) suggest that there are four conditions that need to be developed during the incubation phase. These are outlined in Table 8.2.

Table 8.2   Incubation phase – checklist for facilitators

Conditions	Possible actions
Comfort zones	Encourage honesty and acknowledge feelings. Assure members that confidentiality will be respected. Give plenty of positive feedback. Use narratives during early phase to encourage sharing and disclosure. Establish a members' profiling area so that they can get to know each others' background. Support those lacking in confidence.
Commitment and trust	Model honesty. Open debates on commitment. Review needs of community regularly. Follow up members who seem to lack commitment. Model commitment. Accept that some communities will founder due to lack of commitment and that it is not your sole responsibility. Encourage co-dependency.
Collective responsibility and co-dependency	Invite those with expertise to lead on identified activities. Don't feel responsible for all community interactions. Guide from the side and develop the knack of standing back. Use questioning techniques and scaffold activities in such a way as to encourage participants to find their own answers.
Humour	Encourage humour. Initiate humour. Don't stand on dignity. Try to build in fun. Beware of pranksters – they can be saboteurs in jokers' clothing.

During the incubation phase community members start to communicate, develop confidence in their online voice and work together. The group begin to develop trust and often disclose and discuss their concerns. The incubation phase is an important stepping-stone in the life cycle of the community, because unless members develop trust and share their real concerns these may lie at the heart of many barriers to constructive development later on. The facilitator will need to take a pro-active role in supporting and encouraging members to engage actively in open discussions and guided activities. Paired activities that require members to share information and experience and begin to tackle work-related problems can work well at this stage in the life of the community. Facilitators need to incubate their communities during the early phase, taking care to respect comfort zones and not to challenge members too much too quickly. The incubation phase is about comfort and confidence, and encouraging the community to grow and develop through mutually supportive ways of working.

Phase 4 – Improving performance

This is the phase when the serious business of the community starts to happen. Group members are likely to be working on real, work-based problems and sharing resources, knowledge and understanding. The learning community is performing at its full potential as real-life issues are tackled and the members work collaboratively to develop practical solutions. The speed of work at this phase may be very fast, with messages posted on a daily and sometimes hourly basis. Group members are likely to be engrossed in collaborative work practices and there is often a sense of excitement, as individuals and the learning community are working on the boundaries of current practice.

This stage may include examples of:

- the whole group brainstorming, pooling ideas and resources
- developing and agreeing an action plan
- individuals testing out ideas and asking for feedback
- whole-group synchronous discussions, e.g. face-to-face or in a virtual conference room
- production of draft ideas, reports and products
- creating new knowledge and understanding
- developing innovative work practices
- developing solutions to work-based problems
- creation of new products and by-products
- collaborative project outcomes.

There is often a sense of hard work and a real commitment to achieving community goals. The group is likely to work constructively to share ideas, resources and solutions. There is likely to be evidence of the trust, openness and honesty, and good humour that has been established during the incubation phase. At this stage the group is going to be involved in both sharing and managing information and resources. They may be exchanging information based on their own knowledge and experiences, and there is often a real need for this information to be managed. This is particularly important in very active communities when large numbers of postings can lead to information overload. The provision of summaries, outline reports, action plans, etc. can all help to manage the information that is generated during the improving performance phase. At this stage, the level of intervention by the facilitator will drop as the community is self-managing and, to a certain extent, self-sufficient.

Phase 5 – Implementation

The purpose of most work-based learning communities is to support improvement practices in the workplace, and communities that are successful lead to changes both in the workplace and to the participants' professional identities. The implementation phase involves transferring learning from the community to the work situation. This can be in the form of a product or outcome or of changed work practices, e.g. implementation of personal transferable skills and practitioner expertise. Some communities work towards implementing a single project or improvement practice, whereas other communities have a much more strategic and dispersed impact on the workplace.

Phase 6 – Community closure or change

The learning community may come to the end of its natural life, e.g. as a result of achieving its initial goals. This may result in the community's closure or its evolution into a new community with a new goal. If the learning community closes, it may go through the traditional rituals of closure, e.g. reflection on the life of the learning community, celebration of achievements, party (face-to-face or virtual), exchange of personal contact details. These enable the members of the community to complete their business and say their goodbyes.

At this stage the facilitator may be required to become more active than during the previous two phases (improving performance and implementation). The facilitator may be involved in initiating and supporting closure activities, or in helping members move to a new community. In one learning community facilitated by Allan and Lewis (2005) the community had come to the end of its life cycle, i.e. it had achieved its goals, and members indicated that they wanted the community to continue. It was agreed to e-mail all members after four weeks to re-establish the community, but when the time came there were no replies to the e-mail, suggesting that the community had closed and individual members had moved on to new activities.

If the learning community evolves into a new community, then it will start the life cycle again with an initiation process. This may be extremely brief and take place over a few days as members discuss the 'new community' and re-establish themselves with a new goal and direction. Alternatively, there may be a series of discussions and negotiations with the employing organization. The new community may involve different members, e.g. a mixture of people from the 'old' community and new members. In this type of situation the induction and incubation periods are vitally important if the 'new' community is to work effectively and not break down into a series of cliques. The facilitator is likely to be very active in its establishment and in supporting it through the community life cycle.

The ending of a virtual learning community needs careful management to make sure that a series of processes occur. It is important to ensure that the learning process is consolidated, and members often find it helpful to spend time reflecting on their development. The group process needs to be completed and this often involves reflecting on the life of the community, celebrating strengths and successes, acknowledging weaknesses, and discussing the end of the community and the need for individuals to leave it and move on to the next stage. In some organizations the transactions and transcripts produced by the community will be harvested for new knowledge and archived. It is up to the facilitator to ensure that community members have a sense of reaching an ending and have no unfinished business, and that there is time to complete the closure process in an unhurried way.

This concludes the description of the life cycle of a community of practice. Table 8.3 provides an overview of the phases in the life cycle.

Mentoring

Earlier in this chapter the concept of 'peripheral participation' was mentioned, and associated with this is the idea that an experienced practitioner, who is perhaps a core member of a community of practice, will help to support the development of new and less experienced members. One process that is commonly used for individual career development is that of mentoring. Mentoring, which is 'learning by association with a role model', is an important way of gaining support in the following areas:

- moving from one role to another
- dealing with a specific issue or problem
- developing skills for a particular task or project
- training support and development
- professional contacts and networks
- career and professional development.

Essentially, a mentor is a friend and someone who will support an individual's

Table 8.3   Summary of the virtual learning community life cycle (adapted from Lewis and Allan (2005))

Phase	Foundation	Induction	Incubation	Improving performance	Implement-ation	Closure or change
Key features	Framework for learning community is established. Agreement reached with ILS managers. Infrastructure including ICT is set up.	Individuals join the learning community and are introduced to it.	Social activity. Creation of comfort zones. Encouraging co-dependency. Honesty. Trust. Humour. Fun.	Starts work on real-life problems. Collaborative and co-operative work. Learning activities designed to improve work-based practice. Development and testing of new practice/products. Feedback.	Transfer of ideas and practice into the workplace.	Learning community no longer required and is closed. Learning community may fizzle out or it transforms itself into another learning community with different focus/member-ship.
Facilitator's levels of activity	Very active.	Very active.	Very active.	Guiding from the side and moving towards periphery.	On periphery.	Facilitates closure or the initiation of a new learning community.
Facilitator's activities	Establishes infrastructure.	Builds trust and confidence. Enables community to develop ground rules.	Injects confidence about practice. Injects ideas. Encourages honesty and trust. Sets up social areas. Sets activities that encourage members to 'open up'.	Designs learning activities and community challenges. Provides structure and support. Makes links with theory, practice and workplace. Gives support and feedback.	Involved in feedback and support. Focus is on practice and sharing good practice. May be involved in project management process.	Facilitates closure, e.g. review, good-byes. Facilitates arrangements to move forward into initiation stage.
Threats	ICT challenges. Appropriate people not getting involved.	Lack of trust. Time pressures. Fear. Working outside comfort zone. Lack of commitment to purpose of community.	Social conflict. Personality clashes. Time pressures. Fear. Lack of commitment to purpose of community. Lack of honesty.	Group dynamics. Low participation. Information overload. Insider/outsider. Saboteurs. Sub-groups. Distractions.	Failure to take responsibility for outcomes. Lack of transfer. Fear of change.	Group stuck. Doesn't want to move forward. Ends abruptly without closure.
Infor-mation and knowledge manage-ment	Creating information infrastructure.	Information transmission.	Information shared and exchanged.	Information management. Collaborative approaches to developing new knowledge.	Knowledge management. Knowledge transfer.	Information transmission and exchange. Archiving of community resources.

personal and career development. Some organizations have formal mentoring schemes and these are typically aimed at new recruits and/or groups of staff who traditionally encounter barriers to their progression, e.g. women or staff from ethnic minorities. Informal mentoring schemes are very common and may be initiated by the mentee, their line manager or a colleague. Typically, staff will identify a mentor within their own organization but some workers, e.g. consultants, find it appropriate to approach a colleague in another organization.

Formal mentoring schemes may be organized by a professional body, e.g. as part of gaining professional qualifications, by employers or as part of a special project, perhaps to support the career progression of particular groups of people. In this situation, the mentors will be selected and offered support by a mentor co-ordinator and this support may be provided via virtual communication tools. Example 8.6 shows a sample discussion group message posted by a mentor co-ordinator.

Example 8.6 Discussion group message from a mentor co-ordinator

Hello everyone,

A few people have asked about getting started with e-mentoring and I thought the following might be helpful. Please don't hesitate to add your own comments or thoughts to this posting.

Getting started

The best way to start is to spend time finding out about each other. You could then move on to discuss the following aspects of your e-mentoring relationship:

- how often you will communicate
- whether you will specify times of communication
- whether you will agree turnaround times for reply
- whether you will have any face-to-face meetings
- whether you will have any telephone calls
- restrictions on electronic or telephone contact on either side.

The mentoring life cycle

It may be helpful at the start to think about the mentoring life cycle, with its sequence of phases:

Initiation phase
Building a rapport – getting to know each other.

Continued on next page

Example 8.6 *Continued*

Goal-setting phase
Setting goals and making plans to achieve them.

Developmental learning phase
Working together towards achieving goals.

Winding-down phase
Reviewing outcomes and evaluating the process.

Dissolving the mentoring relationship
Ending the mentoring relationship; but professional friendship may continue.

Timing
The amount of time spent on each phase will depend on you and your mentee, and the frequency and level of contact you have with each other. The e-mentoring process is scheduled to take nine months, although it may be a shorter or longer period depending on individual pairs.

Introductions
All mentors and mentees will receive an e-mail this week and this will provide you with each other's contact details. It is then up to you to make contact with each other.
I hope this helps you to get started. Does anyone have any questions?

Regards,
Jane

Typically, the mentoring process lasts over a period of several months or even years. It involves a mentee meeting with the mentor, e.g. at three-monthly intervals, and exploring their current situation and career plan. These meetings may take place face-to-face or using virtual communication tools. Figure 8.6 provides an outline of a typical mentoring process involving the phases mentioned in the example discussion group message above.

Headlam-Wells (2004) identified the benefits of a blended e-mentoring process for management development: it helped to overcome feelings of isolation through personal contact and provided access to networking opportunities. E-mentoring was an efficient way of providing management development by saving on time and/or travel costs, although mentor/mentee pairs generally preferred to meet face-to-face and hold telephone conversations, in addition to communicating in a virtual environment. The mentees valued the support, guidance and professional friendship they gained from their mentors and one mentee reported, 'It was

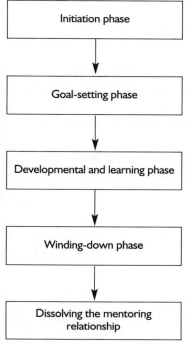

Figure 8.6 Typical mentoring process

good to share with someone trustworthy and supportive.' Mentoring is a two-way process and the mentors benefit too, e.g. Headlam-Wells (2004) stated that the mentor experience was also positive, and it offered mentors an opportunity for personal growth and development, e.g. by learning more about mentoring, and new opportunities for reflection. In addition, it provided the opportunity to 'giving something back'.

Summary

This chapter introduced the concept of communities of practice and distinguished them from communities of interest. The characteristics of communities of practice were outlined and illustrated with a number of practical examples of library and information communities of practice. A case study illustrated the value of membership of a multi-professional community of practice for individuals and their workplace. The five-phase process involved in establishing and facilitating a work-based community of practice was described. The topic of mentoring, which frequently occurs in the context of a community of practice and enables new or inexperienced members to become active members of their community or profession, was also considered.

References

Allan, B., Hunter, B. and Lewis, D. (2006) Four Years On: a longitudinal study assessing the impact of membership of a virtual community of practice, *Networked Learning Conference 2006*, University of Lancaster.

Brown, J. S. and Duguid, P. (1991) Organizational Learning and Communities of Practice: toward a unified view of working, learning, and innovation, *Organizational Science*, **2** (1), 40–57.

Brown, J. S. and Duguid, P. (2001) Structure and Spontaneity: knowledge and organization. In Nonaka, I. and Teece, D. (eds), *Managing Industrial Knowledge*, London, Sage, 44–67.

Cox, A. (2005) What Are Communities of Practice? A comparative review of four seminal works, *Journal of Information Science*, **31** (6), 527–40.

Headlam-Wells, J. (2004) E-mentoring for Aspiring Women Managers, *Women in Management Review*, **19** (4), 212–18.

Hyams, E. and Mezey, M. (2003) Virtuous Virtual: weblogs: the new internet community? *Library & Information Update*, **2**, 36–7.

Lave, J. and Wenger, E. (1991) *Situated Learning: legitimate peripheral participation*, Cambridge, Cambridge University Press.

Lewis, D. and Allan, B. (2005) *Facilitating Virtual Learning Communities*, Maidenhead, Open University.

Salmon, G. (2000) *E-moderating*, London, Kogan Page.

Swan, J., Scarborough, H. and Robertson, M. (2002) The Construction of Communities of Practice in the Management of Innovation, *Management Learning*, **33** (4), 477.

Wenger, E. (2003) *Communities of Practice: learning, meaning, and identity*, Cambridge, Cambridge University Press.

Wenger, E., McDermott, R. and Snyder, W. M. (2002) *Cultivating Communities of Practice*, Boston, Harvard Business School Press.

9 Managing blended learning projects

Introduction

Many library and information workers are involved in managing or working on projects that design, develop and implement blended learning programmes. For example, they may be involved in the development of reusable learning objects, of a new website or portal, or of interactive training materials.

Project management is a key transferable skill (Milner 2007) and it is essential for library and information workers to be able to manage projects and to work effectively within project teams. This chapter provides guidance on project management and covers the following topics: principles of project management; the people side of project management; working in collaborative and multi-professional teams; obtaining financial support; and gaining accreditation for your programme.

Principles of project management

There is an extensive literature on project management. Allan (2004) provides a detailed guide set in the context of ILS, and more general textbooks include Maylor (2003) and Lockyer and Gordon (2005). In addition, funding bodies such as the Joint Information Systems Committee (JISC) provide guidance on project management (www.jisc.ac.uk) and projects that are funded by this body will need to use their guidelines and documentation processes.

The traditional project management literature developed from research and practice in industry and military projects and, as a result, offers an approach that is embedded in the scientific management field. These traditional approaches to project management tend to be concerned with splitting the project into its constituent parts and then managing and controlling the project process in a rather top-down, authoritarian manner. While it is important to approach project management in an organized and logical manner, it is also important to appreciate the importance of people and the management of the relationships aspect of a project.

How does project work differ from the day-to-day work in a library or information department? The characteristics of projects include:

- having a definite start and end date
- being unique and novel to the people involved in the project
- having limiting factors, e.g. time, resources
- having outcomes that usually result in change
- having a single point of responsibility.

If you are involved in a new project, the first question to ask is 'How complex is the project?' Extremely complex projects require the use of project management tools and techniques whereas relatively simple projects can be managed with a plan written on a single sheet of A4 paper. Factors to think about when assessing the complexity of a project include:

- Time issues
  — speed of change
  — time allocated to work on project vs time for other duties, e.g. running the ILS services
- Work issues
  — level of innovation
  — volumes of data
- People issues
  — experience of team members
  — size of team
  — levels of co-operation or collaboration
  — level of project – strategic or operations
  — working across different departments or organizations.

Why do projects go wrong? Newspapers thrive on stories of project failures and examples include projects that have gone over budget by millions or over time by years, e.g. many public-sector IT or building projects. Puleo (2002) identifies some of the more common pitfalls of project management as follows:

- lack of project sponsorship, e.g. by senior managers
- lack of a steering committee to achieve co-ordination and collaboration among people across organizations
- the wrong project manager i.e. someone without the necessary project management, motivational, leadership and change agent skills
- insufficient time for team members to carry out their project work
- lack of co-ordination between the project and everyday services.

Another common error is tackling a project that is so large and takes so long to implement that by the time it is completed the product is redundant because the environment has changed, the user needs have changed and the technology has moved on, bringing with it new opportunities.

The project cycle

A standard approach to project management and one that helps to ensure that typical challenges are predicted and effectively managed is through the project cycle (see Figure 9.1) and each stage in this cycle is outlined below.

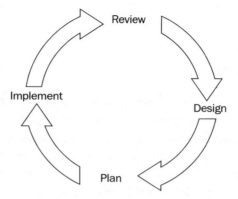

Review

Design

Implement

Plan

Figure 9.1 The project cycle

Design stage

The first stage is to define the project and its scope, which involves developing the original 'raw' idea into a clear project outline. This consists of the following processes:

- identifying the basic aim of the project
- identifying the project outcomes
- checking that there is a match between the project and the organization's objectives
- identifying the project team
- producing a project brief – one side of A4 that summarizes the proposed project
- identifying milestones
- completing a cost–benefit analysis
- completing a risk analysis.

A sample project brief is provided in Example 9.1 and this illustrates the basic information required at the starting point of a project.

Example 9.1 Example project brief

Proposed project title: Use of a weblog to support Knowledge Centre customers.

Aim: The aim of this project is to develop a pilot weblog to support the Knowledge Centre customers.

Outcomes

A pilot Knowledge Centre weblog

A user-evaluation survey

Rationale

The development of a test weblog would enable us to explore a new approach to informing and updating Knowledge Centre customers. Weblogs are becoming a commonly used information source and their use is slowly developing within the company, e.g. the Human Resources director now has a weblog. Developing a weblog would provide the Knowledge Centre with a new communication channel and one that is less formal than our website. It would enable us to disseminate news and ideas in small chunks and also provide links to our website.

Action plan

This action plan assumes that the project starts on 1 July.

Action	Staff	Costs	Deadline
Research and develop test weblog	Rakiya (information officer) Neill (IT officer)	Rakiya – 40 hours Neill – 10 hours	End of July
Pilot weblog among Knowledge Centre staff only	All KC staff	Rakiya – 10 hours Neill – 1 hour All other staff – up to 1 hour each	End of August
Develop weblog based on staff pilot	Rakiya – 10 hours Neill	Rakiya – 10 hours Neill – 1 hour	14 September
Launch website	Rakiya	Rakiya – 1 hour per week	Starts 15 September – 15 December
Evaluate weblog	Susan – information officer Rakiya	Susan – 12 hours Rakiya – 3 hours	Starts 15 November – 15 December
Decide future of weblog	Knowedge Centre management team	Management team – 1 hour each	Management team meeting 18 December

Costs: No substantial costs. Main cost will be staff time (see above). Other costs will be for consumables.

Milestones: Launch website – 15 September; decide future of weblog project – 18 December.

Risks: These relate to key staff, e.g. Rakiya; if she became ill during the project period, this would delay the project. Ensure that Susan is kept informed throughout the programme so that she can pick up the reins if required.

In addition to this information it is worthwhile thinking about some of the basic principles that may underpin the blended learning programme or activity. For example, it involves thinking about the overall make up of the programme or activity and deciding on the type of blended learning programme that will be developed. This involves considering the different aspects of a learning programme that are presented in Chapter 1, Figure 1.2 and explored in Chapter 4, which considers the overall design process of the blended learning programme.

Project planning

The next stage is producing a project plan. For large and complex projects the plan is likely to expand on the project brief and contain the following information:

- aims, outcomes, milestones
- detailed list of the tasks that need to be completed and the time each task will take to be completed; this may be presented as a Gantt chart (see below)
- network diagram or PERT chart (see below)
- week-by-week 'to do' list
- staffing requirements
- risk analysis
- contingency plans.

Many organizations have their own template for project documentation, so this is worth checking out before you produce your plans. If you are working on a very simple project, the project plan is likely to be a simple action plan.

Using computer software such as MS Excel or MS Project to manage the project plan and finances is common practice. There are two important outputs used in the planning stages. The first of these is a Gantt chart (Figure 9.2), which is commonly used as a means of enabling the project team and others to understand the organization of the project over time. A Gantt chart, so called because it was developed by Henry Gantt, presents the project as a series of tasks mapped onto a diary or calendar. In the absence of a computer-produced Gantt chart it is very simple to create one on a whiteboard or flipchart paper.

The next part of the planning process is to produce a network diagram which shows the logical relationships between the different tasks (Figure 9.3). Specialists in project management differentiate between network diagrams, PERT (Programme Evaluation and Review Technique) and critical path diagrams. At a very basic level, a network diagram shows the logical relationships between tasks, rather like a special flow chart that illustrates relationships between tasks, e.g. it will show which tasks can only start when a previous task is complete and which tasks can take place in parallel or at the same time. The critical path is the pathway through the network where, if any, of the tasks on the pathway takes longer

Tasks	Week 1	Week 2	Week 3	Week 4	Week 5	Week 6	Week 7	Week 8
1 Produce project brief	▓							
2 Produce plan		▓						
3 Agree workloads		▓						
4 Produce detailed module plan			▓					
5 Obtain feedback			▓					
6 Design prototype				▓				
7 Obtain feedback					▓			
8 Develop resources					▓			
9 Integrate text and resources							▓	
10 Obtain feedback						▓		
11 ...								▓

Figure 9.2 Example Gantt chart

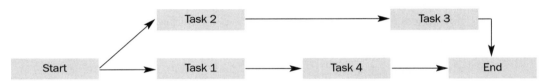

Figure 9.3 Network diagram

than expected to complete, then the whole project will be delayed and deadlines will not be met. Project management software such as MS Project is particularly useful because it identifies, in red, the critical path through the project.

An important aspect of the planning stage is to estimate how much time it will take to complete each task. A useful equation for calculating the time to complete a task is given below. The equation works out an average taking into account the best or most optimistic time, the worst or most pessimistic time and the average time.

Estimate of time taken to complete a task $= T_{(estimate)}$

$$T_{(estimate)} = \frac{T_{(pessimistic)} + (4 \times T_{(average)}) + T_{(optimistic)}}{6}$$

Worked example
Estimate the time taken to create a 'blank' weblog

Time $_{(pessimistic)}$ = 12 hours
Time $_{(average)}$ = 5 hours
Time $_{(optimistic)}$ = 3 hours
Time $_{(estimate)}$ $= \dfrac{[12 + (4 \times 5) + 3]}{6} = 5.8$ hours

At the planning stage it is also worthwhile thinking about how you will communicate with the team and stakeholders throughout the project process. It is important to identify how you will find out about people issues, project progress, significant constraints, and existing or potential problems.

Implementation

At the implementation stage, work on the actual project starts and this involves putting the project plan into action. If the aim of the project is to produce a new blended learning programme, then it is at this stage that you will start to work through the design process outlined in Chapter 4. The implementation stage involves monitoring the following:

- People issues
  - project team, e.g. staff motivation and morale
  - project team – development and training
  - project team – providing an appropriate working environment, e.g. one that supports creativity
  - other stakeholders, e.g. responses to the initiative
- Project process
  - tasks started and completed
  - creep in project time (tasks that take longer than estimated)
  - slack in project time (tasks that take less time than expected)
  - existing and potential problems
- Resource issues
  - project finance – match between anticipated expenditure and real expenditure
  - external environment
  - new developments, e.g. in internet technologies, that the project team need to take on board.

If you are managing a complex project, then it is worthwhile thinking about how you will keep up-to-date with project activity. This normally involves setting up reporting systems to enable you to keep track of progress. In the types of projects that ILS staff are involved in, monitoring the project is likely to be through a combination of talking informally with individual team members and of informal reporting systems. The latter may be as simple as asking every team member to e-mail the project manager about their progress once a week.

Project completion and review

The last stage of the project involves:

- checking to ensure that the project outcomes have been met
- dealing with loose ends e.g. late invoices
- project review
- disseminating the project outcomes, e.g. via the ILS website, conferences and other activities
- producing and disseminating project reports
- handing over the project to the team who will maintain it as part of the day-to-day services within the library
- celebrating.

Complex projects will require detailed evaluations and reports. A simple approach to reviewing small-scale projects involves asking team members and stakeholders to answer the following questions:

- What worked well?
- What could be improved?
- What did you learn?
- What will do you differently next time?

The people side of project management

Although the traditional project management literature tends to focus on technical aspects of projects, the people side is vital if the project is to be successful. Nowadays library and information workers may find themselves working in a variety of project situations, ranging from small, in-house teams through to multi-skilled teams and collaborative teams made up of workers from a variety of professions and organizations.

Managing and working in a project team involves focusing on and working with individuals, the team and the task. If you are the project manager, you will need to know the individual team members and their strengths and weaknesses. You will be involved in action planning, giving and receiving information and feedback from team members, e.g. through e-mails or phone calls, and providing them with help and support as required. An important aspect of team work is motivation and you may be required to spend some time motivating and supporting staff.

Traditionally, large and formal projects are managed through a series of teams:

1 Steering group. This provides the overall strategic direction for the project and includes individuals who can champion the project throughout the organization, e.g. senior staff, directors.
2 Management group. This group manages the operations of the project and resolves significant problems. It is likely to include the project manager and some key team members, and it may contain staff from other departments associated with the project, e.g. IT department.

3 Project team. This is the operational team that carries out the work and resolves problems. It reports to the management group.

This is illustrated in Figure 9.4.

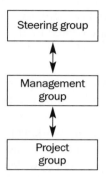

Figure 9.4 Project management structure

The other group of people who need to be considered are the stakeholders, e.g. all the staff within the organization, ILS staff not involved in the project, students or end-users, etc. As project manager, it is worthwhile to identify the stakeholders and think about how you will communicate with them about the project. On very large projects, the project manager may want to set up a formal stakeholder panel or group as a means of establishing two-way information flow about the project.

Working in collaborative and multi-professional teams

> Partnership is one of the most complex and difficult ways in which to work. When it works even reasonably well, however, it can bring some of the best results for the end-user.
>
> (Dakers, 2003, 47)

Library and information workers have always had a tradition of networking and collaborative working both within the profession and with other professional groups. A scan of the current ILS literature reveals that many information workers are now involved in developing and delivering a wide range of services through partnerships. For example, in post-16 education many library and information workers come together in collaborative teams with academics, technologists and educational developers from their own and other educational organizations. The development of blended learning programmes frequently involves working across organizational boundaries and across organizations. This brings a range of benefits and challenges, as outlined below.

What are the benefits of working in partnership? Informal discussions with some directors of library and information services and with project managers produced the following list:

- Enhanced access to people, resources and organizations.
- Enhanced ownership – projects that are set up to tackle specific problems collaboratively are owned by the partners, and this means that the project outcomes are more likely to be accepted and owned by the partner organizations.
- Enhanced quality – the involvement of a wide range of people who bring their different professional perspectives can enhance the quality of the project experience and outcomes. Individual partners may be more willing to take on new ideas and working practices as a result of the partnership.
- Increased exposure to new ideas/approaches – working in multi-professional teams can help partners to widen their outlook and obtain a broader understanding of their work and its context.
- Improved use of resources – partnership working can enhance access to resources and result in more efficient use of them.
- Enhanced motivation – being part of a successful partnership can boost morale and help individuals to develop new enthusiasms for their work. However the opposite may also be true!
- Continuous professional development – working on a collaborative project provides individual workers with the opportunity to develop their knowledge and skills. Development of professional communities of practice (see Chapter 8). Partnership working brings learning opportunities for the different partners and this can be the result of 'enforced' reflection on our own perspectives and working practices in comparison with those of our partners.

Despite these benefits there are some challenges to working in and leading collaborative or multi-professional teams. Sullivan and Skelcher (2002) identify and explore the life cycle and social processes involved in working in partnership and they present their model as a series of consecutive stages:

1 Pre-conception – the potential partners, agencies and individuals become aware of the possibility of working in partnership and the potential benefits and needs to do so.
2 Initiation – individuals come together and explore the potential of working together in partnership.
3 Formalization – the partnership is formalized by implementing an appropriate governance structure and/or committing to a project bid.
4 Operation – the project is put into action and partners work together to achieve the project goals.

5   Termination – the project closes or transforms itself into another venture.

This model provides a useful template for exploring and facilitating collaborative arrangements and its structure is similar to that of the stages of team development (see Chapter 6) and of community of practice development (see Chapter 8). As with the team development model, it is perhaps an over-simplification. Some potential partnerships will not move beyond the pre-conception stage and may stall at the initiation stage. Others may transform into a new venture during the formalization stage, when individuals develop a better understanding of their context and the project potential. Overall, this model does help to provide team leaders with guidance on how to facilitate a project that involves working in partnership, and the concept is explored later in this chapter.

Leading and managing the partnership team

The literature on partnership and collaborative working provides a set of characterics that distinguish effective partnerships from those that are not effective and, perhaps, fail. Effective partnerships tend to demonstrate the following characteristics:

*   clear project goal and objectives
*   project goal and objectives shared by all partners
*   all partners have made a commitment to the project
*   trust and respect among different partners
*   project process is transparent and agreed by all partners
*   project action plan is realistic and takes into account the needs of the partners
*   partners share the workload and give each other support
*   clear and open communication between partners
*   partners give and take constructive feedback
*   clear framework of responsibility and accountability
*   partners invest time into the partnership and their relationships with each other.

This set of characteristics provides a project manager with a 'to do' list for managing both the partnership team and the project. The following list identifies some of the reasons why partnerships fail:

*   Domination of the partnership by one member or organization. If one dominant partner takes over, this can lead to resentment by other members. It may lead to individual project members not feeling part of the team and withdrawing from the project.
*   Cynical members. Some partners may be cynical about the project, its

funding, or working in partnership. This may have a negative effect on the project and team working, and result in a self-fulfilling prophecy.

- Rotation of members. This is a problem if one or more partners are represented at meetings by different members of staff during the life of the project. It means that the project team rarely gets beyond the formation stage and there has to be constant repetition of previous discussions in order to enable the new members to catch up.
- Previous history. Sometimes the past history of relationships between partner organizations or individuals can have a detrimental effect on the whole partnership. This is particularly true if members use the current project to sort out old scores and battles.
- Unequal distribution or work or project responsibilities. If a small number of people take on the majority of the work, this can lead to them feeling resentful because they are 'carrying' other team members. It can also mean that other team members begin to lose ownership of the project.
- Added bureaucracy. Working in partnership can add another level of bureaucracy to the project work. Partnership working tends to involve more meetings and careful documentation of events. This can often take up more time and resources than necessary.
- Different cultures. A potential problem area is the different cultures and working patterns of project partners. For example, a partnership involving members from the business and academic communities may experience tensions as a result of differences between the cultures of the two sectors. Unless these are respected, unnecessary conflict may develop in the project.
- Inexperienced project manager. The appointment of a project manager with little experience of working on projects, across sectors or in an intensely political context can sometimes lead to the demise of a project.
- Political interference. Political interference in the project, e.g. by senior managers, directors and elected members, can lead to problems for the project manager and team.

The initial stages of a partnership are probably the most crucial ones in terms of creating a strong foundation for effective working. The greater the number of partners and the more complex the project, the greater the amount of time and attention to detail that needs to be paid in the initial stages. Dakers (2003, 47) identifies the length of the lead time in setting up and running projects and states 'organizations considering this complex level of collaboration should allow significantly more lead time than for projects with fewer partners. No doubt we will produce the results to time, but all be somewhat greyer for it.'

As with any team or group enterprise, the first few meetings of partners may involve the following processes: introductions; surfacing expectations, hopes and fears; creating the vision; building the objectives; and agreeing the action plan. The process of surfacing expectations is a simple yet very important one. Asking partners what they expect as part of being on the project team will enable similar and also different expectations to be aired and discussed. It will also help to prevent theoretically small issues becoming inhibitors in the project process. Another important area to explore is each other's thoughts and underlying assumptions about blended learning. My own experience is that if you have four or five different practitioners in a meeting, they will each have differing understandings of what blended learning entails. Time spent surfacing and talking about individual assumptions and pre-suppositions is helpful and can prevent misunderstandings later in the project process.

Once a project team is established, it is vitally important that all members and partners are engaged with the project. This is one of the key roles of the project manager, who must create and maintain a 'glue' that holds the project together. The complex team 'glue' may consist of either informal or formal processes and these can be divided into 'soft' or people-centred approaches and 'hard' or procedural and documented approaches. These are outlined in Table 9.1.

Table 9.1 Types of complex team 'glue'

Soft	Hard
Shared goals(s)	Minutes of meetings
Shared values and beliefs	Contracts
Common concerns and deeper convictions	Terms of reference
Meetings and social networking	Project schedules
Informal communications, e.g. e-mail or phone calls	Use of project management tools, e.g. Gantt charts
Informal feedback	Reporting regimes, e.g. reporting back to senior managers
Good will	Funding regimes
People, e.g. project managers and project team members	Legal requirements

Both types of project team 'glue' are important. Effective project managers ensure that the project glue is in place and will spend time on both the 'soft' and the 'hard' glue. If the project runs into barriers or problems then the formal arrangements such as contracts and regular meetings may become vital in sorting out the situation and moving the project forward.

Many partnership or multi-professional teams involve working across organizational boundaries, and this means that the team may operate as a virtual or blended team. Sometimes virtual-team work takes place entirely via e-mail. Virtual environments such as virtual learning environments, organizational intranet sites or online collaborative project sites (see Chapter 2) are increasingly used to mediate communications within the team. The development and facilitation of a virtual project team is similar to that of a community of practice as outlined in Chapter 8. As well as the project glue identified in Table 9.1, it appears to be particularly important to develop trust in virtual teams (McConnell, 2005). Boden and Molotch (1994) suggest that it is important to 'upgrade' from virtual to other means of communication, e.g. phone or face-to-face, if you are dealing with difficult situations; they call this the 'compulsion of proximity'. This suggests that project managers need to spend time developing trust within the virtual and blended team, and they may need to take 'time out' to communicate with each other by other means.

Obtaining financial support

Many library or information workers now bid for funds to support their learning and teaching projects. They may apply for funding from their department, their organization or from a national agency such as a professional body or a government or other funding organization. Tanner (2003) writes: 'Recent UK research has shown that in the period 1997–2000 "only 32 per cent of archives, 3 per cent of libraries and 30 per cent of museums had not submitted bids for projects worth over £10,000".' The competition is real and fundraising is a skill that all librarians have to learn. The bidding process is summarized in Figure 9.5. The first stage is to identify a potential project, perhaps singled out during the strategic planning process within the ILS or in response to a particular problem or challenge. It is useful to outline the idea in a project brief, as discussed earlier in this chapter and illustrated in Example 9.1 (page 204).

Identification of a potential project and commencement of work on project brief
Identification of a potential source of funding
Obtaining the necessary documentation
Checking potential funder's requirements and criteria
Checking with parent organization that these meet its aims
Identifying a senior manager who will support the funding application
Identifying a single individual who will be responsible for the project
Carrying out research within the sector
Carrying out research within the bidding organization
Setting up or calling together a bidding team
Producing a draft funding application
Checking out queries with the funding organization
Obtaining feedback and guidance from colleagues
Editing and redrafting the funding application
Obtaining approval from own organization to submit the funding application
Submitting the funding application within the time scale identified by the funding
    organization.
Receiving outcome of selection process
If successful, start project; if unsuccessful, obtain feedback from funding organization and
    use it to help you become successful in your next application

---

Figure 9.5 Summary of the bidding process

The next stage is to identify potential sources of funding and this often requires considerable research. Keeping up-to-date with possible sources of funding is a challenging task and beyond the scope of this work. However, in the area of blended learning, organizations in the UK that regularly fund projects include HEFCE (www.hefce.ac.uk), the Higher Education Academy (www.hea.ac.uk) and JISC (www.jisc.ac.uk). In addition, if you are developing a blended learning project for a specific group of end-users, e.g. scientists or lawyers, publishers or specialist professional bodies may be a source of financial help. If you are working with young people, there is a range of organizations, including voluntary organizations, and initiatives that may provide access to funding. Sometimes, individual philanthropists may offer grants.

Currently there is a diversity of sources of funding and the types and availability of funds are constantly changing. Funding opportunities change over time as the priorities of funding organizations change, as does their access to funds. This means that anyone who is considering bidding for funding must do extensive research to identify current sources of funding and their up-to-date, detailed requirements. Many information workers make use of specialists for current information and advice on funding matters, e.g. local authorities typically employ specialist staff in their economic development units who have expertise in funding and funding applications, while universities often have a centralized research and development department that provide access to this type of information. In addition, individual consultants in this field provide services and expertise in funding applications.

Experience of the bidding culture suggests that the process can be extremely time consuming and resource intensive. Much time can be spent in getting to grips with a particular bid – reading all the relevant paperwork can be heavy going, and writing a succinct bid that meets the needs of both the funding organization and the ILS and its stakeholders can consume vast amounts of time. Information workers need expertise or access to expertise in writing bids. While public sector organizations can provide this support to their departments, smaller and independent organizations may need to contract the services of a consultant to develop their funding application. The actual bidding process produces 'winners and losers' – for those who are unsuccessful in obtaining a bid after they have invested much time and effort, it can be a very demoralizing experience. Winners may suddenly find that they need to get a project up and running in a matter of weeks, often while still fully engaged in their full-time job role.

Developing a bid

Once you have identified a potential source of funding you will need to obtain the documentation that outlines its funding programme(s) and requirements. Such documentation is normally available via the internet and many funding organizations require submission of electronic funding applications. If you obtain the documentation from the funding organization's website, then it is worthwhile monitoring the website regularly so that you can pick up any additional information, e.g. more detailed explanations of requirements, or changes in submission dates.

It is vital to check the funding organization's small print and to ensure that you and your project will fit its requirements. Otherwise you may find that you have wasted time preparing a project bid for a funder who will not consider your application because you don't fit its criteria. If you are uncertain about the requirements, contact the funding organization by phone or e-mail. Many funders organize special meetings or launches for new funding opportunities and these are well worth attending because they provide an opportunity to find out more about the funder and what it is looking for.

You need to ensure that the proposed project fits into your own organization's or department's aims and objectives. This will ensure that you have support from within your own organization for the project. It is vital to gain the support senior managers. Initially 'selling' your idea to one manager is often a good strategy, which can then be followed up by ensuring that the project proposal is discussed and (hopefully) supported by the senior team. You will need to identify someone who will take responsibility for putting together the funding application.

The basis of all good funding applications is research, and you will need to demonstrate to the funding organization that your application is based on knowledge of current good practice and thinking. Many funding applications require you to demonstrate knowledge of your current context and the ways in which your project will make a difference. This means being aware of relevant current government policy and activities within your particular sector (e.g. public library, higher education), your area of interest (e.g. reusable learning objects, repositories, training end-users, internationalization, supporting diversity) and across the profession as a whole. This research will enable you to link your application to current thinking and activities, and help you to identify gaps that your project may fill. In addition, it will help you to develop the appropriate language to use in the funding application.

If your organization, e.g. university, some public sector organizations, has an organizational structure that will work with you in putting together your bid, you will be able to get advice on what is required for your application. If your organization doesn't have this structure you may find it helpful to organize a team that will take overall responsibility for the application. This team may include: a person with overall responsibility for producing the application, individuals who are interested in and enthusiastic about the potential project, technical staff, finance staff and potential project champions.

You will also need to do research on your proposed project within your organization. The purpose of this research is to start thinking through some of the practical aspects of the project and to answer questions such as:

- Who will become involved in the project?
- Where will the project take place?
- Is there an enabling infrastructure?
- Is there an appropriate administrative infrastructure?
- Is there an appropriate ICT infrastructure?
- What financial systems are in place that the project will need to use?

Initial meetings may be held with appropriate directors and managers, e.g. the human resource manager, finance director and administrative manager. In these meetings you may want to show them the project brief and explain the basic ideas underlying the project. Find out what you will need to do to put the project in place, e.g. if it takes your organization six months to recruit a new member of staff this will have implications for your application.

Costing the project is a relatively straightforward process. You will need to identify all the likely costs and present them in a suitable manner. Many organizations have their own guidelines and rules for costing projects and it is worthwhile contacting the finance department before you start. The list of headings which you will need to consider is as follows:

- staff
- durable equipment
- software
- consumables
- printed materials
- subscriptions
- external assistance, e.g. consultant, trainers
- printing
- travel and subsistence
- miscellaneous
- VAT.

Staffing is likely to be a major cost and it is important to calculate it using realistic figures. Normally staff costs are calculated pro rata of the annual salary plus overheads. The overheads are the costs to the organization of employing a member of staff, typically 20–30% of the gross salary. It is important to know your own organization's rules before calculating the staff costs. If your project is going to last more than a year, any likely pay rises (e.g. cost of living or performance-related increases) will need to be included in the costings.

The other project costs will need to be calculated and included in your project plan. In the UK, project managers need to determine whether or not VAT can be claimed on purchases. The rules for VAT are complicated and change over time, so obtain up-to-date specialist advice on this subject, e.g. from your finance department. Some funding organizations ask for a business plan, which is another name for the project budget. In a business plan you should outline projected costs, anticipated income and cash-flow projections, e.g. income and expenditure on a monthly basis.

The next step is to produce an initial draft funding application, and this is a key stage in the funding application process. You will need to circulated the draft application, obtain feedback on it and then work on and polish it until it completely matches the requirements of the funding organization. This is a lengthy process and the draft will go through many iterations before it is ready for submission. Questions or issues that arise during the feedback process and meetings of the bidding team need to be taken to the funding organization. The more clarity that you have about its expectations, the more likely that you are to meet them.

Obtaining feedback and guidance from colleagues is an important part of the bidding process because it will help you to sharpen up your application and include a range of ideas and perspectives. Send copies of your draft bid to colleagues (both within and outside your organization) and ask them for feedback. If you have specific queries or concerns, it is sometimes appropriate to use an e-mail discussion list to obtain further information or advice. However, it does mean that you may be allowing your competitors to know your plans. Remember that if individuals are generous with their time and experience in helping you to put together your bid, it is important to thank them and to repay their work 'in kind' at a later date.

Continue editing the funding application. Keep checking back to the requirements of the funding organization to ensure that your application doesn't drift and develop in directions that don't meet the requirements of the funding organization. Once the application is ready you will need to obtain approval from your own manager and/or organization before sending it off. Many funding organizations require that the funding application is supported by a statement of commitment from a senior member of staff such as a chief executive officer, principal or director.

The next important step is to submit the funding application within the timescale identified by the funding organization. It is vital that you submit the application on time. This sounds obvious but it is worth knowing that with many large national or international funding processes, applications that are even one minute late will not be considered. If you are submitting your application electronically, it is always a good idea to submit it 24 hours before the closing date as this will allow time to sort out any unexpected technical difficulties. Keep the receipt or acknowledgement of your application.

Different funding organizations will inform applicants of the outcome of the application process over different timescales and by different means, e.g. phone, e-mail or letter. This information should be provided in the details of their requirements. It is best practice not to contact the funding organization until after their deadline for informing applicants about the results of the bidding process has passed. Numerous phone calls from worried applicants before this deadline are a great source of irritation and a time-waster for the funding organization.

Many project applications are unsuccessful, and it is worthwhile obtaining feedback from the funding organization. This will help you to learn from the experience and, hopefully, submit a successful application next time. Do remember to thank those people who have contributed to your funding application. If you are successful, then you are likely to move into the next stage of the project management process, i.e. project planning, which is outlined earlier in this chapter.

Gaining accreditation for your learning programme

This section is particularly relevant to ILS in the education sector who are interested in gaining accreditation for their blended learning programme or module from their parent organization, e.g. a higher education institution, or from an awarding body such as the Open College Network (www.nocn.org.uk).

What is accreditation? Accreditation means that the programme or module has been formally approved by a recognized educational establishment or awarding body. If you are developing a programme or module and think that it is suitable for accreditation, the first step is to contact the appropriate people, e.g. in a university this is likely to be the quality office, and to obtain details about the accreditation process.

The next step is to follow the accreditation process, which is likely to mean that you develop and produce a set of documents that meets the accreditation body's requirements. If you followed the design process outlined in Chapter 4, you will have already prepared much of the information required for formal accreditation. As with the process of bidding for funding, the accreditation process involves reading a set of detailed documents and completing a set of forms so that you provide the correct information in an appropriate manner. Example 9.2 provides a typical sample module outline form, and this contains the information that will have been generated during the design process outlined in Chapter 4.

Example 9.2 Pro-forma – approval of a new module

A	Module title and code (if known)			
B	Credits			
C	Level			
D	Prerequisites			
E	Constraints			
F	Rationale			
G	Aims and distinctive features			
H	Learning outcomes			
I	Learning and teaching strategy			
J	Arrangements for revision and private study			
K	Methods of assessment			
L	Methods of reassessment (if different from K)			
M	Programme – module learning outcomes – assessment mapping [desirable]			

Programme outcomes	Module outcomes	Asessment method 1	Asessment method 2	Asessment method 3

N	Estimated number attending module		
O	Indicative content		
P	Indicative learning resources		

You will need to identify the academic level of the programme or module and the number of academic credit points that are associated with it. The number of academic credit points awarded to students completing a programme or module is associated with the number of learning hours that are normally required to successfully complete the course. Typically, in the UK, ten credit points at level 4 (undergraduate first year) are awarded for 100 student learning hours. One of the easiest approaches to understanding the system is to look at the existing documentation for a module or programme that you know well. This will help you to gain a sense of what is required.

From a project management perspective, if you are considering gaining accreditation for your programme or module, then you need to include this process in your project management plan. As with other tasks, it will take time and it needs to be integrated with other aspects of your project plan. You will need to research the requirements of the awarding body and fit into its processes and timescales. If you are new to this aspect of educational development work, then it is worthwhile attending relevant staff development activities. You may find it helpful to talk to colleagues who have experience of this process and to the staff who manage the overall process.

Summary

This chapter has provided an outline of the project management process involved in managing a learning innovation or blended learning project. It summarizes the standard project management cycle: design; plan; implementation; completion and review. The people side of projects involves working with and communicating with the project team and stakeholders. Working in collaborative and multi-professional teams is particularly challenging, and this chapter has emphasized the importance of developing project 'glue'. Finally, this chapter has explored the challenges (and time) involved in obtaining financial support for projects, and also gaining accreditation for your blended learning programme.

References

Allan, B. (2004) *Project Management*, London, Facet Publishing.

Boden, D. and Molotch, H. L. (1994) The Compulsion of Proximity. In Friedland, R. and Boden, D. (eds) *NowHere Space, Time and Modernity*, Berkeley, LA, University of California Press, 257–86.

Dakers, H. (2003) The BL Reaches Out, *Library & Information Update*, **2** (10), 46–7.

Lockyer, K. and Gordon, J. (2005) *Project Management and Project Network Techniques*, 7th edn, Harlow, Prentice-Hall.

Maylor, H. (2003) *Project Management*, 3rd edn, Harlow, Prentice-Hall.

McConnell, D. (2005) Examining the Dynamics of Networked E-learning Groups and Communities, *Studies in Higher Education*, **30** (1), 25–42.

Milner, C. (2007) Project Management: a key transferable skill, *Impact*, **10** (20), 23–5.

Pauleen, D. and Yoong, P. (2001) Facilitating Virtual Team Relationships via Internet and Conventional Communication Channels, *Internet Research: electronic networking applications and policy*, **11** (3), 190–202.

Pilling, S. and Kenna, S. (eds) (2002) *Co-operation in Action: collaborative initiatives in the world of information*, London, Facet Publishing.

Puleo, L. (2002) Some of the More Common Pitfalls of Project Management, *Accounting Today*, www.electronicaccount.com/Accounting Today/ [accessed 31 August 2007].

Sullivan, H. and Skelcher, C. (2002) *Working Across Boundaries*, Basingstoke, Palgrave Macmillan.

Tanner, S. (2003) Next Generation Management, *Library & Information Update*, December, www.cilip.org.uk/cgi-bin [accessed 12 May 2007].Index

Index